Contents

Prologue

In a world where business lurches from crisis to crisis and scandal to scandal, where ordinary people see their savings wiped out through the unscrupulous and largely risk-insulated decisions of executive and managers, and where governments are compelled to intervene and prevent further collapse and loss, there is a desperate need for a new way of *thinking*, a new way of *doing* and a new way of *being* in business. A fundamental shift is required to reconsider profit and shareholder-centric outcomes as the solitary motive in business. Innovative ways are to be found that will bring the responsibility to society, community and the environment to the centre, and focus attention on what business can and should do to positively influence these.

A new ontology at the base of business thinking will affect decisions and improve conditions for the broader society. This book explores a number of methods and models that can influence and facilitate such innovation and the discovery and establishment of such an ontology. There are guiding questions and other tools which culminate in an online test and companion workbook to assist you in your quest.

A conversation between a Giraffe and Hyena

Hyena (sniggering): Hey Giraffe, you look funny when you chew sideways like that.

Giraffe: That's part of the skill you need when eating branches with long thorns. I don't want an unexpected lip piercing from a three inch thorn.

Hyena: So what are you doing here by yourself?

Giraffe: Just thinking.

Hyena: About what?

Giraffe: About how badly the world needs a new ontology.

Hyena: A whaaaat?

Giraffe: Ontology

Hyena: What's that?

Giraffe: An ontology is a way of being and doing.

Hyena: Huh? Don't make me sorry I asked.

(Giraffe sighs an exasperated sigh with a slight shake of the head)

Hyena: Don't treat me like I'm stupid!

Giraffe: I can't make the words "being" and "doing" shorter or simpler.

Hyena: Okay, then give me an example, so I understand.

Giraffe: You often use that big tree that fell over to cross the stream, right?

Hyena: I do.

Giraffe: And you can see the fish swimming around looking for food. Sometimes they are chased by Crocodile.

Hyena: Yes, what about them?

Giraffe: Well, their ontology, their way of being and doing, is to live in water. It's all they know. They don't even realize that they are in water. To them it's normal, the way life should be and, in their belief, it's how everyone lives. If you were to drag one of them out onto the river bank it would very quickly realize that things are different and that it's no longer in water. They can't breathe air like we do, they can only breathe underwater.

Hyena: Really? They can't breathe air? That doesn't sound right.

Giraffe: Well, they have a special way of taking air out of the water around them. Just like we can't breathe under water, they can't breathe on dry land.

Hyena (somewhat dubiously in that "yeah, right" kind of way): I see. But what does that have to do with ontol… ontol… whatsisthing?

Giraffe: Ontology

Hyena: Yes that.

Giraffe: Well, fish can't be any other way. They can only BE in water. That's their only way of *being* and *doing*. And the whole world – all of us – animals and humans, have our own unique ways of *being*.

Hyena: So it's the stuff we know.

Giraffe: No – not knowing; that's something different. We use "being" kind of like a verb.

Hyena: What's a verb?

Giraffe: A verb is a doing word. Here, "being" is an action.

Hyena: Oh. So then your ontology is about how you are being – when being is a doing word not a… being word.

Giraffe: Yes. Ironically, you got it perfectly right.

Hyena: Are you trying to make me feel bad?

Giraffe: No, I'm trying to enlighten you.

Hyena: There you go again, big words!

Giraffe: I'm trying to make you understand more clearly, about the world needing a new ontology.

Hyena: So why do you think the world needs a new ontology? What's wrong with the way we are "being"?

Giraffe: Because the world is in trouble. From up here, I can see further and more of what's going on. I can see there is fire before anyone can even smell the smoke. The way we're carrying on can't last, and something's got to give. It's going to break, and when it does we will have real problems.

Hyena: (Laughs hysterically)

Giraffe: What's so funny?

Hyena: Do you remember the time Elephant was trying to pull that branch of marula fruit off the tree? He pulled and pulled and when the branch broke and the tree snapped back, you just saw monkeys flying. I thought I was going to tear my fur I laughed so hard.

Giraffe: I remember. Those monkeys were really angry, and some were pretty badly beaten and bruised.

Hyena: So are you saying the world is heading for another broken branch?

Giraffe: Yes, but this time it won't be just a branch or a tree. The whole world is at stake and no-one will be laughing.

Hyena: Why so dramatic?

Giraffe: Because it's a real problem that we're not being responsible, taking responsibility for how we act and behave towards one another. We take whatever we can get, more than we really need without thinking about the smaller animals that can't reach. Humans are the same. Take and take with no thought of the consequences.

Hyena: What's wrong with that? It's survival of the fittest.

Giraffe: Well, of course you would say that. Your ontology as a hyena is exactly that. You sneak up and steal Lion's food when he's not looking.

Hyena: Because I can get away with it.

Giraffe: But you take more than you need and more than you can eat.

Hyena: Like I said. I can get away with it.

Giraffe: Well it's not right and not sustainable. We should all be accountable to everyone else. It's not that hard to do and in the end everyone will benefit.

Hyena: Are you saying that the world is using a Hyena ontology?

Giraffe: Exactly. And it's time for a new one. A Giraffe ontology.

—

Hyena: So… what is a Giraffe ontology? What's so special about it? How is it different?

Giraffe: Do you really want to know or are you just asking to argue?

Hyena: No, I really want to know. You made it sound so serious.

Giraffe: Very well then. A Giraffe ontology is based on unselfish caring, sharing and responsibility.

Hyena (yawns): Sounds boring. Where's the excitement in that?

Giraffe: No doubt the idea of sharing and caring doesn't appeal to your killer instincts. But as I already said, the Hyena ontology isn't working, so the world will have to be prepared to change the current attitude.

Hyena: And how will that happen? Where do you start?

Giraffe: We start by teaching a focus on consciousness.

Hyena: What does being awake have to do with it?

Giraffe: Not awake, *aware.*

Hyena: Aware?

Giraffe: Yes, in this case consciousness means awareness. When we are aware of the danger of fire we can move. When we are aware of the world around us, we can change direction, follow a different path.

Hyena: So you start by making everyone aware of the problem.

Giraffe: Correct, and the solution. And why it's important to understand both the problem and the possible solution.

Hyena: And why is it important?

Giraffe: Because we have to work together, cooperate honestly and get organized.

Hyena: I see.

Giraffe: I believe that if we show everyone the value of doing what is right, for the right reason, and everyone *gets* it, the situation will improve for all of us. The new path is very exciting and is full of promise.

Hyena: But how do we know what the new path is? Where should we go?

Giraffe: This may sound a bit strange but you find the path by walking it; even if it's not yet there or you can't see it.

Hyena: How can we follow a path that isn't there?

Giraffe: That's part of the adopting and holding on to a new way of being. It may not make sense immediately and we have to be brave and dare to do something in a very different way. Like an explorer charting a new area.

Hyena: But we are all so used to doing things the way they've always been done. How do we know that we will find the path?

Giraffe: Correct, change isn't an everyday thing. But creating the path where it isn't, by walking it, is all about the opportunity for something new – new prospects where everyone benefits and, in the process, you sometimes have to break through some thick brush to get there.

Hyena: But won't it be very higgledy-piggledy?

Giraffe: At first it will. But you will see that we will, in time, become organized in a new way, instinctively.

Hyena: Find the path by walking. Imagine that. Sounds like something the old Owl would say.

Giraffe: There is something very important about creating the path by walking it.

Hyena: What's that?

Giraffe: We have to stop believing in the old ways of doing things and stop thinking that there is only one straight route to get to a new place.

Hyena: That's not so easy.

Giraffe: It is if we change what we believe the result should be – until now there has always been a focus on only one result; the way it has always been done. But why should we only do things the old way? What if we allow ourselves the freedom to imagine a new result, a new outcome?

Hyena: So you're saying that if we focus on a new *result* it would be easier to let go of the old beliefs.

Giraffe: Exactly.

Hyena: It's worth a try.

Giraffe: It's more than just worth a try. It's important that we change things and look after the bottom of the pyramid.

Hyena: The bottom of the pyramid? What pyramid?

Giraffe: It's a figure of speech. Picture the world and all that live in it as a pyramid – the king of the jungle at the top and the small animals at the bottom. The power and money is concentrated in the upper part and the big base at the bottom has little money and no power. This is how the Hyena ontology has shaped it. Survival of the fittest, as you called it earlier.

Hyena: Yes, the Hyena way.

Giraffe: If we want the world to work better and reflect, what I call, Giraffe values, we need to start taking care of the bottom of the pyramid. We have to live in a way that is sustainable, equal and inclusive, and start working together.

Hyena: Smaller words Giraffe, please!

Giraffe: Let me explain it this way. Rats and ants react in a different way when the water rises and they're trapped. The rats will frantically clamber all over one another, pushing each other down, fighting to get to the top. And that way most will probably drown. The ants will hold hands and together float to the top. That way they all survive.

Hyena: Crafty.

Giraffe: Indeed – and it shows the value of working together. It's like when humans do business. It should be business FOR society and not business BEFORE society.

Hyena: I like that, it's clever.

Giraffe: But it must also be sustainable, and before you ask, sustainable is used so much today that it's lost some of its meaning, so let me give you the real meaning. Sustainable simply means that we use our resources in such a way that we don't run out and that we leave enough for our children, their children and many generations to come.

Hyena: Yes, I always hear about sustainable this and sustainable that and it gets confusing.

Giraffe: So, I want the world to stop using Hyena values and adopt Giraffe values.

Hyena: What are they?

Giraffe: The values we all still have to create together, but I can tell you what the principles are.

Hyena: Really Giraffe…

Giraffe: The starting points

Hyena: Okay, and they are?

Giraffe: As I said already: **sustainability**, **inclusiveness**, **fairness** and most importantly, **caring generosity** that takes us away from the I-want-more greed. If life is about give and take, then there is far too much taking and not enough giving.

Hyena: So where do the values come from?

Giraffe: The values are a product of the new path; the new way that we invent together

Hyena: It's all very exciting. Let the journey begin!

1 Introduction

Increasingly managers, politicians and the wider public have started agreeing that the never-ending story of misbehavior, unethical behavior, fraud, poor service delivery, etc. mainly in business, are unworthy of the 21th century. For years the corporation was the cornerstone of our economic system – stable, trustworthy, providing growth, and creating employment. All, of course, for the advancement of society. Arguably, corporate and business development has contributed to the increase of wealth, at least in certain parts of society and parts of the world. At the same time, this often had negative effects on other parts of society and in other parts of the world. However, until roughly a decade ago, we were not aware of the scandals and brutalities that we have come to know over the last decade, perhaps starting with the Enron case as the most noticeable instance. Books have been written about these scandals, analyses made, corrective measures taken, but not much seems to have changed. The Libor manipulation in the UK, the latest in a long sequence, goes beyond imagination. Why is it so difficult to change? Do we have an interest in change in the first place? Who are we, and what can we change to?

These questions are what this book will deal with. What are the assumptions supporting our current business management model? Are those assumptions the correct ones? Are profit and shareholder value exclusively the drivers of business, or are these merely outcomes, though important ones? What if **values** would be the driver? Isn't the motivation of any entrepreneur to bring to the market something that nobody yet delivers and that clients need and are waiting for? Something that adds real value to the lives of customers? What is the value added by a company? What do you add to society, to the economy? A difficult question, perhaps, so let me state it differently. If you go bankrupt tomorrow, what will we be missing, what will society be missing? And if society is missing nothing, why does your business exist in the first place? Indeed, companies often lack values, value added meaning and purpose. And meaning and purpose motivate people and employees, not profit and shareholder value.

Once we have explored the purpose of business, we will delve deeper into the mechanism of management. Most of what business schools teach is based on a set of assumptions that can and should be questioned. Business management is for the most part based on a very mechanical concept of a company. That company will perform in an ideal way provided that we correctly assemble a certain set of elements. We can make decisions and apply formulae to impact any of those elements, and that will produce a clear and uniform outcome. We presume causal relationships to be everywhere in the company. If I invest 10% more in marketing, my market share will increase by 2%. If I recruit 10 more people I could raise my revenue by 20 million. If I dismiss 50 people my costs will go down by 10%, etc. However, practice shows that this does not work. We never get these clear-cut outcomes and we excuse this by claiming that we always deal with a number of unknowns, but that their impact is minimal. We grossly ignore the role of human beings in this. We ignore that people are non-linear and dynamic in their thinking and that they do not follow a path where there is a neat relationship between cause and effect. People are networked, interconnected with many other people, inside and outside the company. The outcome of decisions that impact that network can often not be anticipated at all due to the dynamic workings of the network. You cannot say with certainty how people are influenced in their behavior as a result of singular decisions.

Some will argue that all of this is the domain of courses like human resources management and organizational behavior. And that is true, but only in theory. It is already a gross oversimplification to assume that human resource management and organizational behavior are isolated disciplines. It is to be brought into a more broad conversation about business management. In fact, since we work with human "material" everywhere, human resources and organizational behavior are really foundation courses. Since your company is a network and the market is a network, it is crucial to understand the mechanics of the network. A network cannot be deconstructed into basic elements so that, if they could be optimized individually, the entire network would be optimized. A network can only be "optimized" or managed if we accept it as a complete network, a holistic structure. For this we have to use a holistic approach to management. Such a holistic understanding of management and business is developed in this book, including tools to apply this in practice.

A last crucial element is the focus of management. If the company's drivers are values and no longer purely financial concerns, then what should a manager focus on? What should receive principal attention? I argue that the answer to that question is innovation, innovation as a driver for continuous change. What do we need to do in order to be close to our clients, to deliver value under conditions they desire? In order to answer that, we will need to be "innovative". We have to be alert, to continuously monitor improvement, explore new ideas, and find new business models and new insights. It is a way of "being" in an ontological sense, being resilient, alert, aware, empathetic and translating that into new products and services, or at least improved products and services.

In this we focus on the role of the manager: the manager as a values-based innovator. Companies and the society are in great need of leaders who are able to refocus companies and organizations in their main task of creating and contributing wealth to society, adding value to society by doing meaningful, purposeful and inclusive business. Business has to have clients and ideally that should be anyone regardless of social standing or economic factors. We cannot exclude those with lesser means and who cannot pay for expensive products because we only cater to the top of the pyramid. And talking about innovation, can we design products for the bottom of the pyramid? Why do we still design 80% of our products for 10% of the people? When are we going to design 80% of the products for 80% of the people? It is then that we will have inclusive business that contributes to the development of the economy whether rich or poor, mature or emerging. Then, business will show its real power for good, which it certainly hasn't shown as yet. There is hope. Everything we need is already there. We just have to change focus correctly. Therefore, this book will deal with the following issues: values, network functioning, leadership and innovation; A whole new approach to business and leadership.

Some current thinking about values

In the first part of the previous century, Management by Instructions (MBI) was what was then called the scientific way of management. From that time the evolution of the behavior of markets and also our understanding of this evolution, has fuelled further evolution in our managerial thinking– especially in terms of increasing complexity, uncertainty and speed of change. The 1960s, for example, gave rise to the still popular Management by Objectives (MBO) model. MBO developed alongside ideas on the role of the group and of group thinking: the idea of matrix organizations, project groups, sales teams, etc. This understanding of organizations and its accompanying, sometimes guerilla-like management style, has contributed to economic success over the last few decades. More recent, has been the emergence of Management by Values which continues to have a slow uptake. Nevertheless, as this book illustrates, there is a growing demand for more human, purposeful and meaningful orientation of business. Where does it all lead?

Dolan et al (2006) suggest that the following four interconnected trends are increasing organizational complexity and uncertainty, and contributing to situations where the MBO approach reaches its limits:

1. The need for quality and customer orientation
2. The need for professional autonomy and responsibility
3. The need for 'bosses' to evolve into leaders/facilitators
4. The need for 'flatter' and more agile organizational structures.

In terms of quality and customer orientation, we are confronted with the issue that in today's markets, value-adds have become a question of continuation, or let's call it survival. A highly developed customer expectation can only be met either by a product or service that adds real value – something which no-one else offers – or by a price competitive offering which of course, in the long run, may not be viable for the company to maintain. Consider the simple question that I mentioned earlier which in practice does not seem to have a simple answer: what is the value added by your company? What would the market, the economy and society miss if your product or service is no longer there (e.g. if you went bankrupt)? Are companies truly able to state the value they add to society and if they can't, how could companies be managed to realize any values? If they do not have them, why do they exist in the first place from an economics point of view, other than simply for making an individual profit? Maybe there is no answer yet, since many are still looking for the perfect answer.

The need for professional autonomy and responsibility is one that has to do with the re-focusing of human skills on the human (and the mechanical skills on the machine). The more technology progresses, the greater the need for humans to make decisions and to use technology to best realize their potential. Successful companies today seem to clearly understand the need for the human dimension in management. In a networked structure, whether company or economy, the intense interaction of individuals can only produce emergence if those individuals have autonomy, are responsible and have the necessary professional skills. A soccer team will only function if all players are professionals (they are properly skilled at playing soccer), they have autonomy on the field and they are willing to take their individual responsibility in the game. There is no other way to manage a soccer team, nor is there any different basis for a company.

Success needs to be based on 'bosses' that evolve into leaders and/or facilitators. We will develop this further. Leadership is related to communication and, as Dolan et al suggest, instructions are the management tools of 'bosses', objectives are those of administrators, and values are used by leaders.

Though many are convinced of the need for flatter organizations, very many traditional organizations are oriented towards hierarchical control with:

- Those who direct and think (or are supposed to);
- Those who control the ones who produce;
- Those who produce.

Some 'bosses', but only a few first-class ones, continue to be necessary, but not as controllers of irresponsible operatives. Rather, their role in line with Dolan et al's research, should be to transmit values, facilitate work processes and allocate and co-ordinate resources.

The scenery of values

As already argued, the approach of "shareholder value only" belongs to the mainstream managerial paradigm that is increasingly being called into question. With less and less time to lose, people cannot afford the luxury of continuing to think in a paradigm that hardly questions the "negative" side-effect of its own ontology, let alone its impact on all living beings, including ourselves and nature. The framework of a short term business view, ignoring the devastating impact of our consumerism on our environment and our own wellbeing, is no longer tenable.

On 27 January 2008, we learned that at least one trader in France was responsible for the loss of 5 billion euros for Societe General. It wasn't the first time in financial history that this happened. Nick Leeson's actions in 1995 had devastating consequences for Barings Bank. While searching online, I found this short paragraph, part of a much larger article.

*"The collapse of Britain's Barings Bank in February 1995 is perhaps the quintessential tale of **financial risk management** gone wrong. The failure was completely unexpected. Over a course of days, the bank went from apparent strength to bankruptcy. Barings was Britain's oldest merchant bank. It had financed the Napoleonic wars, the Louisiana purchase, and the Erie Canal. Barings was the Queen's bank. What really grabbed the world's attention was the fact that the failure was caused by the actions of a single trader based at a small office in Singapore".*

I would like to draw your attention to a small detail in this paragraph. *"The failure was completely unexpected."* Even though I am not a financial specialist, I, and others around me, already believed and knew that this could happen. It does not require some "psychic superpower", looking into the future. It is a straightforward application of the dynamics of a (complex) financial market.

ING bought Barings for a symbolic price and later sold it off again, for an appropriate profit.

It's hardly surprising that this can happen since it is a realistic outcome of a systematically incorrect assumption of reality. Everything that has to do with options and futures is, by definition, part of a completely artificial world that is created, and that can continue to survive without any underpinned economic reality. It is a virtual world that has created its own reality, its own goods and services that are pure "belief" products. There is no longer any links with real companies, markets, economic dynamics, etc. A downward economy contains an equally large potential for profit as an upward market. It reaches the same kind of "virtuality" as the divide between the reality of a soccer game and its huge (virtual) economic potential, both connected to the value of top international soccer players and to their competition. At that point the comparison ends: with soccer, the ball, the lines of the playing field and the goal posts do not change during the match; in financial markets they do.

Former French president Nicolas Sarkozy, then French Minister of Internal Affairs, said during a speech to students and staff at a French Business School the following: "…*whatever one could say about capitalism, it, at least, never made victims.*" I still want to believe that he wanted to be truthful. I still hold on to the idea, the impression, that he wanted to express his true feelings, ideas and vision based on his experiences and assumptions. I heard what he said and felt upset, angry and could not believe my ears, since our need for honesty, integrity and the knowledge of some truthful facts was not fulfilled. Was his speech based on values?

We wish and hope to continue our search for reason, for truth, for an open vision and for meaning. We hope never to forget to search for facts, for clarity and for reasonable questions in every situation and for every institution. We do not need to be out-of-the-box thinkers to be able to know, to experience, that capitalism never existed in the first place as a pure model, and that secondly, it had, and still has, some very negative impacts on the well-being of people (child labor, exploitation in low income countries, arms trade, etc.) Capitalism creates victims through the diamond trade, arms trade, trade in alcohol, tobacco and other drugs, wars over energy resources, etc. One does not need to be a communist to see this. What else does Enron illustrate?

The Netherlands had their own Enron, called Ahold, an international retailer. Many small (private) investors lost money; many employees lost not only minor investments but their jobs as well. Ahold faced bankruptcy. Before they entered troubled waters everyone wanted to do business with Ahold – suppliers, accountants and financial specialists of the foremost banks. The General Manager, who was responsible for the eventual disaster, was once elected "Businessman of the Year". They too operated in the same illusionary (or artificial) "world" based on finance and financial values expressed by the share value. In general it was believed (and it still is) that this business model, this management style, should be "the" example for the rest of the world. It does not recognize the existence and the diversity of other business models elsewhere in the world that might be based on other, sometimes more ethical, assumptions. When Ahold went bankrupt, former friends wanted to distance themselves from the former "Businessman of the Year". Unconditional friendships are rather rare in business.

We sometimes see a strange separation between private life and the business environment and Kofman (2006) clearly states that this separation is the cause of much "un-ethical" or "non-responsible" management behavior. The manager can at the same time be a parent or grandparent and they will discuss with their children and grandchildren the importance of honesty, integrity and ethics. At the same time they do not hesitate to act irresponsibly, creating disasters in the organization they help manage and lead. Some go so far as to say that today's managers do not incur any risk any more. At their recruitment they negotiate a golden handshake for the moment the company wants to dismiss them. Poor results or not, significant bonuses are paid out every year. Where is the link to the risk that these so-called managers run? What would justify their extremely high salaries?

Arguably large amount of money is unfairly "earned" by non-equitable trade, child labor, unsafe working conditions, unfair legislation and regulation, unfair competition, fraud in the construction sector, and that seems to take place in most countries. It is almost location and culture independent; but it is paradigm dependent. Changing this attitude therefore needs an evolved managerial paradigm.

Europe and the US have had some interesting cases. Well known and respected managers of large multinationals were accused of insider trading which is illegal in most countries. The challenge is to find evidence for inside trading. In respected financial institutions, trading by employees is not permitted. But how can one exclude insider trading by a family member or friends of managers that have key positions in those financial institutions? They can easily share their knowledge in a very profitable way. Despite the strict laws and regulations in this matter, it is the fundamental paradigm that governs "management" (and its supporting ideology) that makes this unethical activity possible and even underpins it. Banking became, like many other industries, a self-referential system. Inside the system it works highly efficiently, by using "jargon" that only the insiders understand. The outsiders do not understand what happens in the system and are therefore excluded from the supreme insider possibilities. Insider trading need not be deliberately unethical behavior; it can be nothing more than a logical consequence of the self-referential system of contemporary banking.

A few decades ago, you would have had "owners" of small organizations who knew all the people they worked with. They knew that they needed the ideas and creativity of all the other people in the company. They felt responsible, not only for all their family members, but also for the people they worked with. They considered them to be an extended family. They had a vision. They would have been able to answer the question of the value added that their organization brings to society. They were committed to the organization and the people they worked with. They did not hide behind hierarchy, protocols and the like. They were their company.

The present shareholders of an organization are no longer the "owner-managers" of the organization. There are now shareholders on the one hand and managers on the other. They have different goals, means and ideas. Shareholders do not necessarily need a vision or a mission. They keep a distance from the organization and the people that work in and for the organization. They are much more interested in managing figures, and obviously certain figures interest them more than others: share value, dividends, etc. If they believe that the organization will do worse in the future, they will leave "the sinking ship" without hesitation, long before the water becomes visible to others. Some would call this recklessness that gives no thought to the impact on other stakeholders of the company. A number of acquisitions offer dreadful examples of this, such as the recent breakdown and takeover of certain renowned banks.

It seems that true feelings of empathy are minimal. Currently empathy, respect, a peaceful mind, and love seem to be separated from what we consider business should be. Talking about peace and love is in many parts of the world something you do in private and not in public, especially not in the world of business. In business, the prevailing belief seems to be that the analytical, isolated mind is superior and separates us from our heart, since minds are much more effective and efficient. But what do we call effective and efficient? Shareholder value only? Return on investment only? Short term (financial) results? Continuous competition?

But what if, as I will argue later, it is not possible to separate mind and thoughts from the rest of the body? What are the consequences of false hypotheses and assumptions? What price might be paid for these (wrong) mindsets? What about poverty, starvation, humiliation, aggression, child labor, abuse and other cruelties? It could be that our reason can deal with all of these but what about feelings and health? Could this be why people in many organizations and corporations avoid talking about love, compassion, empathy and peace? Could it be that the decisions made by corporations could be completely different if they would not exclude compassion? Is this what people fear most in business? And what is the cause of the many burnouts?

The separation of the owner-manager into an owner (as shareholder) and a manager did not only change the purpose and the method for the shareholder, it also changed them for the manager. As Whittington wrote in his award-winning book in 1993 "*What is strategy and does it matter?*", managers have invented a new type of skill in order to justify the role of the manager. In the era of the owner-manager, the role of that owner-manager was clear: He or she was the leader who committed to the vision of the company, who committed first and who functioned in a co-creating mode. In the absence of that commitment and given that the manager takes a technocrat's role (i.e. managing on behalf of someone else), a new skill was necessary to justify the role and position of the manager: that became *strategy*. Gradually, strategy disconnected from purpose, meaning, commitment and involvement. A manager is hired, negotiates his golden handshake upfront, has a high salary with a multitude of bonuses and runs no risk. The risk-return logic of entrepreneurship has become one of "administration" (we indeed train managers to become masters in business "administration"). The conclusion of Whittington is devastating: after having explained what strategy is, it appears, to him, not to matter.

At the 250th anniversary celebration of the Sara Lee Corporation, the former mayor of New York, Rudolph Giuliani, and some celebrities tried to convince the other invitees of the great importance of shareholders for managerial success. We did not observe any further interest from those anniversary speakers in any of the other stakeholders. The four classical production factors (land, labor, capital, knowledge) were reduced to one.

Everyone is interrelated and we do not want to judge them for what we would call a short term vision. Nevertheless this short term vision causes many problems. Enormous amounts of money are invested in advertisements and marketing campaigns to make sure that as many people as possible consume products and use services that are not only unnecessary, but which may even have negative side effects (such as health-related issues with certain types of food, drinks or other prescription drugs). In many European countries, Christmas sales are seen as the most important instrument to measure the confidence of buyers in the national economy. Will we ever be able and courageous enough to re-think growth? We hope that in a new paradigm this might be possible.

But it is not as difficult as it appears. When asked once how one could know what was good or bad (in a business school and in business per se), I could only quote my wife who always says: "Good is what you comfortably talk about to your children and grandchildren and bad is what you avoid talking about to your children and grandchildren." Thus, the simple question is "What are you doing in your professional life, and are you willingly talking about the details of what you do and how you do it to your children and grandchildren?" Let that be the simple rule to start with.

Some examples

Is values-based leadership new? No it is not. It just deserves to become more center stage, more mainstream; more the *talk-of-the-day* and *teach-of-the-day* in business schools. It is a difficult change, not largely due to the content but because it essentially speaks to deep-rooted assumptions in management education. It relates to the "doing" and eventually the "becoming" of the leader. And where new concepts are easy to assimilate, new behavior and a new "being" is much more difficult and challenging to work on. However it is the cornerstone of the change we need. Let us look at some examples of people that have shown what it means to be a values-based leader.

We start with the political slant to values-based leadership and while some obvious examples are the likes of Gandhi, Desmond Tutu and Nelson Mandela, I'd like to talk about **Jim Joseph**. He is the former ambassador of the USA in South Africa and for many years led a leadership program both in the USA and in Cape Town, South Africa. In his book "Leadership as a way of being", he reflects on those courses in the following words. *"There is a need for a new kind of leader – a transformative leader who is capable of understanding the profound moral and ethical dilemmas of the global environment, who has a vision of a higher purpose and seeks to inspire, motivate and gain the commitment of others to carry out that vision. There is a need for leaders who are comfortable with ambiguity, who are aware of themselves and others, leaders who seek to serve before they wield power."*

1. Through the broad experience of his career, he developed the following 12 lessons. It is possible for a leader to be humble without being docile, strong without being arrogant and still exert great influence;

2. Leaders who seek power to disperse it rather than simply concentrate it have a very special attraction and appeal;

3. The leader must be capable of learning from those he/she leads and must be capable of doing so without losing respect or influence;

4. The value-driven leader who needs consensus in order to act is likely to be most effective if he/she is willing to help shape that consensus rather than simply respond to it where it can be found;

5. The leadership style that works best for me is leadership that seeks to elevate and empower others. It seeks to engage the whole person in ways that satisfy higher and nobler needs;

6. Despite the continuing dominance of hard power – economic muscle and military might – in exerting influence and pressing one's will on others, I have found that soft power – moral messages, exemplar behavior and respect for other cultures – is likely to develop goodwill and establish relationships that are far more enduring;

7. Leadership is likely to be far more effective when it appeals to people's better nature;

8. While we seek to change the practices of the adversary, it is important that we maintain respect for his/her humanity;

9. In times of rapid change, zealots emerge claiming one truth and one theology. The challenge for the leader is not to use his/her values to proclaim absolutes but to help others cope with ambiguities;

10. An organization is what it rewards. It is not so much what it says in its mission statements, or even in its code of conduct, as it is what it rewards its people for being;

11. There are no hard and fixed absolutes about either managing or leading. To be rigid and play only by the rules on your organization chart or the theories of some guru is to miss the opportunity to meet people where they are. People-centered leadership recognizes the uniqueness of each individual and seeks to unleash the magic within;

12. Every leader does not have to be a superstar. Many apparently ordinary people are quiet leaders who make extraordinary contributions. They may not be seen as giants in the grand scheme of things, but the superstar could not accomplish anything without them.

These are some wise lessons of a wise man, referring mainly, but not exclusively to values-based leadership in politics.

Particularly in the African context, mining is important business, with a lot of "baggage". David Gleason (et al, 2011) interviewed **Mark Cutifani**, CEO of AngloGold Ashanti who shows strong similarities to much of what I will further develop as values-based leadership. In the following paragraphs Gleason, Nkomo and De Jongh reflect on the interview with Cutifani.

Cutifani has an established record at various previous places of employment as being a man who tirelessly strove to improve safety records. In defining what Cutifani and his management team wanted for AngloGold Ashanti – which is to create the leading mining company – the first of the values agreed on was safety. In Cutifani's view, the subject of safety is the start of any conversation in the industry because the inherent risks of the business permeate the lives of all involved.

Cutifani approaches sustainability from an angle that is different from what most others would consider it to be, but completely in line with how I define it. He believes that sustainability is synonymous with every company's efforts to make valuable contributions to the communities in which it operates and therefore, to society as a whole. "*Firstly, in the mining industry, or in any industry, if you are not about creating a better society, then I don't think you are about creating a sustainable business. At the end of the day, if we don't create value for the communities and the societies in which we operate, we don't have a future*". Cutifani emphasizes how critical it is for mine managements to be seen to be contributing meaningfully to the upliftment of the communities in which they operate.

Motivation is a two-way interaction. It is about: "*...reacting and interacting with people and motivating and inspiring and understanding and adjusting... your job is to make sure that the world, in terms of what we are trying to achieve, is absolutely clear to them. And by the way, the clarity of your vision comes from the conversations you have with the people who help you understand what the issues are and what the frustrations are. So it is a virtuous circle in terms of the conversation*".

And about ethics: "*I think ethical behavior is a value judgment as well. I think you have also got to be careful when we talk about morals and ethics. We should be very careful about the judgments we make about somebody else's ethics or morals… and my view is, if you are not prepared to disclose it, then don't do it: a very simple rule*".

(And the same rule we mentioned earlier, about talking to your children and grandchildren.)

In summary, Cutifani thinks that first and foremost, sustainability is a long-term societal and community engagement. Secondly, he believes that an organization's strategy must be centered on its people. The third pillar is shared values, to be understood as enduring principles. A shared vision and strategic alignment make up the last elements of his successful strategy.

Dick Dusseldorp, founder of Lend Lease in Australia, is another example of a values-based leader (see Clark, 2002). Dick Dusseldorp, in the words of Jack Mundey (in Clark), was an exceptional property developer and builder. He was not only concerned with the shareholders, but was equally concerned with the rights and privileges of his workers. Dick Dusseldorp gave dignity to his workers. He gave them continuous work in what is often an uncertain and turbulent industry. According to Bob Hawke (in the same book), Dusseldorp can be properly described as a man "before his time". He was an innovative and creative thinker – a man of great vision. His underlying philosophy of consultative co-operation and the equitable sharing of the fruits of enterprise was at the core of his extremely successful business career. He almost single-handedly changed the ethics, work practice and tender procedures in the construction industry in Australia, into a transparent process. By doing so he was driven by a clear set of values.

In Clark's words, he believes that Dusseldorp would probably be branded, in today's terms, an early pioneer of "social capitalism", for he built Lend Lease around the value of creating a community of common interests between its key stakeholders – getting them to transcend their traditional conflicts and divisions and work together toward a mutually beneficial goal. While employees and shareholders of Lend Lease were at its center, this web of common interest also embraced the corporation's clients, its professional associates and suppliers, as well as the broader community in which it operated. It was a philosophy that manifested itself in every aspect of Dusseldorp's approach to business – from the project and labor management strategies he employed to enable buildings like the Sydney's Regent Hotel to rise in double-quick time, to his engagement with community and public sector planning interests on urban development projects in Canberra. Such an approach, in his view, was not only the most sustainable way of doing business; it was also the most profitable. As companies today look for ways to meld precisely these two goals, the way Dusseldorp went about achieving them becomes much more than historical interest (all according to Clark).

Raymond Ackerman made Pick n Pay great: a leading retail chain in South Africa. Deep in the days of Apartheid, Ackerman felt that the system was unfair to black people and he broke the law in order to create better working conditions for his workers, far beyond what was common practice then and beyond what was legally allowed, including housing privileges and the like. Ackerman is known as a fighter for the rights of the consumer and few companies can claim to have done as much for their people as Pick n Pay has. More than 60% of its managers and supervisors are black and where most companies have been practicing this since the early 1990s, Ackerman has practiced this for well over 40 years (Bell, 1999). Long before it was either fashionable or necessary, Ackerman simply believed in promoting people on merit. He did everything that would allow him to satisfy his deep-seated corporate impulse to help the little man.

Ackerman was primarily a father of four children, but at the same time a father to the business, father to its people. In the 1970s and 1980s Ackerman favored social involvement and combatting all things detrimental to the consumer's interest. He took on successive ministers in his effort to seek departures from oppressive laws, which was not an easy thing in the Apartheid years. Often his focus was on his own people, pushing black and colored staff through the barriers of job reservation or residential segregation. Ackerman had to pay a price for this behavior, particularly amongst right-wing Afrikaners, with sometimes lengthy boycotts of his stores. For the good of his clients he would be fighting monopolies, cartels, and governmental price controls (such as on petroleum and agricultural products). Though Pick n Pay has not been able to successfully expand beyond South Africa, Ackerman is yet another example of a values-based leader. He himself relates this to the fact that although the company is highly professional, it is also very idiosyncratic in its ethos (Ackerman, 2010).

Two more examples, of companies this time, hopefully gives a good overview of what values-based leadership means today, while still being successful. Dutch **Oikocredit** is one of the world's largest sources of private funding to the microfinance sector. They also provide credit to trade cooperatives, fair trade organizations and small-to-medium enterprises in the developing world. The company was created by the Council of Churches in the Netherlands with the belief that the world's poor can build better lives for themselves if only they were given a chance. Through no choice of their own, 1.4 billion people in the world live in poverty. They don't lack ability, they lack opportunity. The company is active in microfinance and social investing. They had 520 million Euros invested (in 2011) and, at the time of publishing, they had 26 million clients.

Oikocredit's mission is guided by the principle of empowering people. The most effective and sustainable way of assisting those in need is to provide them with the opportunity to help themselves. They challenge people (and groups) to share their resources through socially responsible investments and by empowering disadvantaged people with credit. For them, all people are created equal. Thus they extend credit to marginalized people irrespective of their faith, culture, age or gender and favor the initiatives of women, as they are the backbone of their families and thus society as a whole. Oikocredit provides a mechanism for meaningful sharing. In the cooperative culture of Oikocredit, people's initiatives and participation are central to all acts and policies.

The underlying principles of the **Tata Group,** and their approach to sustainability are described in the book they published themselves: Code of Honour (2010). According to Kishor Chaukar (managing director of Tata Industries at the time of publication), they practice the belief, in line with the founder's ideas (Jamsetji Tata), that in a free enterprise the community is not just another stakeholder in business, but is, in fact, the very purpose of its existence. Jamsetji's philosophy had two pillars. The first is "Corporate Sustainability". The second pillar is "Code of Conduct" – the belief system, the values and the ethics. These two pillars are there to support and reinforce Tata's aim to improve the quality of life in the communities in which they operate and to build trust with the people they deal with.

Code of Honour details the Tata group's focus around corporate sustainability in terms of: governance, employees, environment and the community. It highlights the Tata commitment to causes that stretch beyond business: social development, research and education, employee wellbeing, and the environment. The group is involved in helping to create and sustain livelihoods by backing grassroots organizations in a multitude of fields and in practicing ethical business principles.

The examples above are by no means the only values-based leadership instances in the world. The ones mentioned here were chosen to describe different sectors: retail, banking, mechanical construction, building and mining.

Some questions to consider

This book is not just about new content, new concepts and ideas. It is about a new way of doing, since eventually this new doing is going to lead to you becoming a different being, possibly a values-based leader. This book is as much a workbook as a textbook. So let's start with some reflection exercises. After having read this introduction, I would like to invite you to reflect on the following eight focus areas in respect of your own company, organization, NGO. Do this in writing, and it might we worthwhile to keep a little notebook for all the "to do" things in this book. It will allow for easy revision and learning later on.

Wherever company is mentioned, you could consider any type of organization: a cooperative, a club, an NGO. In case you are not able to answer a question, I invite you to think through the question, and consider how your company could do things differently from how they are presently doing them. What would be the impact and/or advantage of this different way of thinking?

1. What are the values that your company or organization announces, and according to you, what values are lived up to? Give examples of actions and activities of the company that show the realization of those values.

2. Does your company really value diversity? What do they understand by diversity and why do they value it? What examples can you give to illustrate your answer?

3. Is your company and your management living within paradoxes, ambiguity and complexity, or is the purpose of the company to reduce all this and come up with straightforward actions? Is your company able to leverage complexity to their advantage? Can you give examples of any of the statements you make?

4. What is the company's personal development policy, program, or tools used? Does it, and how does it, link into the values? Can you give examples?

5. Are there any personal well-being programs and/or actions? Can you give examples?

6. Does your management show leadership? *How* does it show it? What does leadership mean in your company?

7. Does your company have an individualistic evaluation system, or a team evaluation system? Could you comment on this question from your perspective?

8. How would you evaluate the company's financial performance? Could you suggest changes in the financial policies that would be more aligned with the values?

9. How does your company organize, support and reward innovation? What does your company understand by innovation?

10. Does your company have programs on sustainable performance, and what do they understand by that? Does your company have programs on social responsibility and what do they understand by that?

11. Does your company have an active knowledge management policy, and what do they understand by knowledge and knowledge management?

12. Does the company have a formal (organizational) learning strategy? What actions do they undertake to realize it?

While these questions may be difficult to answer now, the process of this book and the full Cassandra©
test at the end will facilitate a deeper understanding of business model innovation for your company
and in your unique situation.

2   What drives people, organizations and companies?

The paradigm of consciousness and leadership

> *"Science cannot solve the ultimate mystery of nature...because in the last analysis we ourselves are part of the mystery we are trying to solve....*
>
> *When you change the way you look at things, the things you look at change."*
>
> *– Max Planck, Nobel physicist*

2.1   Some key concepts of a new ontology

The ideas proposed in this book are based on a new paradigm, or at least a less mainstream paradigm, explained in earlier work (Baets and Oldenboom, 2009). As a basis for formulating a new paradigm for understanding complex systems in general and management in particular, as well as to develop an adequate research model, I first summarize some fundamental concepts, often developed in other sciences than those of economy, management or social sciences, but equally applicable in complex social systems. These concepts are explored further throughout this book but initial insight into them will give context to their relevance as we proceed.

- **Holism:** The approach developed and proposed is contained in the holistic paradigm and in the way it is used here, draws from Ken Wilber's (2000) theories. He defines **holism** as an eternal dynamic interaction between four "spheres": two external (individual and collective), and two internal (individual and collective). They are as follows: The mechanical (external) individual sphere; the mechanical (external) collective sphere; the internal collective sphere (common values), the internal individual sphere (emotions and consciousness). See diagram in Chapter 5. Clearly, in reductionist and rational approaches, the external individual sphere receives all the attention. "Classical" ecological scientific movements are especially interested in the collective, but always external, sphere. More recent scientific interests attempt to go beyond that, by including more values and emotions (slowly introducing the concept of consciousness). Holism, as defined by Wilber, is evidently founded on a **constructivist** approach i.e. **the way people create meaning through individual constructs.** Constructs are filters we use to create order and meaning.

- The proposed ontology fits clearly the reality of the **sciences of complexity** in the definition of physical chemist and Nobel Laureate, Ilya Prigogine's study of dynamic non-linear systems. In particular, he was always very interested in two important aspects: the role of time and behavior far from equilibrium. He illustrated the constructive role of time, as expressed in the principle of the irreversibility of time, in complex processes. This principle illustrates why in complex systems it is not possible to extrapolate the future from the past. Complex systems are extremely sensitive to the initial conditions. Minimal changes in these conditions can have major influences on the further development of the process. Finally, Prigogine identifies the most productive state of a (complex) system as one that is far away from equilibrium – "order at the edge of chaos".

- John Holland, a pioneer in artificial life and agent systems, has developed a complex adaptive systems approach (CAS) called **agent based simulations**. This approach simulates the interaction between different agents and, consequently, simulates **emergent behavior** in those kinds of systems. An agent, according to Holland, is a mini software program. Each agent has characteristics. It is necessary to define the field of action (the limits of the system) and to identify a minimum of interaction rules (and exchange rules). Then it is necessary to make the system iterate and simulate the dynamic interaction of those agents. The agents meet each other, interact, exchange (and so learn) and, step by step, form a global behavior with qualities that emerge from the interaction itself.

- **Synchronicity,** according to Wolfgang Pauli, appears in all the sciences and the techniques in which simultaneity (two events happening at the same time) plays a role. It is necessary to take into account that this is not about causal coherence, from cause to effect, but about **coincidence** as occurring together in time. This has to be considered as potentially useful, even if we cannot explain the more profound cause of the simultaneity. We must remember that we always speak of a synchronicity if the events concerned happen in the same period of time. The relationships therefore, to use Jung's words, become **a-causal**.

- The implication of these observations is that the phenomenon of **"entanglement"** (**non-locality**), including a real activity at a distance, is not simply epistemological. It is, in effect, ontological by nature (Polkinghorne, 1990) and can be called **"a quantum interpretation"**.

- Sheldrake and Bohm (1982) broached the subject of **"implicit order"** as something like solid ground underneath time, a totality from which each movement is projected in explicit order. For everything seen, there is something in implicit order at the origin of this projection. If there are many repetitions of an event then behind it is a built constant component. A sort of (fixed) link is born. Through this process, the forms from the past can continue to live in the present. This is more or less what Sheldrake calls **morphogenetic fields**, created by **morphogenetic resonance**.

- **Ayurveda** considers the human being as a self-organizing system composed of many simple elements which are, when taken independently, very stupid, but which together form a formidable **distributed intelligence**. In parallel, a company can be considered a network of "simple" elements which "know" what they must know to be able to form effective networks with others.

- The ontological nature of this quantum structure forces us to look again at our approach to organizations and their management, and on a wider scale, at our economic theory. **The understanding of management must therefore be based on the "carrying along" of quantum structures, synchronicity, morphogenetic fields and individual space for self-organization.**

2.2 Consciousness: the fifth floor (dimension) in the house of knowing (what is the "hard" and the "easy" problem?)

Key to our understanding of management is consciousness, in this sense awareness, and in particular the role that consciousness plays in organizations (see Baets, 2008, for a more contextual overview). In her interesting interview series of a number of neuroscientists and philosophers, Susan Blackmore (2005) identifies two main schools of thought around consciousness. The one school is based on the idea that the brain is a coder/decoder (neuronal actions) and hence, the challenge of consciousness study is to understand how the brain deals with issues like feeling, color, senses, etc. These scientists study brain operations and they consider the problem of consciousness residing in the physical world.

The second school of thought attempts to understand the "first person" perspective. They try to explore how things feel, and they accept that one's "internal movie" has color, music and feelings. According to those scientists, consciousness cannot be reduced to a fixed space-time environment. The study of consciousness for those scientists cannot be conducted via classical "third person" research tools. Let's develop a few of these ideas further.

Bernard Baars (1988 and 1997) accepts that being conscious is activating the best or winning combination of neurons (as opposed to being not conscious). He refers to the theatrical metaphor developed in the Vedantic scriptures and ideas of Plato. Consciousness is what is in the bright spotlight area of the stage. The thalamus is the machinery. This view on science denies emotions. But aren't emotions part of consciousness?

Francis Crick (1994) claims that the hardest problem is understanding how qualia are generated by the brain. Qualia are instances of subjective consciousness that describe the perception of the redness of red, the taste of wine or the sensation of sand between your toes. Daniel Dennett eventually suggests (as befitting a real behaviorist) to get rid of qualia altogether. For Dennett, it is all about behavior. For Crick, being conscious or not conscious has everything to do with brain activity. Consciousness and awareness go hand in hand.

Dennett (1987, 1991, 1996, 2003) is one of the best known opponents of the brain activity school, but at the same time, he pays a great deal of attention to behavior. Subjective experience is hard to understand; it is a point of view, a reflective capacity. People have powerful seductive intuitions that are just wrong. From a third person perspective, you approach consciousness from the outside, not from the inside. According to Dennett we are put into a physical world, where there is no mystery. To him, dualism, the conviction that mental activity is separate from the physical human, is hopeless. Dennett is an absolute materialist and argues that one cannot trust common sense. The point is to categorize the phenomenology of consciousness and explain it. But he does agree that first person research is useful in the stage of discovery, not in the context of justification. But aren't we still in the stage of discovery? Do we have any reasonable understanding yet of how to explain consciousness from a third person perspective? And if not, should we not start with some more explorative research?

Patricia Churchland (1986, 2002) and Paul Churchland (1984, 1996) express the view that we have not made real progress in understanding consciousness, since we do not truly know how information is coded in the brain. For them, consciousness is all about how the brain performs the coding. For them, the brain builds a model and there is a difference between inner and outer (dualism). Though one would possibly put the Churchlands in the first school of thought, they also have interesting ideas that open doors to a more quantum interpretation. According to them, there is more than just wave theory in sound. Heat of a coffee cup is similar to mean molecular kinetic energy, but it is not just correlated. There is something akin to neural correlation, or a better description would be "interconnectedness". Sensations are energies and this "energy" interpretation of consciousness opens doors for a non-causal model of understanding.

Koch (1999, 2003) refers to illusion and the fact that sometimes we see and sometimes we don't. This possibility to see "different" is what he calls consciousness. It is an experience; it is not just what we see, but the feeling that goes with it. It is not the retina that makes the difference, but that which gives rise to the subjective feeling. However, he feels that the only way ahead would be to get the neural correlation right.

Searle (1992, 1997, 2004) takes an interesting middle ground but does not make much progress. Consciousness only exists as something experienced, enjoyed, hence it has a first person ontology. We now try to have an epistemologically objective science about a domain that is ontologically subjective. That is a real dilemma. If we explore the synchronization of massive neuron firings over large areas of the thalamo-cortical system, would this get us anywhere close to understanding consciousness? Searle continues to be positioned between the concepts of the brain mechanism creating a system of rational agency, and the presupposition of freedom of experience.

Ned Block (1997) defines consciousness as the Technicolor phenomenology "what it is like". He defines phenomenological consciousness on the one hand, and access consciousness on the other. The latter form, involving the unconscious, vivid image states, etc, is suppressed. But he admits that studying the phenomenological consciousness alters that same consciousness. This creates issues around the research methods used. According to him, you can have phenomenology that is not completely part of us, just as much as you can have observations that do not connect.

According to Chalmers (in Lanza, 2009) however, the so called "easy" problem of consciousness is to explore:

- The ability to discriminate, categorize and react to environmental stimuli
- The integration of information by a cognitive system
- The reportability of mental states
- The ability of a system to access its own internal states
- The focus of attention
- The deliberate control of behavior
- The difference between wakefulness and sleep

The easy problem is about control and which part of the brain does what. It is about finding mechanisms. Understanding this "easy" problem would not bring us any closer to explaining consciousness or understanding how we transform seeing into experiencing: What is the feeling of the color red? Why is working with one person more motivating for me than working with another? How does the architecture of a building make me feel happy, energetic or depressed?

Biocentrism (Lanza, 2009) squarely brings up the fundamental problems that remain in the acceptance of an "external" reality and defines seven principles that link up the observer and the role of consciousness in the experience.

What we perceive as reality is a process that involves our consciousness. An "external" reality, if it existed, would – by definition – have to exist in space. But according to Lanza this is meaningless because space and time are not absolute realities but rather tools of the human and animal mind. Our external and internal perceptions are inextricably intertwined. They are different sides of the same coin and cannot be divorced from one another. The behavior of subatomic particles – or even all particles and objects – are inextricably linked to their being an observer present. Without the presence of a conscious observer they exist at best in an undetermined state of probability waves. Let us therefore explore the researchers of consciousness that share this view on what consciousness is, before making an attempt to define consciousness and design a measurement approach.

David Chalmers (2004, 2009) is widely known for his attempts to understand consciousness from a first person perspective. How do things feel? Consciousness for him is subjective data. The hard problem according to him, is understanding subjective experience. The processes in the brain are not the feeling itself. Descartes, with his *cogito ergo sum* – I think therefore I am – has in a way defined consciousness: the mind (this overwhelming energy and power) creates consciousness. The connection between brain processes and conscious experience is, according to him, certainly not causal. Consciousness cannot be reduced to a fixed time-space concept, but it is a fundamental feature of the world.

For Chalmers consciousness is a non-physical thing interacting with the physical world. It gives life meaning and it gives life the interesting room for value. This interpretation of consciousness finds an ontological home in quantum mechanics.

Stuart Hameroff (Hameroff et al, 1996, 1998, 1999) supports the Chalmers idea. Consciousness is fundamental to the universal part of our reality, like mass or charge. It is just there. According to him, if qualia -individual instances of conscious experience – would exist, they would exist at the lowest level of existence; at the Planck level where space-time is not smooth any more but quantized. At this fundamental level, qualia are embedded as patterns in this fundamental granularity of space-time geometry that makes up the universe. It is suggested that platonic values in mathematics as well as ethics and aesthetics were embedded there. We know two sets of laws: the Newton laws at the macroscopic level and laws of quantum mechanics at small scales. How small is small? Where does the collapse of the wave function happen? All this has to do with consciousness.

Ramachandran (1998, 2004) considers qualia as equal to consciousness. Qualia deal with the experience of the redness of red. But qualia need a *self* that knows that it knows, and that it is required to know. Qualia are linked to the spinal cord experience, but at the same time grow over the simple feeling of pain, for instance. The self is able to hold a "*meta-wareness*".

Roger Penrose (2002) argues that our minds do non-algorithmic things anyway. They have an *other* logic (a particular collapse of the wave function). There is a type of quantum computing taking place in the brain. He refers to this as quantum computing in microtubules (a protein structure). For Penrose, consciousness is quantum processing. For example, when you are presented with a restaurant menu, you filter according to your preferred dishes, and, when you make your final choice, a collapse in the quantum wave function occurs. Quantum coherence and entanglement may be essential features of life. Consciousness dances on the edge between the quantum world and the classical world. The more we are in contact with the subconscious world of enlightenment, the happier we can be. The universe at the Planck scale is non-local, it exists holographically, indefinitely.

LaBerge (1985, 1990) sees consciousness as having a fractal nature. For him lucid dreaming is consciousness since dreams are experiences. The physical reality is only a hypothesis that allows communication. In an awakened state only 25% of the viewers see things like the change of an actress in a movie or the gorilla in the basketball video. Any approach to consciousness must entail questions of self-transformation; we have to understand the experiences. Metzinger (2003) goes a step further. Consciousness for him, as opposed to all other states, is a physical one, a biological and chemical one which is known from the outside, from a third person view. The first person view is one that is rooted in experience, but he suggests that the most adequate way to research this would be via correlates. That is what I will develop further in this book. Understanding consciousness requires training in order to see experience without the "self". The *self* can be very misleading. One should strive for introspection without attempting to relate it to the known or familiar, and without creating theories. But this goes against the tradition of Western neurosciences. Metzinger questions whether indigenous wisdom, more soul related wisdom, would be all that wrong. For him demystification of society can lead to "desolidarization" of society and classical science offers little defense against that. Shouldn't we be more interested in conscious culture, conscious ethics and possibly a conscious organization?

O'Regan (2011), an influential experimental psychologist, states that people should give up the idea that consciousness is a single thing that emerges from some brain process. Our continuous perception of the world is an illusion; if there is nothing there, you wonder what there is (like the light inside the fridge). The firing of nerves couldn't possibly be the cause of visual experience. Experience is not simply in the brain, but it is something the brain can do. Experience is observing something new, it is movement, it is action, at least for the more perceptual forms of feeling (for "feeling happy" that might be a different story). Redness is how you move the eye; there is nothing really red. For O'Regan, it is all about brain capacity and about focus, not about brain function. We get little bits of information from external sources and then create a rich internal representation which becomes our experience. It is all part of an activity, not a simple transfer. Small changes are often not observed. There is no real seeing, but only interrogation, and that creates the image. The "I" is merely a social construct. This view on consciousness allows us to move into a workable understanding of consciousness in organizations, and opens doors not just to measure or represent consciousness, but equally to work towards a more conscious organization.

Varela (1992) sees that consciousness research is ruled out on a behavioral level for scientific political reasons. There is a methodological issue with science that relates to the scientific tradition. Buddhism, for instance, does allow the reporting of feelings very precisely. Hence science should go a different route if it is to understand consciousness. Consciousness feels so personal, is so singular and given our embodiment, is a neurophenomenological issue. Furthermore, people's consciousness develops in relation to the consciousness of others. Velmans (2000, 2003) builds on the concept of embodiment. Consciousness is not in the brain but is embodied with outside embedding, and it consists of real energies. For reductionist scientists, consciousness has to be a state of the brain. It is a fundamentally dualistic concept but this still does not resemble simple experience.

In fact, this second school of thought suggests that consciousness is a new kind of dimension, a first person sensation that cannot be understood with classical third person research (that cannot be understood in a Newtonian paradigm). Third person research is based on reductionism, measurement, and inside-outside understanding of reality and rationality. Third person research typically takes place in a three dimensional Newtonian reality of absolute time and space. But scientists (and in particular quantum mechanics) suggest another type of reality – a quantum reality (Baets, 2006) that is based on non-locality, synchronicity and entanglement. This is a world of waves being a multitude of possibilities until measurement (or observation) collapses the wave into a particle – a particular state created by observation. (Polkinghorn, 1990) It is the observer – you and me – that seems to create at any given moment, out of all the different possible states, the one that is chosen. Out of all the different possible sounds, we select the one we like most in a piece of music. From all the different possible sensations the color red can give, we chose that one that we like most in a given situation.

These scientists give meaning to the research done by the Bogdanovs (Bogdanov and Bogdanov, 2006) who explore the very basis of nature: what happens beyond the Wall of Planck? Since the Wall of Planck is the smallest possibly value in nature, this discovery is mathematical. Their exploration suggests the existence of a fifth dimension that could be a fourth dimension of space expressed in imaginary (complex) time. Beyond the Wall of Planck and hence also before the Wall, time and space would come together. This would be the world in which things "are" (time and space independent). This state, being the fifth dimension, could be a state of consciousness. This definition of consciousness would perfectly fit the definition that some old traditions (like Ayurveda) give. All understanding is constructed on a number of levels of understanding. In classical sciences these different levels are: mathematics, physics, chemistry, biology and psychology. In noetic sciences (www.noetic.org) those levels are: fractal algebra, energy physics, vibrational chemistry (both based on quantum mechanics), noetic biology (interconnected cells) and energy psychology (perceptions and energy fields). In an ancient wisdom tradition like Ayurveda, those levels are: matter form, ether and astral body, energy level, desire, capacity to think (conceptualization), intelligence and intuition, and finally consciousness. Consciousness is described as the highest state of being, the highest floor of knowing; the ultimate being.

In this definition of consciousness third person research will not be able to clarify what consciousness is, let alone how it would influence corporate behavior, happiness, etc. This understanding of consciousness would mean that within the classical three dimensional Newtonian world, things cannot have a consciousness. At the same time, consciousness cannot be Newtonian.

It is clear that consciousness is a multi-faceted concept that is of crucial importance for a better understanding of the link between organizations and their well-being. In this book, I would like to focus on Hameroff's "definition" which at least comes closest to being a definition. For him, consciousness is fundamental to the universal (the *everything*) part of our reality, just like mass, or a charge: it is just there, which in a way is Chalmers' idea. If qualia are fundamental to consciousness, they must exist at the lowest level of existence; at the Planck level where space-time is not smooth any more but quantized. One could refer to it as granularity at a fundamental level. In nature, there are two sets of laws. If Newton's laws apply at the macroscopic level and the laws of quantum mechanics apply at small scales, then the question is how small is small, and where does the wave function collapse? This question is related to consciousness. Again, consciousness is a form of quantum processing where choices are continually made, as in the restaurant menu example. Eventually this can be measured and visualized by a combination of algorithmic and non-algorithmic processes. Consciousness spans the quantum world and the classical world.

If we wish to research consciousness as defined here, we will either have to use different research methods (possibly still to be developed; first person research methods) or use a measurable proxy for consciousness using adapted research methods. The measurable proxy we argue for is "coherence", as worked out in some detail. As will be discussed in more detail, "coherence" is the impact or consequence of consciousness on the individual level.

2.3   Coherence as proxy for consciousness

According to McCraty and Tomasino (2006), the most common definition of coherence is "the quality of being logically, integrated, consistent and intelligible", as in a coherent argument. A related meaning is "a logical, orderly and aesthetically consistent relationship of parts". If we refer to people's thoughts (or speech) as coherent, we say that the parts seem to fit together. They are not uttering meaningless nonsense or presenting ideas that don't make sense as a whole (Ho, 1998). Coherence, hence, refers to wholeness and a global order; out of the interaction of elements, a whole emerges. Coherence includes the idea of local freedom and global cohesion (Ho, 1998). Interestingly, in physics, the concept of coherence is also used to describe the interaction or coupling among different oscillating systems in which synchronization is the key idea in this concept. This definition of coherence perfectly fits our quantum ontological framework described earlier.

Most of the known scientific research on consciousness and conscious states of mind links consciousness with coherence (on a brain and/or body level). Lehrer et al (2003) report on a UCLA study of Buddhist monks meditating on generating compassionate love. This study exhibited increased coherence. Another study of Zen monks found that the more advanced monks tended to have coherent heart rhythms, while novices did not. Lutz et al (2004) report on a study of long-term Buddhist practitioners. They found that while the practitioners generated a state of "unconditional loving kindness and compassion", increases in gamma band oscillation and long-distance phase synchrony were observed. The authors suggest that this increased gamma band oscillation reflects a change in the quality of moment-to-moment awareness. The characteristic patterns of baseline activity of this group were found to be different from a control group. More research on consciousness, coherence and body impact can be found on, amongst others http://www.mindandlife.org/, and http://www.mum.edu/tm_research/welcome.html. Coherence on a body level – and I will discuss this further – seems to be a reasonable proxy for consciousness. Coherence, as we develop it here, is a concept that is measurable within a classical paradigm. Coherence is seen as an optimal psychophysiological state: a dynamic systems view of the interrelations between psychological, cognitive and emotional systems, and neural communication networks in the human organism. This is the definition of coherence that *HeartMath* has used to build their research tool (http://www.heartmath.org).

The feelings we experience as "negative" are indicative of body states in which "life processes struggle for balance and can even be chaotically out of control" (Damasio, 2003). By contrast, the feelings we experience as "positive" actually reflect body states in which "the regulation of life processes becomes efficient, or even optimal, free-flowing and easy" (Damasio, 2003). Research (Fredrickson, 2002; Isen, 1999) has shown that positive emotions and attitudes, beyond the fact that it makes you feel pleasant, have a number of objective, interrelated benefits for physiological, psychological and social functioning. Coherence is a particular quality that emerges from the connections between the parts of a system or from the connections among multiple systems. The latter is particularly what we would measure in the organizational analysis (using neural networks).

The HeartMath Institute has developed a theoretical framework and tool to visualize coherence inside the human brain/body system. Psychophysiology refers to the inter-connectedness of the physiological, cognitive and emotional systems, and human behavior. It is now evident that every thought, attitude and emotion has a physiological consequence. In more specific terms, they examine the natural fluctuations in heart rate, known as heart rate variability (HRV). HRV is a product of the dynamic interplay of many of the body's systems. Short-term (beat-to-beat) changes in heart rate are largely generated and amplified by the interaction between the heart and the brain.

Research on adults has documented a wide array of effects of positive emotions on cognitive processing, behavior, health and well-being. Positive emotions have been found to broaden the scope of perception, cognition and behavior (Fredrickson, 2001, 2005; Isen, 1999), thus enhancing faculties such as creativity (Isen, 1998) and intuition (Bolte, Goschke and Kuhl, 2003). Moreover, the experience of frequent positive emotions has been shown to predict resilience and psychological growth (Fredrickson, Tugade, Waugh and Larkin, 2003), while an impressive body of research has documented clear links between positive emotions, health status and longevity (Blakeslee and Grossarth-Maticek, 1996; Danner, Snowdon and Friesen, 2001; Medalie and Goldbourt, 1976; Moskovitz, 2003; Ostir, Markides, Black and Goodwin, 2000; Ostir, Markides, Peek and Goodwin, 2001; Russek and Schwartz, 1997; Seeman and Syme, 1987).

By contrast, research has shown that negative emotions such as frustration, anger, anxiety and worry lead to heart rhythm patterns that appear incoherent – highly variable and erratic (McCraty et al, 1995; Tiller et al, 1996).

When certain positive emotional states, such as appreciation, compassion, or love are intentionally maintained, coherent heart rhythm patterns can be sustained for longer periods, which also leads to increased synchronization and entrainment between multiple bodily systems. The HeartMath institute calls this *psychophysiological coherence* or *entrainment* (Tiller et al, 1996). Childre and Martin (1999) have developed a method for quantifying heart rhythm coherence.

In summary, psychophysiological coherence is a distinctive mode of function driven by sustained, modulated positive emotions. At the psychological level, the term coherence is used to denote the high degree of order, harmony and stability in mental and emotional processes that is experienced during this mode. Physiologically speaking, coherence is used here as a general term that encompasses entrainment, resonance, and synchronization – distinct but related phenomena, all of which emerge from the harmonious activity and interactions of the body's subsystems. Thus, the greater the degree of emotional stability and system-wide coherence, the greater the facilitation of cognitive and task performance. This hypothesis, tested extensively by the HeartMath Institute is called the *heart rhythm coherence hypothesis.*

A series of tools and techniques, collectively known as the HeartMath System, provide a systematic process that enables people to study and self-regulate emotional experience, and reliably visualize the psychophysiological coherence mode (Childre and Martin, 1999; Childre and Rozman, 2002, 2005; McCraty, 2003; McCraty and Childre, 2004; McCraty and Tomasio, 2006).

Coherence-building interventions have also been found to yield favorable outcomes in organizational, educational, and mental health settings (Arguelles et al, 2003; Barrios-Choplin et al, 1999; McCraty et al, 2001; McCraty et al, 1999; McCraty and Childre, 2004; McCraty and Tomasio, 2004).

2.4   Some practical implications

Some authors have compared organizations to neural networks (Khalfa, 1994; Caverni et al, 1991; Ehrlich et al 1993; Maturana and Varela, 1984). Maturana and Varela have observed in biological colonies that the colony reacts as a group, very much like a neural network (our brain) reacts. When a group is confronted with a problem, in parallel, different members of the group will be consulted, who in turn then consult other members. There is a great deal of cross consulting. Just as the brain has a learning capacity, biological colonies (companies) also show learning behavior. Consciousness is the outcome of a learning process of interacting "agents" which, in the case of a company, are the employees. Connectionist systems (like neural networks) are based on the assumption that knowledge and eventually consciousness are built dynamically. Understanding organizations as an interacting living network of individuals, out of which certain qualities like consciousness emerge, creates the necessary framework for studying emergent processes (like consciousness or coherence) in companies using artificial neural networks (Baets, 1998).

The link to a wider systems thinking approach of any research design or organizational design and, in particular, the systems qualities of neural networks, can be understood as follows. Complex living systems, such as human beings, are composed of numerous interconnected, dynamic networks of biological structures and processes. The recent application of systems thinking in the life sciences has given rise to the understanding that the function of the human organism as an integrated whole is determined by the multi-level interactions of all the elements of the psychophysiological system. The elements influence one another in a networked way, rather than through hierarchical or cause-to-effect relationships. Abundant evidence indicates that proper coordination and synchronization – i.e. coherent organization – among the different networks of any biological activity is critical for the emergence of higher-order functions.

The operationalization of a "first person" research concept of consciousness (or according to some other authors, a fifth dimension research concept of consciousness) needs to be developed further.

Literature review

Angelo J, The spiritual healing handbook: how to develop your healing powers and increase your spiritual awareness, Piatkus, 2007

Arguelles L, McCraty R and Rees R, "The heart in holistic education", Encounter: Education for Meaning and Social Justice, 16 (3), 13–21, 2003

Arthur B, "Positive Feedbacks in the economy", Scientific American, Feb 1990

Baars B, A cognitive theory of consciousness, Cambridge University Press, 1988

Baars B, In the theatre of consciousness, Oxford University Press, 1997

Baets W, "IT for organizational change: beyond business process engineering", Business Change and Re-engineering, Vol 1, Nr 2, 1993

Baets W, Organizational Learning and Knowledge Technologies in a Dynamic Environment, Kluwer Academic Publishers, 1998

Baets W, Complexity, Learning and Organizations: a quantum interpretation of business, Routledge, 2006

Baets W, "A-causality, consciousness and organisations", in Momo S, Consciousness & Development, Spandanews 4, 2008

Baets W and Oldenboom E, Rethinking growth: social intrapreneurship for sustainable performance, Palgrave, 2009

Bangcheng L and Zang Z, "The mediating effects of team efficiency on the relationship between a transactive memory system and team performance", Social behavior and personality, 38 (7); 865–870, 2010

Barrios-Choplin B, McCraty R and Cryer B, "An inner quality approach ot reducing stress and improving physical and emotional wellbeing at work", Stress Medicine, 13 (3), 193–201, 1997

Barrios-Choplin B, McCraty R, Sundram J and Atkinson M, "The effect of employee self-management training on personal and organizational quality" (Publication Nr 99–083), HearMath Research Center, Institute HeartMath, 1999

Baumann M and Bonner B, "The effects of expected group longevity and expected task difficulty on learning and recall: implications for the development of transactive memory", Group Dynamics: Research and Practice, Vol 15, Nr 3, 220–232, 2011

Benefiel M, Soul at work: spiritual leadership in organizations, Seabury Books, 2005

Blakeslee T and Grossarth-Maticek R, "Feelings of pleasure and well-being as predictors of health status 21 years later", retrieved from http://www.attitudefactor.com/PWItecharticle.htm, 1996

Blackmore S, Conversations on Consciousness, Oxford University Press, 2005

Block N, The nature of consciousness: Philosophical Debates, The MIT Press, 1997

Bogdanov I and Bogdanov G, Avant le Big Bang, Livre de Poche, 2006

Bolte A, Goschke T, and Kuhl J, "Emotions and intuition : Effects of positive and negative mood on implicit judgments of semantic coherence", Psychological Science, 14 (5), 416–421, 2003

Brown W and Ryan R, "The benefits of being present: Mindfulness and its role in psychological well-being", Journal of Personality and Social Psychology, Vol 84, Nr 4, 822–848, 2003

Burr D, "Experiments with a connectionist text reader", Proceedings of the First International Conference on Neural Networks, Caudill M and Butler C (Eds, Vol 4 pp 717–724, SOS Printing, 1987

Caverni JP, Bastien C, Mendelsohn P, Tigerghien G (Eds), Psychologie cognitive: Modeles et Methodes, Presses Universitaires de Grenoble, 1991

Chalmers D, "The two-dimensional argument against materialism", in McLaughlin B, Ed, Oxford Handbook of the Philosophy of Mind, Oxford University Press, 2009

Chalmers D, "How can we construct a science of consciousness?", in Gazzaniga M, Ed, The Cognitive Neurosciences III, MIT Press, 2004

Childre D and Martin H, The HeartMath Solution, Harper San Francisco, 1999

Childre D and Rozman D, Overcoming Emotional Chaos: Eliminate Anxiety, Lift Depression and Create Security in Your Life, Jodere Group, 2002

Childre D and Rozman D, Transforming stress: The HeartMath solution to relieving worry, fatigue, and tension, New Harbinger Publications, 2005

Chopra D, Quantum healing, Bantam books, 1996

Churchland Patricia, Neurophilosophy: Towards a Unified Science of Mind-Brain, MIT Press, 1986

Churchland Patricia, Brainwise: studies in neurophilosophy, MIT Press, 2002

Churchland Paul, Matter and Consciousness: a contemporary introduction to the philosophy of mind, MIT Press, 1984

Churchland Paul, The engine of reason: the seat of soul, MIT Press, 1996

Cottrell G, Munro P and Zipser D, "Image Compression by Backpropagation: an example of extensional programming", Advances in Cognitive Sciences, Vol 3, Ablex, 1987

Crick F, The astonishing hypothesis: the scientific search for the soul, Scribner, 1994

Damasio A, Looking for Spinoza: Joy, sorrow, and the feeling brain, Mariner, 2003

Danner D, Snowdon D and Friesen W, "Positive emotions in early life and longevity: Findings from the nun study", Journal of personality and social psychology, 80 (5), 804–813, 2001

Dennett D, The intentional stance, MIT Press, 1987

Dennett D, Consciousness explained, Back Bay Books, 1991

Dennett D, Darwin's Dangerous Idea: evolution and the meaning of life, Simon & Schuster, 1996

Dennett D, Freedom Evolves, Viking Adult, 2003

Dolan S, Garcia S, and Richley B, Managing by values: a corporate guide toliving, being alive and making a living in the 21th century, Palgrave, 2006

Ehrlich MF, Tardieu H, Cavazza M (Eds), Les Modeles Mentaux: Approche cognitive des representations, Masson, 1993

Fletcher and Goss, "Forecasting with neural networks", Information and Management, Vol 24, nr 3, March, pp 159–167, 1993

Frawley D, Ayurveda and the mind, the healing of consciousness, Lotus Press, 1997

Fredrickson B, "The role of positive emotions in positive psychology: The broaden-and-build theory of positive emotions", American Psychologist, 56 (3), 218–226, 2001

Fredrickson B, "Positive emotions", in Snyder C and Lopez S (Eds), Handbook of positive psychology (pp 120–134), Oxford University Press, 2002

Fredrickson B and Branigan C, "Positive emotions broaden the scope of attention and thought-action repertoires", Cognition and Emotion, 19 (3), 313–332, 2005

Fredrickson B, Tugade M, Waugh C and Larkin G, "What good are positive emotions in crises? A prospective study of resilience and emotions following the terrorist attacks on the United States on September 11th, 2001", Journal of Personality and Social Psychology, 84 (2), 365–376, 2003

Giacalone R and Jurkiewicz C (eds), Handbook of workplace spirituality and organizational performance, Sharpe, 2003

Hameroff S, Kaczniak A, Chalmers D (Eds), Towards a Science of Consciousness I, MIT Press/Bradford Books, 1996

Hameroff S, Kaczniak A, Chalmers D (Eds), Towards a Science of Consciousness II, MIT Press/Bradford Books, 1998

Hameroff S, Kaczniak A, Chalmers D (Eds), Towards a Science of Consciousness III, MIT Press/Bradford Books, 1999

Hay L, Heal your body, Hay House 1988

Ho M, The rainbow and the worm: The physics of organisms, World Scientific Publishing, 1998

Isen A, "On the relationship between affect and creative problem solving", in Russ S (Ed), Affect, creative experience, and psychological adjustment (pp 3–17), Brunner/Mazel, 1998

Isen A, "Positive affect", in Dalgleish T and Power M (Eds), Handbook of cognition and emotion, (pp 522–539), John Wiley & Sons, 1999

Khalfa J (ed), What is Intelligence, Cambridge University Press, 1994

Koch C, Biophysics of computation, Oxford University Press, 1999

Koch C, The Quest for Consciousness, Roberts & Company, 2003

Kofman F, Conscious business: how to build value through values, Sounds True, 2006

LaBerge S, Lucid dreaming, Ballantine Books, 1985

LaBerge S, Exploring the world of lucid dreaming, Ballantine Books, 1990

Lad V, Ayurveda: a practical guide: the science of self healing, Lotus Press, 1993

Lanza R (with Berman B), Biocentrism: how life and consciousness are the keys to understand the true nature of the universe, Benbella Books, 2009

Laszlo E, Grof S and Russell P, The consciousness revolution, Elf Rock, 2003

Lehrer P, Vaschillo B, Lu S, Eckberg D, Edelberg R, Hamer R, "Heart rate variability biofeedback increases barorefelx gain and peak expiratory flow", Psychosomatic Medicine, 65 (5), 796–805, 2003

Levinthal and Rarrup, "Crossing and apparent chasm: Briding mindful and less-mindful perspectives on organizational learning", Organization Science, 17(4), 503–514, 2006

Lipton B, The biology of belief: unleashing the power of consciousness, matter and miracles, Mountain of love, 2005

Lodewijk and Deng, "Experimentation with back-propagation neural networks", Information and Management, Vol 24, Nr 1, pp 1–8, 1993

Lutz A, Greischar L, Rawlings N, Ricard M and Davidson J, "Long term meditators self-induce high amplitude gamma synchrony during mental practice", Proceedings of the National Academy of Sciences USA, 101 (46), 16369–16373, 2004

Marques J, Dhiman S and King R, The workplace and spirituality: new perspectives on research and practice, Skylight Paths, 2009

Maturana H and Varela F, The tree of knowledge, The Biological Roots of Human Understanding, Scherz Verlag, 1984

McCaslin W, Justice as healing: indigenous ways, Living justice press, 2005

McCraty R, "Heart-brain neurodynamics: The making of emotions", (publication Nr 3-015), HearthMath Research Center

McCraty R, Atkinson M, Lipsenthal L and Arguelles L, "Impact of the power to change performance program on stress and health risks in correctional officers", (report Nr 3-014), HeartMath Research Center

McCraty R, Atkinson M, Tiller W, Rein G and Watkins A, "The effects of emotions on short-term heart rate variability using power spectrum analysis", American Journal of Cardiology, 76 (14), 1089–1093, 1995

McCraty R, Atkinson M, Tomasino D, "Science of the heart: Exploring the role of the heart in human performance", (publication 01–001), HeartMath Research Center, 2001

McCraty R, Atkinson M, Tomasino D, Goelitz J and Mayrovitz H, "The impact of an emotional self-management skills course on psychosocial functioning and autonomic recovery to stress in middle school children", Integrative Physiological and Behavioral Science, 34 (4), 246–268, 1999

McCraty R and Childre D, "The grateful heart: The psychophysiology of appreciation", in Emmons R and McCullough M (Eds), The psychology gratitude (pp 230–255), Oxford University Press, 2004

McCraty R and Tomasino D, "Emotional stress, positive emotions, and psychophysiological coherence", in Arnetz B and Ekman R (Eds), Stress in health and disease (pp 342–365), Wiley-VCH, 2006

McCraty R and Tomasino D, "The coherent heart: heart-brain interactions, psychophysiological coherence, and the emergence of system wide order, (publication Nr 06–022), HeartMath Research Center

McCraty R and Tomasino D, "Hearth rhythm coherence feedback: a new tool for stress reduction, rehabilitation, and performance enhancement", in Proceedings of the First Baltic Forum on Neuronal Regulation and Biofeedback, Riga, Latvia, Nov 2004

McTaggert L, The intention experiment: use your thoughts to change the world, Harper Element, 2008

Medalie J and Goldbourt U, "Angina pectoris among 10,000 men. II. Psychosocial and other risk factors as evidenced by a multivariate analysis of a five-year incidence study", American Journal of Medicine, 60 (6), 910–921, 1976

Metzinger T, Being no one, Bradford Books, 2003

Moskovitz J, "Positive affect predicts lower risk of AIDS mortality", Psychosomatic Medicine, 65 (4), 620–626, 2003

O'Regan K, Why red doesn't sound like a bell: understanding the feel of consciousness, Oxford University Press, 2011

Ostir G, Markides K, Black S and Goodwin J, "Emotional well-being predicts subsequent functional independence and survival", Journal of the American Geriatrics Society, 48 (5), 473–478, 2000

Ostir G, Markides K, Peek M and Goodwin J, "The association between emotional well-being and the incidence of stroke in older adults", Psychosomatic Medicine, 63 (2), 210–215, 2001

Parker D, "Learning logic", Intervention Report S81-64, File 1, Office of Technology Licensing, Stanford University, 1982

Penrose R, The Emperor's New Mind: Concerning Computers, Minds and the Laws of Physics, Oxford University Press, 2002

Polkinghorne J, The Quantum World, Penguin, 1990

Pribram K, Languages of the brain, Brandon House, 1971

Pribram K, Brain and perception: Holonomy and structure in figural processing, Lawrence Erlbaum Associates, 1991

Radin D, Entangled minds: extrasensory experiences in a quantum reality, Paraview Pocket Books, 2006

Radin D, The conscious universe: the scientific truth of psychic phenomena, HarperOne, 2009

Ramachadan V, Phantoms in the brain, Harper Perennial, 1998

Ramachadan V, A brief tour of human consciousness, Pi Press, 2004

Rosenberg M, Non-violent communication, Puddle Dancer Press, 2003

Rummelhart D and McClelland J, Parallel Distributed Processing: Exploration in the Microstructure of cognition, Vol 1 and 2, MIT Press, 1986

Scharmer O, Theory U, Society of Organizational Learning, 2007

Schlitz M, and Amorok T, Consciousness & healing: integral approaches to mind-body medicine, Elsevier Churchill Livingstone, 2005

Schlitz M, Vieten C and Amorok T, Living deeply: the art and science of transformation in everyday life, New Harbinger Publication, 2008

Searle J, The rediscovery of the mind, Bradford Books, 1992

Searle J, The mystery of consciousness, The New York Review of Books, 1997

Searle J, Mind: A brief introduction, Oxford University Press, 2004

Seeman T and Syme S, "Social networks and coronary artery disease: A comparison of the structure and function of social relations as predictors of disease", Psychosomatic Medicine, 49 (4), 341–354, 1987

Sejnowski T and Rosenberg C, "Parallel networks that learn to pronounce English text", Complex Systems, Vol 3, pp 145–168, 1987

Sheldrake R and Bohm D, "Morphogenetic fields and the implicate order", ReVision, 5:41–48, 1982

Simon D, Vital energy: the 7 keys to invigorate body, mind and soul, Wiley, 2001

Svoboda R, Ayurveda: Life, health and longevity, Ayurvedic press, 2004

Tiller W, McCraty R and Atkinson M, "Cardiac coherence: A new, noninvasive measure of autonomic nervous system order", Alternative Therapies in Health an Medicine, 2 (1), 52–65, 1996 research, 7, 140–150, 2006

Varela F, The embodied mind, MIT Press, 1992

Velmans M, Understanding consciousness, Routledge, 2000

Velmans M, How could consciousness experience affect brains, Imprint Academic, 2003

Venugopal V and Baets W, "Neural networks and statistical techniques in marketing research: a conceptual comparison", Marketing Intelligence and Planning, Vol 12, Nr 7, 1994

Wallace B, "The Bhuddhist tradition of Samatha: Methods for refining and examining consciousness", Journal of Consciousness Studies, 6 (2–3), 175–187, 1999

Weick K and Putnam T, "Organizing for Mindfulness: Eastern Wisdom and Western Knowledge", Journal of Management Inquiry, 15:275, 2006

Weick K and Roberts K, "Collective mind in organizations: Headful interrelating on flight decks", Administrative Science Quarterly, 38: 357–381, 1993

Weick K and Sutcliffe K, "Mindfulness and the quality of organizational attention", Organization Science, Vol 17, Nr 4, July-August, pp 514–524, 2006

Werbos P, Beyond Regression: New tools for prediction and analysis in the behavioral sciences, Masters thesis, Harvard University, 1974

Wilber K, A brief history of everything, Gateway, 2000

Literature review

Tollefsen D, "From extended mind to collective mind", Cognitive systems

3   Emergence in emerging markets (the mechanism)

Exploring an interconnected world, as we suggested in earlier chapters, immediately makes the link to biology and the lessons we can learn from biology. Ecosystems, life itself and nature are interesting models of interconnectedness. The interactions that take place between different elements (be it amoebas, cells, animals in a colony, the process of photosynthesis, etc.) on different levels of existence suggest some ideas to explore in order to improve our understanding of the interconnectedness between people in markets and companies. In this chapter, we consider some biological concepts that challenge the study of values-based leadership, and more broadly for human behavior within the context of groupings.

Does self-organization exist?

The answer to this question opens revolutionary possibilities for business. The relevant research for the answer comes from biology in general and neurobiology in particular. While Maturana and Varela are perhaps the best known representatives for the perceptual innovation known as self-organization or autopoiesis, the concept has been applied by several others in different domains and in different ways.

In their work, the two neurobiologists did not examine the systems from the perspective of genes or species, but from the simplest biological element, the amoeba. For them, the amoeba has a central role in each living being, and so Maturana and Varela studied how co-operation between these amoebas creates (complex) behavior. Each amoeba has individual autonomy at the center of a certain organism, and what appears to happen is that the living system basically functions in a mechanical fashion. In effect, the total behavior of the system is generated by its elements and their interaction. As a result, observers find themselves entirely outside the system, and therefore, perceive the unit as well as the environment. The elements of a system each react uniquely in interaction with other components. Each declaration of a living system cannot therefore be based on either the idea of the goal, the direction or the final function. In this layout the systems seem to be autopoietic, they are circular, self-productive, self-conservative but also self-referring.

Here we have a few points of reference to see how people collaborate in a company or an organization. Accept for a minute that the purpose of a company is to create value for the market, value that is not yet available in that market. That could be the vision, longer term perspective and focus of the company. However, a company cannot be anything other than a collaboration of a number of individuals who are trying to attain their own individual goals and who employ a certain number of rules of interaction. If that was the case then it is remarkable, for such a system creates its own order and self-maintains in a good state (like our bodies) on the condition that no artificial order is imposed (something we could call an organization). By contrast, scientific management does precisely that. We impose an organization which we will then control if the requisite results are to be attained. This might be a reason for corporate failure.

Questioning organizing and observing theories

At this stage we must develop our understanding of the process by asking key questions: What does autopoiesis need to be true? What conditions must be satisfied to produce this self-production and self-organization? The answers lie in the theory. All perceptions, observations and experiences occur via our body (our senses) and our nervous system. The body then plays the role of the medium of transport. Once in the system, therefore, it is impossible for human beings to have a pure description of anything that is independent of themselves. Each experience is always a reflection of the observer. There is no object outside the field of the observer; instead this observation belongs only to them.

What is therefore true in an autopoietic system and how can we face up to knowledge and truth? What does truth signify? Who supports autopoiesis in maintaining a system in a good state? The survival of the system becomes a key criterion for measuring knowledge and success. Each approach that aims to be scientific can only clearly describe what the observer sees. In effect, the observer plays a crucial role. The comparison with the external world makes no sense. Therefore, the methodology and the manner of leading our investigations are specific. They cannot be detached from the view of the observer. In a company situation, each truth can be just as precious, and just as important, as another. It is not certain that the manager has more reason or a better understanding than someone who is closer to the company process, or to the customer.

Consequences follow from this. Autopoiesis really says more about the observer than the subject (or should it be object) which is observed. In the case of autopoiesis, at least, that is clearly accepted but what about other scientific paradigms? An ulterior consequence is, of course, that any absolute claim of objectivity cannot be made, by whatever approach. All of this had already been confirmed by Gödel's theory. Both belief and theory are pure human constructions, which then construct a reality instead of being a reflection of an existing reality. For this reason we sometimes speak of a paradigm of radical constructivism. Remember constructivism? How we make meaning of things to create order from randomness and chaos, in order to make sense. Reality is created and not perceived. Constructivism as research paradigm is gaining increasing support in social science research, but is also subject to a lot more discussion in the classical sciences.

Theory in action: computers, law and linguistic animals

Self-productive ideas have been successfully applied in the construction of self-generating computer applications. The application manipulates itself to be in an optimal situation at all times; in this case we are talking about genetic software. A telephone switchboard, for example, must at any moment of the day deal with a volume of swiftly changing traffic. We can easily imagine making a program which takes into account the multitude of possibilities but, in practice, that appears rather difficult. We can develop a software program which manipulates itself in relation to specific volumes of traffic that the switchboard intercepts. We do not produce a program that resolves the specific problem, but rather a program which uses ideas of self-reproduction.

Without expressing a value judgment, this chapter observes the same processes elsewhere in practice. The legal system, for example, organizes itself in the best manner to assure its survival and the survival of its practitioners, rather than an expressed aim such as enabling justice. For that the system is going to reproduce itself and establish its own frame of reference. In order to make the legal system more efficient, a common language (the law) and a number of procedures are created. The professionals of the legal system – judges, lawyers, etc. who work within it, know the language and procedures. Common understanding and efficiency advances inside the legal system. But the citizens that are only seeking justice (and have no *a priori* interest in the survival of the system itself), don't understand the jargon and ceremonies around their – for them – very simple request. To outsiders, the insiders become extraterrestrials. To the insiders the outsiders don't understand the importance of the survival of the system.

We have already mentioned the idea of self-reference as a strong, but potentially destructive, idea. By analogy with the legal system we can regard each human being (a society, an organization, a meeting, etc.) as an autopoietic system.

People seem to be "linguistic animals" (and that refers to communication and interaction in a network) who do nothing other than play the game that could be called the "practice of artificial living". Human experience as an observer is not only crucial, but is more important than what really happens in the world. The role of language and communication is core. All understanding happens through language and its representation but, in addition, all communication with others in a network takes place through language.

The number of misunderstandings in the world, within the same group of languages, is symbolic in relation to this central aspect of interaction. Even in the center of the same group of languages, the Dutch and the Flemish, for instance, use the same words differently. Sentence structure is different which leads to the gathering of the same ideas in a different way. The network of ideas that a speaker tries to transmit is a function of the construction of sentences, even the sequence of sentences. But also, from the listener's side, how they make sense of the phrases determines the understanding of the message received. Communication is constituted by a network of agents (people) exchanging a network of thoughts with, perhaps, some hopes of being able to learn something, develop knowledge or get something done. In order to reach a real understanding of communication, we should not ignore common intention.

For facilitation of communication we create formal languages (a set of rules). These languages have the intention to standardize and therefore facilitate communication. However, they do not grasp the common intention and by formalizing the exchange of ideas, they sometimes obscure common intention. Children who communicate between themselves in different languages, without speaking those languages, may consequently make far fewer mistakes in the formal language and seem able to conceptualize more rapidly.

It seems evident that the messages children want to transmit are easier than those politicians wish to transmit. Here too, we immediately fall into the positivist trap: if we can measure, then we can know. But it would now seem that communication is not at all organized in the same way as thoughts are.

Is non-verbal communication not equally efficient and less structured?

Does the extreme order help the process of communication, compared to a higher intensity of communication? If everyone in a Spanish café seems to be talking at the same time, and no-one seems to be listening, is the communication less significant and less precious? Do similar interlocutions lead to not-so-good decisions? Do we always have the intention of rational exchange, or do we use language for emotional connection? And would the latter be less value adding in communication? An example of disordered but effective communication is "open comms" in a live television broadcast which could, to an outsider, appear to be complete chaos. However, this communication is perfectly ordered to the insider where, being able to communicate to everyone from camera operators, sound technicians, commentators, and a host of technical operators, is vital to the success of the production. It is a highly ordered chaos focused on a very definite outcome – delivering the live sports event with most relevant sights and sound to the viewer.

Cognitive connections and artificial intelligence

Contemporary cognitive psychology seems to illustrate a good number of these ideas. A great deal of research is done around language and interlocution, showing that language and action are tightly linked. Language is our "existence in the world". Language is really the entire thinking of humans. Even on the subject of language, we *think* about language, *using* language (a good example of self-referencing). Knowledge is not linguistic representation because it is possible to distinguish between different things beyond language. Language is, in fact, a social act. Organizations are therefore networks of recurrent interlocution constructed between individuals and groups of individuals. This thinking has parallels with a certain re-orientation in the developments in artificial intelligence.

The reigning paradigm of objective observation and the associated possibility of drawing up optimum rules, led to the research of "machines based on rules" in expert systems. The assumption is that all decision processes can be captured in rules. While these expert systems have known moderate success, the achievement of the objectivist orientation of artificial intelligence has certainly been over-estimated. Current developments lead in two rather different directions. One goes in the direction of research, which can be regarded as the search for self-learning behavior of systems (emergent behavior), and makes use of connective structures. This development is seen in artificial intelligence in particular. The connective structures are structures where many simple tightly-connected elements and communication make sense out of chaos. In practice, this involves such techniques as neural networks or networks of agents.

The second direction in current research also builds on the self-learning behavior of systems. In this case, it is perhaps better translated as constructing behavior, based on "enacted" technologies. "Enaction" here refers to what Varela calls "enacted cognition" as an actor "enacts" a theatre play. An amateur asked to play the role of Hamlet might try but would be unlikely to achieve a satisfying theatrical outcome. If an actor is asked to play Hamlet, he does not 'play' Hamlet, he becomes Hamlet. Each evening he re-creates another Hamlet. Maybe the two find each other in the character of Shakespeare. A manager can no longer 'play' the role of manager. A manager can simply 'enact' his role. He 'is' his role and it is therefore very difficult to learn this 'behavior'. You become a manager by experience. You cannot teach someone to become a manager and, as will be argued later, something which is based on skills and competence cannot be taught anyway.

Developing knowledge: pathways, platforms, communities

For this reason, the personal development path of a manager is so crucial. Only a "learning" manager will be up to playing the role of the spider in the web, the inspirer and creator of good conditions for others. The manager must and should strive for continuously improving himself in this task. Operations or instruments only have a very limited utility and can never play a driving role in dynamic situations. Worse still, they can therefore never have a general validity.

The vision is the glue that keeps the network together; a kind of weak force that gives basic stability to the network and prevents the network from disintegrating. The absence of this glue or vision will remove that basic centrifugal force. It is this vision, this glue should be values-oriented if we wish to move towards values-based leadership.

Knowledge is only knowledge if it offers a reasonable representation of action and creation. Otherwise it is only possible to speak of information. In this case therefore, the use and the analysis of communication (conversations), as well as a strong focus on the support of communication (by platforms, for example) only gives the context within which the actors create knowledge. To illustrate: the "communities of practice" experiment carried out by numerous companies, seem to conform well to this preoccupation. That experiment was not uniquely led by artificial intelligence.

Nevertheless, the interest in dynamic re-creation in two directions appears in artificial intelligence research. Things are not fixed, but are produced afresh each time. If someone is asked their age, the information is not stored somewhere particular in the brain. Each time the question is asked, the person is going to produce the reply again. This seems inefficient from the point of view of a recurrent question, but it is, in fact, the case. On the other hand, a question is rarely truly repetitive, even if it is asked using the same words, since in the majority of cases it is looking for another signification. The intonation, for example, is often a clue to the question and the expected answer.

This dynamic reproduction as an approach therefore leaves open the possibility to reply very quickly (and differently) to similar or slightly changed questions. For an authentic, real-time conversation this principle is therefore a lot better and more efficient. Furthermore, if the brain would need to store all possible information in order to be able to answer all possible questions, it would need significantly more storage capacity (and hence a larger head to accommodate that). From a rational and positivist view of the conversation, this seems an aberration and an error of thinking. Language in general plays an important role in this research. The research methods themselves are more self-learning. The general validity of the observations is less declared; something which is done more quickly in classical science.

Contemporary theories of artificial intelligence regarding how to think about the subject of reasoning, offer a different attitude. They take more distance from earlier, rather positivist approaches. Possible interaction between reason and the soul are looked for, which was unthinkable before in cognitive psychology. Reason (intelligence) is considered a behavior: behavior is what counts. The link between the brain and reason (intelligence) is broken: reason is not only present in the brain but in the whole body (distributed intelligence). We are referring here to the concept of "embodied mind". Reason, the brain and intelligence are considered less and less to be like a computer, which refers to the thinking of the machine behind reasoning. The interpretation, which is generally always vigorous becomes, in effect, more and more based on shifting sands.

Intelligence is strong in the organization of "the next step". It is weaker in the planning of a number of next steps (multiple) and weaker still in the execution of subsequent multiple steps. Intelligence is the organ of control for an autonomous agent. The structure was formed in a descending manner or by a combination of various elements. A common example of a combination occurs when different people sit around a table. The result is in effect, a structure built up by a network of different elements (people).

In addition, intelligence is something continuous and not only a sort of metaphor for a machine which functions with zeros and ones. Intelligence does not function with numbers and symbols but with vague notions like tall, taller, smaller etc. Intelligence reacts to these sensations, which can be translated into sensorial perceptions. Then all of that is translated into information. It is not the action on the senses themselves which creates information, but the liaison of a specific perception with the existing network of perceptions, and information. Sensorial perception, action and knowledge go together and that is summarized in the notion of "enacted cognition".

Biology lessons and enacted cognition

Self-organization and self-production are concepts which are strongly embedded in neurobiology; concepts which, when translated into social systems, receive more and more attention but which are radically different from the tradition of western management. In this tradition, everything must be organized and controlled, based on whichever intellectual tradition it is inspired by. But, in practice, that does not work and can lead to frustration.

Through Varela's concept of enacted cognition, it is possible to see how intelligence re-combines old information and experience to produce new actions. Intelligence is positioned in a diffuse way in the whole body, but it seems that, even if the modules are independent, they collaborate through connections between each other. These notions undermine what is used most of the time as a basis for our management, especially specifically concerning structure and control. In particular, it raises one crucial question: can a social system be organized from outside?

From enquiries into the behavior of autopoietic systems, the answer seems to be no. Instead, it appears that each system, even if examined from the simplest components, can only organize itself, replicate itself and assure its own survival. Although this could be taken as negative at first glance, it represents an undeniable strength. Systems do not necessarily need a tight direction with a lot of complicated rules, at least if we dare to give back the control and the direction to the system itself. Therefore, the shocking conclusion for traditional management is that intervening in such a system should probably be avoided.

Just as people are often not aware of the self-organization within themselves, management of large companies are largely not aware of the self-organization within the company. Many subsequent re-organizations directed from "outside" or "above" into traditional organizations actually risk destroying the very organizational fabric that has allowed it to operate as an integrated whole. However, careful experiments in certain companies seem to indicate how more self-organized management could succeed.

In practice, how can this relate to knowledge management? Or to put it in more specific terms: how might knowledge be organized in a "self-searching" and preferably self-finding way (as opposed to the branch structure implemented in very large databases)? Groups responsible for the conception of new products seem to be more creative and efficient if they have more liberty. This is not to claim that nothing can be learned from the past with regard to successes and errors, on the contrary. However, the difference is that the lessons learned from previous experience are not translated into typical outcomes such as the "ten commandments of innovation". Instead, they are used rather like stories from which, according to individual interests, advantages can be extracted.

The gift of learning and learning to walk

The potential of learning, in itself, in companies is an interesting gift. More and more companies try to provide a more flexible range of training and support better linked to the profiles of particular individual roles. They seek to provide "just-in-time, just-enough" learning, based on the development of necessary managerial competencies. Other research, including our own (Baets, 2005), has illustrated that workplace learning is a very effective and efficient way of continuous learning. This is particularly marked if it is related to the development of managerial competencies. E-learning by itself (without speaking of classical e-teaching or of distance or correspondence learning), is a promising development through which a manager, while doing her or his job, is supported by the learning environment. To those who want to learn, it will offer potentially effective support, adapted to their needs. Such situations also abolish the classical teacher role, which is designed to transmit to classes of pupils how the real world is (or should be). Those who want to learn find what they want and need to learn, and then learn by doing (and therefore learning). All these developments are promising, on condition that the organization has the courage to relax control at all levels.

This does not translate into saying that everyone just does anything they want, and then see what happens. Let's use Alice in Wonderland as an example. If, effectively, employees do not know where they or their organization wants to go, then each path is equally relevant and good decision-making is difficult. Nor can organizations be too rigid with direction as in western management's tendency to make the paths to follow fixed. That leads to problems when these paths change – as they quickly do in current conditions of rapid change – and organizations forget the need to adapt and change themselves, because they concentrate on the destination to reach instead of the path to follow.

Alice's choice was made impossible because she didn't have a final destination. And that is what values are in a company. Values-based leadership is based on the values that a company would like to reach. We will talk a bit more about values in a later chapter. But the role of values is not to replace profit, or even shareholder value in business management. The role of values is to be the lighthouse, the desired destination not just for the company, but for each and every employee of that company. Values as the lighthouse add a dimension to business management that we just don't have today. And in the absence of those values as a longer term, sustainable purpose we are almost bound to rely on short term goals, like profit and shareholder value. If there is no longer term perspective, we can only manage the short term. If, however, we are able to agree about the values driving our business, they become the lighthouse for the mechanism of emergence, as described in this chapter.

From an autopoietic perspective, the path that leads towards the goal will be created by walking it, in the network of employees. As Antonio Machado says: *Caminanto, no hay camino, se hace camino al andar* (Wanderer, there is no path, the path is made by walking). In many cases it requires the hacking of bushes and branches to form the desired path. The path is also forged through the negotiation of obstacles such as large boulders, streams or cliffs. Management, or organizational strategy, must be concentrated on the goal to reach and then to share ideas with the network of employees. In practice, that does not often happen. Strategy is often considered a secret and so employees cannot even help management to attain the goal. Alternatively, the strategy often appears to be short term oriented. The agents in the network each have their own preferences and capabilities. In the interaction with other elements of the network they can walk on the path leading to the goal by different small steps. If the goal is clear and realistic, the path could be adapted each time it is necessary, and sometimes this could be very often. Knowing the goal, employees can take individual responsibility in contributing to this network of walking paths.

The search for an underlying theory (1): chaos and order

As already noted, certain contemporary disciplines challenge the tradition of western management and its propensity to organize and control. Another understanding of the functioning of social systems is possible and can give us other ideas for management if we are able to observe from another paradigm. Is there therefore a paradigm which is scientific (based on scientific discovery) and which provides a vision of social self-organization?

In seeking to ground this vision theoretically, this book found inspiration in what is known as the theory of complexity and/or chaos. Scientists starting effectively from a positivist paradigm, but with an open-mindedness which lets them truly see, have made remarkable observations. A number of them, for example Prigogine, have received the Nobel prize for their research but very often their knowledge remains essentially within their own circle of researchers in hard sciences. Only during the last few decades have we gradually seen what their theories, especially their application, can mean for social systems. This aspect orients us towards "the search for an underlying theory".

Look at the chaos of daily life, a point of common contact where writers and readers can supposedly agree. But how does it work? Chaos is clearly present at times, but fortunately we also regularly have order. Certain things often play out in a well-organized way. The administration is organized, the trains are well organized and planes leave more or less on time. Isn't that order? And how does chaos play a role in that? Is there a theory of chaos? As we have already stated, positivism goes perfectly with the Cartesian attitude. It is, however, in the positivist sciences that the first doubts emerged. As early as 1903, Poincaré made a remarkable observation.

> *"Sometimes small differences in initial conditions produce very large differences in the final observations. A minor change in the former can cause a tremendous error in the latter. The phenomenon is becoming unpredictable; we have random phenomena."*

He could not prove it, but he could clearly see remarkable things happening. During the simulation of certain mathematical models, it was discovered that when very small differences in the initial values appear, big differences could be found in the final results. Poincaré could not explain the cause. Nor did he appear to have the least idea that he was making an observation which would later lead to what became known as the theory of chaos and complexity. It should also be remembered that Poincaré did not have computers at his disposal to experiment rapidly with all sorts of simulations.

It was not until 1964 that Lorenz, an American meteorologist, discovered and identified the problem with supporting data. In between these dates, in 1931, Gödel's theory had sowed confusion by proving that any axiomatic system, let us say a mathematical system of variables and equations, would one day not be up to accepting or rejecting all possible statements. Therefore, there could be no unique perfect model of the world. This discovery was much more than a huge question mark, and represented a new turning point for mathematicians. Mandelbrot's fractal algebra is just one of these new orientations. But Gödel's theory, while adding to its significance, does not give a response to Poincaré's problem.

Lorenz, however, did add clarity. As a meteorologist he worked with a simple system of three dynamic non-linear equations. Dynamic means, for example, that today's temperature is a function of yesterday's. Non-linear means that somewhere there is a variable with an exhibitor. With his system, Lorenz tried to predict the weather. He made a number of observations and simulations on this subject. Lorenz had a computer, which was not common in 1964, and thanks to this computer, Lorenz could clarify what Poincaré had suspected. The use of computers became indispensable to be able to do sufficiently large simulations.

During these simulations Lorenz had to interrupt his research. Since computers did not have screens at the time, they produced a mountain of paper which had to be analyzed. When he wanted to pick up the simulation later, he wanted to use the last value the computer had produced as the initial value of the rest of the simulation. He had, as a good scientist, certain doubt about the wisdom of such an approach. Therefore, instead of taking the last value, he took the result of the previous 100 observations and started the simulation with that value.

During this new simulation of the hundred last steps, he wanted to be sure that everything went as well as previously before going any further. To his great surprise Lorenz discovered something scary. Nothing went as expected. In the first period, he saw little differences appearing, but they were not always the same. They were rather arbitrary. Although the range of discrepancies was at first quite limited, the same values were a bit random. The biggest and smallest values alternated in a previously unknown pattern. But while the simulation continued, he observed some remarkable occurrences. The new simulation seemed to suddenly react in a strange way. The values showed huge differences in the two directions and the differences between the first and the second simulation became bigger than the values simulated. Therefore, these values became incoherent. The whole exercise became totally futile.

Lorenz had hit on what might be described as "the bug of unpredictability". In certain systems it seems impossible to predict. From a certain moment, and we do not really know when that moment is, the system becomes entirely incomprehensible; it displays "chaos". Therefore a prediction can work very well for a certain period, and then suddenly, and seemingly unpredictably, become completely useless.

What happened? Lorenz had certainly entered the correct number. But although he had used the correct number printed on the list, it was not really the same number. It was a rounded figure, compared to the one the computer had used in the first series of calculations. It calculated, for example, with precision up to 16 figures, but only printed 8. Therefore the number with 8 digits after the decimal point was slightly different from the true figure. In real life, calculations are often done with rounded figures, rather than with the precise number, which may include several figures after the decimal point.

It appeared to be a question of non-linearity and of the dynamic characteristics of the system, and so, just like that, Poincaré's worry had a name. Dynamic and non-linear systems cause, by their very structure, unpredictability. A complex system is hereby defined as a non-linear dynamic system.

The search for an underlying theory (2): management paradox

Companies' management constantly confront complex or, in other words, non-linear and dynamic, systems. Is there a phenomenon in management for which the current value will not be dependent on yesterday's value? The current value is, in part, always a function of yesterday's value. The level of this year's salaries is without a doubt a function of the previous year's levels. The market share which you can achieve today is without a doubt a function of the market share achieved the previous month. The phenomena of management are therefore, in consequence, dynamic until proven to the contrary.

In addition, each management phenomenon is not only dynamic but also non-linear, except for the processes which are constructed to be linear, such as production lines. Such processes have been built specifically to do specific tasks in a way that can be checked and controlled. However, even in such carefully planned and created processes, examples abound of control going off the rails (in nuclear plants, for instance). Even in such constructed environments, most of the interesting phenomena, the phenomena that involve people, are non-linear. Market behavior, competitors' behavior, employee collaboration in their daily work and the processes of decision-taking through dialogue, etc. are non-linear and dynamic and, therefore, essentially unpredictable and uncontrollable.

So, a paradox of management is the attempt to direct and control something which cannot be controlled and directed. That would not be so terrible if its failures were unsurprising. In fact, it is impossible for management to guarantee success (in markets and/or dynamic companies) through control and prediction. Consequently, it is called into question as a way of facing up to such dynamic systems. What can a manager's role be if everything is unpredictable and uncontrollable? In essence this is the main question of this chapter: what can a manager do if no control approach works?

One possible response is to adopt a learning approach. The cause of chaos, which intervenes in a system for the same reason as order, is the very characteristic of a dynamic system. The system does not have a problem with that. It does not have a problem containing order as well as chaos, sometimes demonstrating order, sometimes chaos. It is human beings who have a conceptual problem with trying to consider systems as organized entities which are therefore manageable, and who have ongoing practical problems in trying to deal with a complex system with control and prediction mechanisms. In practice, the phenomenon emerges though trying to reach understanding through models. It happens when a manager uses models (even simple ones), or rules of thumb. Those simple models are often linear and non-dynamic, and they cannot deal with the simultaneous presence of order and chaos in a system. Certain mental models of managers, like automatic pilot behavior, are naturally also models.

The phenomena studied in management are continuous and not discontinuous – they constantly change and never stop. But what measurements can be taken? As precisely as possible this should always be a point of discontinuous measurement. We therefore continually approach societal processes which are themselves continuous (market behavior, buying behavior, human interaction) with variables and decisions based on discontinuous measurement. The point of measurement (of observation) is never really correct. Using the phenomenon Lorenz revealed, which we could call "the dependence of initial values", we know that, since the observation is never correct, the simulation is going to produce chaos.

But there is still something else. In practice, we cannot approach a reality which is by definition continuous (e.g., market behavior), other than by a discontinuous approach. In other words, although managers may try to do the maximum and to be precise, observation and data can never be correct. In managerial applications there is no immunity from the virus of unpredictability. Accordingly, the approach advocated by this book aims, to an extent, to incorporate this virus in the model. Any systematic approach will always demonstrate order at certain moments and complete chaos at others.

Characteristics of complex systems: learning from Lorenz's butterfly

At this stage, having established that these observations are not only scientifically important, but also, and especially, that they have consequences for companies (and also for social life, politics, law, etc.), the rest of this chapter looks at what we can learn from the theory of complexity. This theory is not new, but in the management of companies or other general social sciences it is still growing and relatively recent.

This is why it is important to revisit key figures. Through his research, Lorenz, for example, shed more light on what Poincaré had suggested and offered a little more comprehension of the behavior of complex systems. Lorenz captured the dependency on the initial values: little differences in the initial values led to big differences in the subsequent sequence of events. But Lorenz found yet another characteristic of complex systems. Apparently, complex systems can also demonstrate moments of relative calm (stability) in the midst of chaos. Sometimes the simulations revolve around points of attraction, let us say points or fields of local stability, then suddenly change and orient themselves towards a more chaotic sequence of events, then calm down again around another point of stability. This is similar to a magnet placed under a sheet of iron filings, ordering the filings in semi-circles around the magnetic poles. We call these points of local stability "attractors", even "strange attractors", since we do not know when, how or with what strength they attract the phenomenon. Certain complex systems have only two attractors but some other systems have a much higher number of attractors.

The name of Lorenz remains linked to a very remarkable phenomenon in respect to weather forecast systems. In one simple simulation (three equations with three unknowns), Lorenz observed that the phenomenon being studied centered around two attractors. The phenomenon moved around the first attractor one moment and suddenly whizzed off to then settle itself around the second attractor. Next, the phenomenon moved back suddenly to the first and then again towards the second. In fact, in doing that, the phenomenon created a sort of butterfly-shape. This therefore became known as Lorenz's Butterfly after his 1972 paper title "Does the Flap of a Butterfly's Wings in Brazil Set Off a Tornado in Texas?" (cited in Lorenz, 1993, p. 14) It would be comforting to be able to say that such speculations are impossible; that they do not make any sense. In theory, however unsettling, it is possible as simulations show, and practice has, so far, never been able to prove the contrary.

In fact, to the regret of the formidable progress of science, weather is still totally unpredictable more than a few days in advance. So why should it still be necessary to again emphasize that this is also the case in management? Consider the stock market. Do expert analysts know why the stocks do what they do? Is there one person who can do better than the "random walk" in anything other than the short term? Could it be true that the lack of understanding of stock market behavior has a relationship with the manner in which we approach it, and, therefore, with the perceptual glasses used to observe it?

In the 1960s and 1970s we considered the Soviet Union to be the boogeyman which allowed the examination of the world with a certain perspective, a certain pair of glasses. These glasses are not necessarily correct but they perceived what they perceived. However this is also not necessarily true. After the Berlin Wall fell the military and economic power of the Soviet Union could actually be observed. The representation of the Soviet Union as the great danger for the world and development has come to be, at least in retrospect, a little unjustified. In the meantime, this vision served all sorts of goals and justified massive investments in, for example, the arms industry and the defense sector. This, of course, happened to the detriment of other possible expenditure. The point of departure chosen will justify our action. By choosing the glasses, the field of vision is restricted to them or by them.

After the fall of the Berlin Wall, another pair of glasses was required. In the meantime perhaps another pair focused almost exclusively on Muslim fundamentalism. It is a lot simpler to consider the world in terms of huge aggregates, like the free West, the communist world (although now it is a lot smaller), the Islamic world, the problem states (Iraq, Iran, etc.). However, what if the world is just a game played by a collection of individuals, organized or not, in groups at a local level; groups which are linked in various networks where each individual (or group) can continue to live life in the best possible way, with a minimum of rules of behavior? Perhaps the search for theoretical understanding takes place at a too-elevated level of aggregation? The theory of complexity, and notably the work of John Holland on agent-based simulations, provides contrasting points of reference that open other fields of vision.

Characteristics of complex systems: Prigogine, Liquids and Time

Up to this point, two characteristics of a complex system have been identified: it is strongly dependent on initial values and it displays local stable moments around what we call "strange attractors". These can be extended by the ideas of a man who is closely linked with the theory of complexity: Ilya Prigogine, a Belgian Nobel Prize laureate, and professor emeritus of the Faculty of Science at the University of Brussels (ULB). His research was oriented around the dynamics of liquids (fluid dynamics). At first glance, these theories are a long way from managerial thinking. In fact, Prigogine's research on the behavior of liquids during the process of heating discovered dynamic characteristics of liquids in this phase, which in turn led to remarkable conclusions of wider relevance.

Prigogine's best known conclusion, and the most important for the study of complexity, is the principle of the "irreversibility of time". In short, he showed that the future cannot be extrapolated from the past, at least in dynamic systems. The reason is that a dynamic system re-creates itself all the time and can branch off at any moment. A dynamic system develops in a non-linear way and thereby obscures its historic development. It makes reference to the concept of the constructive role of time, what he calls "the arrow of time". Time plays a constructive role in dynamic processes. Over time, or rather as time gradually moves on, something new happens in liquids, something with new characteristics; the initial characteristics are never found again if we stop the heating (or if we cool it down). For example, once a cake is baked it will never again return to being dough. Coffee, once made, will never go back to being granules and water, but it will also again change taste when it is reheated a second time. In the heating process, liquid takes on other irreversible characteristics. Time plays a constructive role. Time contributes to a new creation.

Despite the two great scientific revolutions, the Theory of Relativity and Quantum Theory, most of the thinking in physics is still Newtonian: the space-time couple is seen as a fixed one. In Newtonian thinking, time is reversible and so the future can be predicted from the past and also vice versa, in theory. In fact, the past can be predicted from the future and, therefore, past and future are immutably and deterministically linked. In practice, that is not naturally the case in companies. In fact, no-one has ever succeeded in predicting a market potential, market shares or future relationships between competitors. The financial markets are the most eloquent examples of this failure but, for any dynamic market, it is equally impossible to forecast other than in the short term. The more dynamic a market, the more difficult the forecasting because, in this case, time plays a "more" constructive role.

That does not mean that the past is totally insignificant. The past, and more particularly the experiences of the past, are the raw material for human learning. But the past does not let us predict the future at all (other than in the very short term or in stable situations where forecasts are therefore useless). The characteristics of a liquid, according to Prigogine, are created anew each time. These characteristics are a type of knowledge and consequently knowledge is created anew each time. It is not enough to mix powdered coffee with water to obtain coffee. We have to go through a process using a coffee machine and, in the course of this process, the qualities of coffee are introduced by the dynamic behavior of the system in question.

After Gödel's observations, the principle of the irreversibility of time is the second important phenomenon in the thinking around complexity.

Prigogine also investigated the behavior of systems far from their balance point, far from equilibrium, in comparison with systems close to equilibrium. By way of comparison, and this is in opposition to classical economic thinking, a system in balance is a totally uninteresting system. If it contains all information, it is dead and can therefore not be moved from its balance. In the theory of information, it can be said that the system understands all the information, or contains all information. There is nothing else to add. A society (or company) in balance is therefore a dead society and it is extremely difficult to revive it or innovate. Therefore, a system is interesting if it is not in balance. It is the same thing for a company. Nevertheless, there is also a difference between a system close to equilibrium in comparison with one which is further away.

Prigogine introduced the notion of entropy and the production of entropy. Entropy is an indication of the *amount* of chaos in a system (how much uncertainty exists). A system where entropy is equal to zero is dead and in a balanced position. A system far from balance has a high level of entropy. Prigogine observed that systems far from equilibrium are more interesting because, in this state, many things happen. It is not, strictly speaking, a question of entropy, but rather the production of entropy, the progression (or diminishing) of entropy. This is important to bear in mind, but, for the purposes of this book, there is no need to go further on this point or the detail of Prigogine's work.

Characteristics of complex systems: Holland, the game of life and fitness

How does this apply to management? Well, in mature markets for example, increasing market share is a lot more difficult to acquire than in emerging markets. In dynamic markets (chaotic markets) such as in emerging markets, market share is won more easily simply because the entropy of these markets is higher. Of course, it is also possible to fall a long way, but this is essentially the risk the entrepreneur takes: those who take risks will be rewarded (won't they?). Companies are therefore theoretically encouraged to actively look for markets with higher entropy (i.e. rather chaotic markets). In practice that goes against the thinking which controls and dominates current management behavior. The current preference is to choose the long and rather difficult path of a more stable (and expensive) approach to win market share. The tendency to control everything in management aligns with that thinking. "Controlled growth" with a "calculated risk" typifies the contemporary credo but runs the risk of neglecting market characteristics. In practice, as the subprime mortgage market has only too graphically illustrated, that often does not turn out as expected.

Shifting to discuss new products and new markets, the innovatory force of a company is immediately invoked. Innovation does not go well with a stable company and a culture of strong control. To explore new possibilities necessitates a rather chaotic company culture, a culture with a great deal of entropy, a culture where one can learn and fail. To limit innovation by detailed and defined procedures (as is often the case in practice) becomes a contradiction in terms: the so-called "management" of innovation. To develop beyond this requires introducing new ideas.

Besides the ideas of Varela and those of Prigogine, another major current of ideas related to the theory of complexity is linked to the name of John Holland, the father of genetic algorithms. Indeed, Holland's theories, along with those of Prigogine, are accepted by the majority of people in the Anglo-Saxon world as **the** theory of complexity (although the development of genetic algorithms cannot be seen disconnected from the research of "artificial life", which is closely connected to Chris Langton's work). The research on artificial life highlighted remarkable characteristics of systems, notably the functioning of so-called complex systems on the basis of a number of simple rules. It is possible that a system with simple agents (say people) in which everyone follows their own simple goal (to survive, to add value to society or to do a meaningful job) and where everyone follows rules of simple interaction, produces complex behavior.

Take two simple examples: the flight of birds and the game of soccer. In general, observing birds in flight in a V formation gives the impression of them being well organized. However, the individual behavior of the birds is not very organized. It can be reduced to simple rules such as birds not losing sight of each other while not touching each other. Trying to write a program to simulate this process, based on reductionist ideas and an associated procedural approach, will never succeed. The birds' behavior can never be understood at a sufficiently detailed level. On the other hand, it is perfectly possible to simulate a flight in V formation with the following two rules:

Always keep a distance between 15 and 25cm (6 to 9 inches) from each other. If a bird wants to move away, it can do so until it reaches the 25cm (9 inch) limit when it risks "losing" its neighbor. The 25cm rule links this bird with its neighbor. When the birds risk touching each other, the 15cm rule maintains a sufficient distance between them. We can immediately see the movement in waves of the entire flight. When a flight approaches a post, firstly the 15cm rule keeps the bird at a sufficient distance and pushes it around the post. The 25cm rule prevents them from flying off into the distance. At the other side of the post, the 15cm rule again prevents them colliding and the flight continues on the other side.

The game of soccer has precisely the same qualities. Because it is impossible to understand footballers' dynamic decisions, programming classically, in terms of procedural thinking, does not provide any solution. Once again a few simple rules can provide the solution. They all want to win, remembering that there are therefore 22 players with the same aim – to score a goal. A few simple rules of interaction are determined between them, for example, not to play the ball with your hand – except if you're the goal keeper – not to kick each other, etc. These rules are identical for all 22 players, except there is one difference. Eleven players play in one direction while the other eleven in the opposite direction. What happens now is that these 22 co-operating agents can develop a very complex game, while each one of them has a simple aim (in this case, to score a goal), on the basis of a few simple rules of interaction. This has made football the world's most popular sport.

The coach does not determine the rules or how someone must play. The coach transmits his understanding of the game and shares his experience, after which the players themselves must act.

In a company, the values orientation of the company is what should be the shared goal. People should interact with each other, work together and serve the customers based on a very limited set of simple rules (respect for each other, weekly reporting, etc.). Each employee is an autonomous agent, taking responsibility for her or his behavior (and being accountable for it). The manager is the coach, sharing his or her experience, and motivating the players, the employees, to the best of their potential.

Those same mechanisms can be seen in genetic software, genetic algorithms or "artificial life". It appears that a given network of agents (entities, software, people, etc.) with a certain aim in mind and with a few simple rules of interaction is capable of very complex acts. It is the underlying principle of agent simulations, a development in artificial intelligence for which Holland is in part responsible. These (artificial) agents appear to be able to learn by themselves and to produce behavior which is adapted and geared to learning, like the footballer who gradually acquires experience during his training and playing against different opponents. Accordingly, such a system based on simple rules of "fitness" (i.e., geared to Darwinian notions of the survival of the fittest) can demonstrate a capacity for learning and for solving complex problems. Agents' systems are therefore an imitation of methods of organization noticed in human "colonies" (football players, companies, employees, etc.). The search for rules of decision-making becomes useless. Determining objectives for each individual, linked with rules of interaction, seems to produce the work required.

Two important developments stem from this: genetic software programs as well as genetic algorithms. A genetic software program is software which self-regulates in a way that optimizes the execution of the task in relation to the environment at a given moment. The software of a call center which genetically self-regulates to be able to manipulate the flow of continually changing communication is one example. Another interesting development is the use of genetic algorithms: algorithms which genetically manipulate chains of 0s and 1s to provide a multitude of possible solutions. The different possibilities are compared on the basis of their "strength" (fitness). By constantly manipulating the information and keeping the better solutions, the best solution can finally be found. This system is remarkable in its simplicity and strong in its capacity to resolve complex problems.

The bases of these developments, and the interesting applications which stem from them, have implications. They imply that, where the hierarchical and organized structures are not capable of completely understanding this type of system, it is no longer necessary to look in the classical direction: a number of alternatives already exist elsewhere. Companies, or any kind of network or social entities (society, country, international community) can be considered as agent networks. These agent networks demonstrate emergent behavior (or self-creating behavior) which is produced anew each time by the network (in line with Prigogine's illustrations). The role of a manager of such a network is therefore no longer to provide good solutions (if that was indeed the case before). Instead his or her job is to create the best conditions and circumstances for the network to be able to work freely in the best way possible. These networks are self-creating and self-organizing, and based on principles already found in neurobiology. These networks demonstrate behavior which is sometimes very complex, but the rules of piloting are very simple. The strength is not even in the links in the network (the agents) but more in the quality of interaction within the network itself. Effectively, it is the quality of agent interaction in a company, and not the quality of individuals, which will build the quality of the company. Recruiting very intelligent employees brings nothing to the company if they are not prepared to collaborate.

It is clear that the supervision mechanisms for such networks are different from classical management. What is most important is not what is good or better, but rather how to speed up the process of learning. It is therefore important to learn from mistakes and successes while each time allowing the network the possibility of creating a new space (with the solution). This network must be held as far as possible away from balance, in order to maintain high entropy and therefore creative potential, but that can only be done with good conditions of basic support. The key word is: learn.

The basis of management is learning; but learning that is quicker than competitors with the best support of collaborators in their learning. On the other hand, the more order is sown in the network the more chaos will be harvested. Only a learning human, a human prepared to learn and capable of learning, can play a role in such a network in the best way. The manager is only one element in the network.

Prigogine's work on the one hand and Holland's on the other, was considered by the majority as the theory of complexity (in Anglo Saxon terms). We have also seen in other sciences (such as physics, chemistry or information technology), how evolutions in the same sense are produced, notably with the works of Maturana and Varela in neurobiology.

The autopoietic principle (of self-reproduction and self-organization) conforms perfectly to the character of permanent creation in a system (Prigogine) as well as the emergent behavior of agents in a network (Holland). Neurobiological research is a not negligible fundamental aspect to take into consideration in comparison with what is developed here.

Varela himself made parallels between human organization and the functioning of the human brain (the neural network), which is a very dense network linking billions of 'knots' (neurons). Each neuron is in fact very simple and can only execute very simple actions (yes or no to pass on energy). Connected (in a network), these neurons are capable of marvelous things. The idea of neural networks and their use for understanding organizations has already been studied in my other publications (most of them available on my site and blog, http://www.walterbaets.com, or summaries are to be found in the further literature). This metaphor of the organization as a neural network does not only go well with Varela's theories, but also with the metaphorical aspect of Prigogine's and Holland's theories.

Characteristics of complex systems: Towards a new paradigm

A number of more recent theories seem to forge a strong new paradigm; a paradigm which has a large number of consequences for management and managers. Prediction and control become useless, since they are not realistic in dynamic systems in which they cannot be correctly calculated. As a result, managing some parameters or variables, (and the associated slogan "we can only manage what we can measure"), does not make sense anymore. But what is the role of a manager then? What qualities must a manager have to be a good one? If the manager effectively looked at companies with another pair of glasses (another paradigm) he or she could see things differently. The things that are seen now, but cannot be well understood in the classical paradigm, could suddenly make sense. That opens opportunities to do something with them today, which will be different, without a doubt, from what is done traditionally. Market behavior and the behavior of the agents in the network can be better understood. Everything therefore becomes a question of learning, learning more quickly, learning continuously and inviting others to learn alongside: the learning manager as an inspirer in a learning network.

Applying this new paradigm in companies allows a better understanding. At present it is not applied much. A few research centers and even a few companies follow this evolution with interest but proportionately this is still very limited. Sometimes smaller companies manage to organize themselves in an "organic" manner. These companies seem to open more possibilities for self-creation and self-organization. There are even virtual companies which have succeeded, although in general they are very small.

Characteristics of complex systems: Arthur, Economics, and Returns

On the scientific economics plane, Brian Arthur has been, for several years, interested in the economic theory of complexity by looking at market behavior. He observes things completely differently from traditional approaches. Other contemporary economic thinking is based on a number of simplifying acceptances, none of which are realized in practice. Man is supposed to be entirely rational, possessing all the information, working in a market with a limited number of goods (or services) and a limited number of players. This continues, despite the fact that not many people still believe that buyers are rational, nor that they possess all the information.

This has been further undermined by the spread of the internet. It is not only difficult to possess all the information, but there is a continual "overload" of information. Information is not that important in itself, but rather it is the interpretation of this information which makes the difference. All these acceptances of rational economic man, which seem to be innocent at first glance, are necessary to be able to work with non-dynamic models (or to assume dynamic behavior to be static). Based on knowledge about the faults of a static and linear approach of a non-linear dynamic phenomenon, there can be little hope that these models will give an understanding of real market behavior.

A fourth acceptance of our economic theory is the law of diminishing returns. Under this law, physical goods (or services which are not based on knowledge) are such that if one consumes more of a particular good, then one will obtain less satisfaction (marginally) for each additional unit. Having eaten five tarts, the sixth is not really very satisfying. Or put another way, if one has already seen ten films, the eleventh is no longer as entertaining. The plus-value in question therefore diminishes. The latest new unit produced less of a plus-value than its predecessors. The same is true in the production sphere. If we have the necessary amount of steel in order to produce a car, any additional unit of steel will not create any more value.

This economic theory does not pay attention to the fact that, in an economy based on knowledge, where the products are principally based on knowledge (even if it is not pure knowledge), this law no longer holds. The characteristic of knowledge itself is different compared to the raw material of an industrial product. Knowledge increases in applicability the more one shares it. With products based on knowledge, the pre-financing is very important (the research part) even before the product can exist. Let's take medicine as an example where, at first, investment in research is very important. After this first phase, one can market the medicine, sell, and hope that the revenue repays the initial investment made. The price of the first copy (of the first product) is very high but each following copy is very cheap in "production" (copying). Since the sales price remains the same, each additional unit sold can therefore provide an increasing added value per unit (and not decreasing as suggested in the law of diminishing returns). The first copy of Microsoft Windows cost a fortune to produce. Each following copy costs a few dollars: the time to make the copy and a CD. To return to the earlier example of the eleventh film, the assumed loss in pleasure or utility takes no account of how increasing appreciation of a genre or a writer, can frequently increase viewing pleasure. A delight in Hitchcock movies, for example, often means looking forward to the next or even an early, poorer quality film by the master.

In knowledge-based markets, some reinforcing element appears. It can be caused by "positive feedback", or a market strength which does not lead to a balance, but creates a sort of snowball. At the beginning of home video there were different standards. VHS and Betamax fought a battle where Betamax was really of better quality and price, but VHS won. What happened is that more videos of the VHS standard invaded the market, then more video equipment manufacturers chose the VHS standard, following which, more film makers released films in the VHS format. This snowball led to VHS becoming the market standard. Microsoft's Disc Operating System (DOS) was not necessarily the better operating system for PCs. At the time when IBM chose DOS as their operating system they were far from the standard and far from a product considered as good quality. The IBM decision led many developers to create their software programs using the DOS system. The other PC manufacturers (Olivetti, Philips, etc.) then also chose the DOS system. Windows still works on DOS (though it is well hidden). A more current example in the politico-social sector is the pre-election campaigns for the US presidency. Why did all the new candidates make such huge efforts to win votes in tiny states such as Iowa and New Hampshire at the beginning of their campaigns when, obviously, states like Florida or California would deliver many more delegate votes? The reason is very simple. They hoped to start out with victories, a snowball effect in "funding" to buy more television time, thanks to which they could attract more attention, and then get more financing etc. Often, in effect, this approach really works.

In the world of business, where Microsoft has clearly won the battle of the PC standard, the phenomenon of positive feedback no longer leads to the usual market share of 15 to 20% in industrial leaders' markets. In the knowledge market it is closer to 60 to 80% and effectively, in the Microsoft case, there are even higher percentages. The justice system that only understands the old paradigm, by which it operates itself, very quickly supports so-called allegations in the knowledge market. If Microsoft were divided into several smaller companies, there would very quickly be another majority player emerging in this market. It is the logic itself of these types of markets. A classical approach has great difficulty understanding that; complexity-based theory has no such problem.

This difficulty is not restricted to economics. Western thinking about science and organization in general does not fit easily with the theory of complexity. Although opposed to western philosophical and scientific traditions, complexity-based theories are not only interesting, but could also very well contribute to a better understanding of social phenomena. Managers will have difficulties accepting a number of aspects and the consequences of these theories. But very few concepts of western managerial thinking seem to contribute to finding solutions in a dynamic world. It is systematically difficult to grasp what really happens, and the classical instruments do not always necessarily help towards a better understanding.

How can a manager apply all that? When managerial control puts a brake on innovation, is there an alternative? This chapter has argued that there is, and that it has a direct relationship with learning: how to keep learning as an individual, how to simultaneously stimulate others to learn, and how to create an environment that supports learning? These are managerial attitudes and skills required to cultivate creation and innovation.

Some final questions

Before moving on to the next chapter let us ask a few questions in relation to emergence and complexity.

1. Is the dynamic of your company situated at the edge of chaos? Is the company welcoming the potential of chaos, or rather steering strictly towards stability?
2. How do you reflect on the saying that evolution and progress needs both the new and the extinction of the existing? How does your company deal with this?
3. Diversity in all its facets (gender, ethnicity, interests, languages, cultures) is a prerequisite for the emergence of the new. How would you react to this?
4. Do you agree that radical unpredictability is an essential characteristic of business? Can you comment on the why and the why not?
5. Is the self-organizational capacity of a company an indicator for sustainability? Can you reflect both on the question itself, and on how this impacts your company?
6. In order for self-organization to kick in, people need to have the space and modus operandus of "individual, autonomous agents". Do you agree or not, and can you relate this to the success or failure of your company? Can you give examples?

7. Do you think that agency (action itself) is located at the level of the interacting individual entity (the employee, the buyer, the seller)? Or do you think that action is situated on a more aggregate level? What does this imply for the functioning of your company?

Bibliography and further literature

Baets W, Organizational Learning and Knowledge Technologies in a Dynamic Environment, Kluwer Academic Publishers, 1998

Baets W, A collection of essays on Complexity and Management, World Scientific, 1999

Baets W, Knowledge Management and Management Learning: Extending the Horizons of Knowledge-Based Management, Springer, 2005

Clippinger III J,(Ed), The biology of business, Jossey-Bass, 1999

Gleick J, Chaos: making a new science, Heinemann, 1987

Holland J, Emergence from Chaos to Order, Oxford University Press, 1998

Lorenz E, The Essence of Chaos, University of Washington Press, 1993

Maturana H and Varela F (Eds), Autopoiesis and Cognition: The Realization of the Living, Reidel, 1980

Maturana H and Varela F, The Tree of Knowledge, Scherz Verlag, 1992

Merry U, Coping with Uncertainty, Praeger, 1995

Mingers J, Self-Producing Systems: Implications and Applications of Autopoiesis, Plenum Press, 1995

Nicolis G and Prigogine I, Exploring Complexity, Freeman, 1989

Stacey R, Managing Chaos, Kogan Page, 1992

Stewart I, Does God Play Dice?, Basil Blackwell, 1989

Varela F, Principles of Biological Autonomy, Elsevier-North Holland, 1979

Waldrop M, Complexity, Penguin, 1992

4 Complexity and the quantum field (the organizing principle)

The previous chapter has opened a quest for a new paradigm, or even possibly for a new ontology. If we would like to understand the world differently we may need a new set of basic assumptions, beliefs that we hold about how nature itself functions. It is generally accepted that the world functions according to the laws of nature, originally given to us by Newton. We operate in a fixed time-space concept. Events are causally related and we know with certainty what happened yesterday and how it influenced what happens today. Clearly, however, our relationship with the past is a much easier one than our relationship with the future. We know exactly what happened yesterday; we have little certainty of what will happen tomorrow. In reality, a Newtonian world does not seem to hold if we operate on the level of less rational decision making, emotions, feelings, etc. Nevertheless, our managerial thinking is still heavily based on causal thinking, even though management mainly deals with people issues of different kinds. We claim that we can only manage causalities, the interconnection between cause and effect. But in reality again, what a manager or leader deals with is the interconnectedness of people, and that seems to follow its own pattern of logic.

We have experienced the revolutions of relativity and quantum mechanics in physics during the previous century. How do the findings of quantum mechanics allow us to adjust our basic assumptions on the functioning of companies and markets?

Today, management theory and practice are facing the challenge that thinking about managerial problems in linear and deterministic ways may create more problems than they solve. Strategy studies, for instance, displays a growing interest in learning and organizational flexibility, and it gives importance to distributed cognition and adaptive systems. Management theorists are keenly observing developments surrounding the complexity and chaos theory in science; management researchers are attempting to apply emerging theories to managerial problems.

The idea that many simple, non-linear deterministic systems can behave in an apparently unpredictable and chaotic manner, is not new. It was first introduced by the great French mathematician Henri Poincaré. Other early pioneering work in the field of chaotic dynamics is found in the mathematical literature by scientists such as Birkhoff, Levenson and Kolmogorov, amongst others. More recently, Nobel Prizes have been awarded in this field of research to Prigogine and Kauffman. One of the difficulties for management theory and practice when engaging with complexity theory lies in its attachment to causality.

Complexity, as a growing organizational paradigm in the knowledge-based economy, primarily questions the concept of causality. Despite relativity and quantum mechanics, most physics (and certainly all managerial thinking) is still Newtonian; based on a fixed space-time frame. In the meantime, further developments have taken place in the area of biology (such as the concept of Sheldrake's morphogenetic fields) and mind/body medicine that all seem to point to a merging idea of a quantum interpretation of social phenomena (non-locality, synchronicity and entanglement). Could a-causality form the basis for a quantum ontology of complex systems?

This chapter attempts to explore the essence of such a quantum ontology, which, afterwards, enables the development of a systemic concept of values-based performance and diagnostics that go with it.

The philosophy of quantum mechanics: Challenges and opportunities

The foundational concepts in the complexity realm emerge from such fields as neurobiology, cognitive sciences, physics and organizational theory. New developments in knowledge management such as connectionist approaches to complex adaptive systems for the visualization of emergence give promising results (Baets, 2005). In fact, instead of directional causality, it appears that the networked economy is ruled by synchronicity – appearing at the same time – in line with findings in quantum research. Could it be that the economy and management in general, and the more dynamic aspects of it like innovation, in particular, are indeed based on a quantum ontology?

The insight into complexity that developed over the last decade, and its consequences for management, discussed earlier in the book and in previous publications (Baets, 2006a and b), provides a platform for this chapter to explore the ontological basis of complex systems.

What Prigogine and complexity theory discussed in general, was fundamentally the existence of any causal relationship. In fact he was surprised that despite the two fundamental revolutions in physics in the last century, relativity theory and quantum mechanics, physics still remained mainly Newtonian. That physics presumes a fixed time and space concept in which the future is causally related to the past, is a deterministic view that if certain conditions exist in certain ways there would be a determined outcome. Instead, complexity theory and quantum mechanics show the impossibility of this assumption.

In both the special and the general theory of relativity, the notion of causality, in which a cause precedes its effect, remains intact in the relativistic – subjective and without absolute objective truth – formulations of electrodynamics, mechanics and gravitation. In quantum theory, the usual meaning of causal connection between one event and another is therefore called into question.

The discontinuity versus continuity distinction can be seen as contingently rooted in philosophical commitments and in the physical phenomena studied. By the late 19th century, there were already significant, if not overwhelming, philosophical precedents for the concept of indeterminism or absence of causality (including the possibility of inherent chance) in nature. These opposed the straightforward determinism often associated with classical physics. Soren Kierkegaard believed that objective uncertainty can force one to make a leap into the unknown so that decisions cannot always, even in principle, be based on a continuous chain of logic. For example, one of Hoffding's tenets was that, in life, decisive events proceed through sudden 'jerks' of discontinuities, an idea incorporated into Bohr's view of atomic phenomena (Cushing, 1998).

As Schrödinger concluded: "this means nothing else but taking seriously the de Broglie-Einstein wave theory of moving particles, according to which the particles are nothing more than a kind of "wave crest" on a background of waves" (Klein, 1964). Einstein, de Broglie and Schrödinger shared a commitment to a continuous wave as a basic physical entity subject to a causal description.

There was a split in philosophical outlook along generational lines: on one side was the 'older', essentially classical world view of people like Einstein, Schrödinger and de Broglie; on the other was a radically different, eventually *indeterministic* conception of physical processes engendered by a generally younger generation (Bohr and Born being exceptions here), including Heisenberg, Pauli, Jordan and a new member of the group, Dirac from Cambridge University (Polkinghorne, 1990).

On the standard, or Copenhagen, interpretation of quantum mechanics and, in particular, the Schrödinger equation, there is no longer event-by-event causality, and particles do not follow well-defined trajectories in a space-time background. The theory predicts, in general, probabilities, rather than specific events.

Dirac argues that an intrinsic distinction between large and small is related to the effects produced on an object when it is observed. The act of observing the system – the cat in Schrödinger's famous experiment (Schrödinger, 1935) – has forced the system into a given state (Dirac, 1958).

Beyond causality

This leads to one of the most profound issues in the interpretation of quantum mechanics, especially for our purpose – that of causality (in the sense of a specific, identifiable cause for each individual effect). As Dirac (1958) observes, causality applies only to a system that is left undisturbed. If a system is small, it cannot be observed without producing a serious disturbance, and hence observers cannot expect to find any causal connection between the results of their observations.

In this same spirit, Heisenberg too felt that, since the mathematical structure of quantum mechanics is so different from that of classical mechanics, it is not possible to interpret quantum mechanics in terms of our commonly understood notions of space and time with classical causality (Heisenberg, 1927). This sudden and discontinuous change of the state of a quantum-mechanical system upon observation or measurement, is an example of one of the central and long-standing conceptual difficulties of the standard interpretation. It is termed the "measurement problem".

The Heisenberg uncertainty principle and the lack of absolute predictive power are an inherent feature of quantum mechanics. In principle there is no deterministic scheme to predict the exact future trajectory of an electron. Bohr developed this idea further. Today, this dependence of the outcome of a measurement upon the means used to effect it, is referred to as *contextuality*.

An obvious rhetorical question now presents itself. What does the wave function represent? Is it our state of knowledge of the system (in which case quantum mechanics is incomplete), or the actual physical state of the system (in which case there must be a sudden change of the system upon our observation of it)? Although the system may appear in either of two states (or 'components') before the measurement, nature has (in the image suggested by Dirac) been forced to 'make a choice' when observed. Since the system is thereafter in a definite component, no subsequent interference with the other component is possible. The 'collapse' of the wave function has taken place. An issue of ontology, isn't it?

EPR (Einstein, Podolsky and Rosen; 1935) introduced the deterministic hidden-variables theories. They assume that there is a set of variables, or as yet undiscovered properties of a system, and that the exact space-time behavior of the system is causally determined by the values of these 'hidden' variables. The introduction of such a large number of hidden variables may seem to be a high price to pay to maintain locality and realism. John Bell proved a remarkable theorem in 1965. Simply put, no determinate, local hidden-variables theory can agree with all of the predictions of quantum mechanics. Consequently, it can now be asserted with reasonable confidence that either the thesis of realism or that of locality must be abandoned. Either choice will drastically change our concepts of reality and of space-time (Clauser and Shimony, 1978).

It is generally believed that a causal interpretation of quantum mechanics is impossible, although no proof of this presently exists.

The standard, or Copenhagen, view of quantum mechanics is characterized as requiring complementarity (say, wave-particle duality), inherent indeterminism at the most fundamental level of quantum phenomena and the impossibility of an event-by-event causal representation in a continuous space-time background. So, on the Copenhagen interpretation of quantum mechanics, physical processes are, at the most fundamental level, both inherently indeterministic and non-local. The ontology of classical physics is dead.

The heart of the problem is the entanglement (or non-separability) of quantum states that gives rise to the measurement problem. This entanglement makes it impossible to assign independent properties to an arbitrary isolated physical system once it has interacted with another system in the past – even though these two systems are no longer interacting. The non-separability characteristic of quantum systems can be seen as an indication of the *'holistic'* character of such systems. Some claim the need for a new concept of causality, but it is not clear what that would be. Heisenberg long ago suggested introducing a new class of physical entity, *potentia*, into our theory (and into our ontology).

Eventually, a Bell-type theorem is proven and taken as convincing evidence that non-locality is present in quantum phenomena. Quantum mechanics has undeniably introduced us to non-locality, entanglement and synchronicity; concepts that thus far have not yet been applied in economics, business or social sciences at large.

Extending spirit, the fifth dimension and other implications of a possible new ontology

Earlier work (Baets, 2006) has suggested that an interesting path of exploration might be to go as low as possible on the aggregation level, and work on the level of human emotions of team members to allow innovation to produce itself through the emergence of processes. In fact, we want to explore the quantum reality of management and, by extension, of any other social phenomenon. A double question remains: can you, and how can you, make the concept of, for instance, innovation a holistic one? The answer would encapsulate the personal emotional side. However, on a deeper level, this question can be asked with reference to conscience and causality, and the "seat" of consciousness (as discussed in chapter 2).

At a more grounded level, the questions are: on what level can we find consciousness? Is there something like a collective consciousness, for example, in a company on the subject of innovation? Does everyone have a sort of essential element of incorporated consciousness with a possibility of connection with others at the level of consciousness? These can be directly translated to companies: do consciousness, engagement, and emotions make a difference for a company? Does a company have a "soul", a "consciousness"? Is there a link between this "consciousness" and the success of a company? Are vision, emotions and consciousness linked? More concretely, what determines the choice of a client who has a preference for one company over another? What lets potential clients make a distinction between two companies which essentially offer the same services, for example, two big banks such as BNP and ING, or two consultancy companies such as PWC and Accenture? And finally, can we arrive at an approach, accepted as scientific, that gives at least the beginning of a response to these questions? Although the questions are, of course, a little metaphysical, this does not prevent them from remaining important questions. This chapter will now explore some evolutions in different types of sciences, each interpreting the suggested new ontology.

Once holism, constructivism and emergence are accepted as fundaments of a new paradigm, a paradox emerges, perhaps the most important one in science. Despite the two great revolutions of the previous century – the theory of relativity and quantum mechanics – almost the whole scientific community is still focused on Newtonian principles, that is to say fixed space and time. Science still does very little with the space-time continuum that these revolutions have offered us. In the hard sciences, at least, there are groups of researchers working on this subject. In economic, managerial and social sciences this revolution seems to have been completely side-stepped. Our managerial thinking is still the Marshallian economic thinking of the 19th Century (Arthur, 1998).

At the end of his scientific career Wolfgang Pauli (as described in de Meijgaard, 2002) asked himself how we can know if human cultures can live with a clear distinction between knowledge and belief (an idea, moreover, of Max Planck). For this reason, according to Pauli, societies struggle if new knowledge arrives and puts the classical spiritual values in question. The complete separation between the two can only be a solution in the short term and one of facility. Pauli had predicted that there will be a moment in the near future when all the images and metaphors of classic religions will lose their strength of conviction for the average citizen. In that situation classic ethical values disintegrate and result in a period of hitherto unknown barbarism. He was touched by, and very interested in, what he himself called "background physics" – the spontaneous appearance of quantitative concepts and images in fantasies and dreams. He admitted he also had them himself. Their character was very dependent on the dreamer. Background physics has an archetypal origin and that leads (always, according to Pauli) to a natural science which will work just as well with matter as with consciousness. He was also sufficiently a realist to say that if a researcher in physics has observed a sub-system, the observations are as much dependent on the observer as on the instruments.

According to Pauli, the physical concept of "complementarity" physics (de Meijgaard, 2002) illustrated a profound analogy with concepts such as consciousness and the unconscious. Two extreme cases which can never be attained in practice are "someone with a perfect consciousness" (eastern philosophy suggests that this can be attained uniquely in death, also called Nirvana) and something like a "bigger spirit" which will never be influenced by a subjective consciousness. This "bigger spirit" is what eastern philosophy calls the "consciousness", and western psychology calls "collective unconsciousness". Pauli accepted that physical values, as much as archetypes, change in the eyes of the observer. Observation is the result of human consciousness.

Pauli wrote a book with Jung on this issue (1955). Where Jung talks about defined archetypes as primordial structural elements of the human psyche, Pauli introduced the notion of the "collective unconsciousness". They both believed that humans were moving towards a joining of the psyche and the physical.

Ideas without borders (1): synchronicity

The introduction of the notion of "synchronicity" in this co-authored work is not only interesting in itself, but recurs in other authors and also other disciplines. According to Pauli, synchronicity – being united-in-time, appears in all the sciences and the techniques in which simultaneity plays a role. What must be taken into account here is that this is not about a **causal** coherence (from cause to effect) but about a **coincidence** (being together in time). This coincidence must be considered as useful even if the deep cause of the simultaneity cannot be explained. It needs to be remembered that references to synchronicity are always present if the events concerned occur in the same time period. The concepts of statistics or the theory of probability are of another order. Probability can be calculated with mathematical methods, which is impossible when speaking about synchronicity.

Synchronicity (according to Meijgaard) is considered the basis of many phenomena which are difficult to explain and which are often called non-scientific. However, they will not be considered further in this context. The concern here is that the widening of consciousness and the dissolving of borders is only possible when, besides classical energetic causal thinking, there is also a space kept for **synchronicity and information**. It is to Pauli's great credit that he indicated the necessity to create space for the concept of synchronicity in scientific thinking. Jung speaks about this as the "a-causal" link. Sheldrake later confirmed these ideas with his theory of morphogenetic fields (a collection of cells by whose interactions a particular organ formed).

Pauli and Jung proposed that the classic triad of physics (space, time and causality) be extended with synchronicity to then form a tetrad. This fourth element works in an a-causal manner and is, in effect, the polar opposite of causality. Pauli and Jung believed that these oppositions were orthogonal in time and space.

The idea of an a-causal link – or non-locality – are new concepts which should contribute effectively to the science of management (and specifically to the management of innovation) to be able to make them more concrete. The term "non-local" comes, in fact, from the opposition taken by Einstein against his own grandchild (quantum mechanics). The majority view of researchers (Einstein excluded) concludes that the observation of one particle produces a direct and immediate effect on the second. In effect, there must be a "togetherness-in-separation: against the intuitive (a theory which was moreover refused by Einstein, who called it "spooky action at a distance"). Even Nature seems to attack pure and simple reductionism (Polkinghorne, 1990). The subatomic world can no longer be treated in a purely atomic way.

The implication of these observations is that the phenomenon of "entanglement" (non-locality) includes a real remote activity, not simply epistemological, but in fact ontological in nature.

The Bogdanov brothers (Bogdanov and Bogdanov, 2004) have published an interesting book that summarizes their PhD work (in theoretical physics and mathematics): "Avant le big bang". In their book, which is discussed by many attached to more classical theories, they attempt to take the understanding of the quantum interpretation a step further. Their theoretical work makes an attempt to explore what could happen beyond Planck's Wall ($<10^{-43}$). Not only do they find non-locality, synchronicity and entanglement, but they also find a possible explanation for non-locality. It extends beyond our current acceptance of just four dimensions: three of space and one of time. Indeed they theoretically observe a fifth dimension, which would be a fourth dimension of space, but expressed in "imaginary" time. Explaining the concept of imaginary time would take us too far, and it is extremely mathematical, but it has to do with the famous "i" in mathematics (the square root of a negative number). If they theoretically observe this fifth dimension beyond Planck's wall, it of course also exists before that "wall", which would mean that there is a kind of *interwoveness* between time and space. Time has a space dimension and space has a time dimension. Even if some scientists want to argue with this work the least one can say is that their observation and proof is elegant (even if it were not true). Although, their proof is rather convincing and their PhD juries were mainly Nobel Prize winners.

This development should not be misunderstood as an extension of the search in physics for the string theory. The latter is not concerned with the (Bogdanov) singularity, but accepts Planck's wall as a fact of life.

Interesting also is that speaking about values, the values of interconnectedness, the spiritual connection, the contribution we make to the broader picture, the value added by companies to a wider societal good, etc., seem to be situated on that same kind of quantum level: a lower level of reality, beyond the world of molecules and atoms. Seeing values as these small building blocks – on levels of sub-atomic particles and unified forces theory, where they are elements of comparable nature, and that in interaction with each other, create an emergent reality – opens doors for a different, values-based leadership style.

Quantum interpretations and ways of knowing in complex social systems

One of the illustrations of this quantum concept, and with the goal of doing a thought experiment, is developed in Mitchell's "dyadic model" as he describes it in his book *The Way of the Explorer: An Apollo Astronaut's Journey Through the Material and Mystical World* (Mitchell and Williams, 1996). Stated simply, the concept of non-locality is derived from quantum physics (as explained before). In fact, in the experiments he demonstrated that particles (photons) stay attached in a "mysterious" manner, even if they displace in directions contrary to the speed of light.

The dyadic model is built on the idea that everything is energy. This basic energy is linked to information, or what Mitchell calls structures of energy. The energy and the information form a dyad. The information, in this context, is the basis of the capacity of matter to "know" (and so has nothing to do with information as treated in information systems).

All matter contains a sort of "awareness" or, put another way, a capacity to "know". If not, how can molecules "know" that they must join up with others to form cells? In a subsequent state (a more complex state) it could be that in the human body/brain matter evolves such that it knows what it knows. It is therefore capable of self-reflection.

Another dyad in his model is 'awareness and intention', which equally make up part of the evolutionary process that leads to consciousness. Consciousness and innovation, accepted elements of the energy-information scheme, are the basis of self-reflective consciousness.

The non-locality is illustrated by the famous connection, proven and explained in more detail before, of the "entanglement" between partner photons which are sent in opposite directions. They still stay, however, in a position to immediately ("instantaneously") communicate between each other over large distances. This has a relationship with the "knowledge" of these particles. Humans are equally made up of these sorts of particles.

Ideas without borders (2): morphogenic fields and quantum arts

So how then, according to Mitchell, does such communication function? The groups of particles seem to have special characteristics of resonance and coherence which are evoked by the groups themselves. This resonance includes historical knowledge about universal matter. This idea strongly corresponds with Rupert Sheldrake's observations. The body/brain can receive holographic information in the form of virtual long wave signals. Mitchell's dyad suggests that the particles "know" by their inherent qualities of consciousness and intention. The groups of particles communicate between themselves on the basis of quantum holograms (that Sheldrake calls morphogenetic fields), which includes information about the universe. As the body/brain also works in a holographic way, it can recover this information. Apparently, nature does not lose its memory concerning its own evolution. Mitchell believes that it is intention, or directional attention, which links humans holographically with the signals or non-local long waves.

The greater the experience of satisfaction, the more the consciousness of each cell in the body will resonate with the holographic information engraved in the 'quantum zero point' – the lowest possible state of energy, in an almost resting, but not quite, state (Polkinghorne, 1990) – of the energy field. This phenomenon refers to being 'carried along'. If humans live in harmony with their biological rhythms (all sorts of rhythms), the body is in balance and the person will fall ill less easily. In the material world, it bears witness to a phenomenon of 'being carried along' when two pendulums are put beside one another. Although the movement of the pendulums in the two clocks seems at first to be totally arbitrary, after a certain time, the movements adapt to each other and move in harmony. The two clocks are 'carried along'. In the world of medicine, a lot of these ideas are found in Ayurvedic (holistic) medicine.

This quantum approach of energy, information and communication, suggests causality at a much lower level of aggregation; that is to say, at a quantum level. In effect, it is synchronicity or coincidence rather than causality. This structure allows people to realize what they want to realize – whether it is, for example, to protect themselves against viruses or simply to survive or innovate as in the case of companies. It therefore becomes a question of elementary particles (say, the characteristics of people translated into economic behavior), which are linked in solid networks with all sorts of matter (the context), which in turn, interact with this matter and in doing so become part of the wider energetic field (morphogenetics) which contains knowledge and information. When more members of a team (or a company) are "carried along", their actions will have more success, whether in project management or in product innovation.

Others (Caro and Murphy, 2002) have applied the quantum concept to art and aesthetics. And although this is not the subject of this chapter, it is interesting to see how the same principles of synchronicity, non-locality and quantum structure can be applied in art. The cradle of this quantum movement in arts is in Spain. Caro and Murphy's book includes chapters on quantum art, quantum literature, quantum anthropology and quantum politics. Towards the end of the book the authors suggest that the quantum principle makes more profound sense and they integrate it with the understanding of societal phenomena.

Dalla Chiara and Giuntini (1999) tried to apply quantum logic to the concept of truth and interpretation in art. They firstly dedicated themselves to the subject of poetic force and asked themselves if truth in poetry is less 'true' than observed truth. Where quantum theory and orthodox quantum logic deal uniquely with problems of absolute clarity leaving no place for different interpretations, problems linked to language are evidently more vague. Humans are not clear and neither are absolute notions. What is it to "be honorable"? What is "important"? Quantum logic does not only work with well-defined unambiguous concepts. With these problems, semantic uncertainties are only the result of the fact that the problem is not completely defined in detail. The authors plead for a vague quantum theory (perhaps even to be compared with fuzzy logic). They refer to a piece of music. A piece of music does not only consist of a score, but a mass of different possible combinations between the same score and different musicians' interpretations. It is therefore a combination of senses (emotions) and symbols, but although each combination is possible, each combination is not necessarily good.

Back to biology: Sheldrake and "implicit order"

The illustrations above concern the use of quantum concepts, non-locality and synchronicity, as much in physical science as in the science of language and music. This section returns to Sheldrake's theory which is founded on biology. Sheldrake (1995), who is a well-known Cambridge biologist, is now an affiliated Research Fellow at the Noetic Society. Although his theory is controversial (as is often the case with a new paradigm) it has been validated by considerable research, as his many publications bear witness. As ideas, these theories are entirely in accord with the scientific subject developed up to this point.

In a book which Sheldrake co-authored with Bohm (1982), they broach the subject of "implicit order". Implicit order is something like a ground below time, a tonality of which each movement is projected in explicit order (what is known). For everything visible, there is something in implicit order which is at the origin of the projection. If an event is repeated many times, then behind that is a constant built component. A sort of (fixed) link is born. Via this process, the forms of the past can continue to live in the present. This is more or less what Sheldrake calls morphogenetic fields, created by morphogenetic resonance. If something climbs into 'totality' where neither time nor space is fixed, it could be that things of the same nature will attach themselves to one another, or resonate. Because neither time nor space exists in this totality, things which happen at a particular place could therefore also happen elsewhere, or at least have an influence elsewhere.

These ideas are very much in line with the Bogdanovs' singularity and their observation that a fifth dimension, being a fourth dimension of space, expressed in imaginary time, could exist. Comparing the different "quantum" interpretations in the different sciences seems to converge. The convergence can be understood as an emergent understanding of this quantum world and its consequences.

Although Sheldrake and Bohm's theory, mentioned above, is the scientific topic that Sheldrake vigorously researches these days, his theory of proved morphogenetic fields could also still be very useful for us.

Sheldrake's idea of morphogenetic fields complements the later ideas that Varela (1979) was able to work on before his death. They engaged with how something like resonance could be the organizing principle in networks. Varela's suggestion has become illustrated by Sheldrake's research. In fact, these characteristics identified from morphogenetic fields are completely in parallel with the complexity paradigm. They could just as well be the characteristics of an economic system, a market or a company.

East-West interactions

A last science where holistic concepts are increasingly popular is, without doubt, medical science where many different thinkers are active on this subject. One general area is Ayurveda (the ancient Indian medical science) and, more particularly, somebody like Dr. Chopra (1990) who, with research and experiments, does more and more research into quantum concepts of healing. These experiments also help to provide basics for the approach advocated by this book.

Ayurveda examines holistic man in a different way to our western medical science. Ayurveda looks for a natural balance in the human being. Another startling distinction is that Ayurveda is a preventive medicine so that the best doctor does not have any patients. Not surprisingly and in line with other theories presented here, Ayurveda focuses on energy flows. The human body has its own system of regeneration, its own defense mechanisms, and the art must then be to reinforce all that. The heart, for instance, is seen as an important regulator of those energy flows. A certain illness (like stomach problems or migraines) is always caused by an imbalance. To put back the balance is the message. As the body is a very complex network with all sorts of cells which know exactly what they should know to be able to co-operate with the others (and knowing perfectly with which others), it is necessary to disturb this network as little as possible. For many reasons, the WHO (World Health Organization) has identified Ayurveda as the medical solution for developing populations.

Healthy living and good nutrition are now also credos in the West. Nevertheless, the 'why' of this advice is of a different nature. Ayurveda considers the human body as a self-organizing system composed of many simple elements which, taken independently, are very simple and elementary, but which together form a formidable distributed intelligence. Entirely in parallel, we can consider a company as a network of "simple" elements where each "know" what they should know to be able to manage and form effective networks. The knowledge of a system is found in the community, not in a local element.

The interesting thing is that these theories re-confirm the concepts proposed before. In particular, Chopra's theories concerning synchronicity and non-locality interestingly illustrate the arguments already developed here from a different perspective.

To summarize the essentials of all these theories we can say that quantum reality, which is expressed in non-locality, synchronicity and entanglement, holds the promise of offering new understanding for a more efficient harmony of the concept of causality in management and the economy, and hence in any complex system. Instead of talking about causality, the focus shifts to discussing synchronicity (coincidence).

The key concepts of the new ontology

As a basis for formulating a new paradigm for understanding complex systems in general, and management in particular, as well as to develop an adequate research agenda, this section summarizes fundamental concepts as introduced in chapter 2, often developed in sciences other than those of economy, management or social sciences but equally applicable in complex social systems.

- It is worth repeating that the approach developed and proposed here is inscribed in the holistic paradigm. Holism, in the sense used here, draws from Ken Wilber's (2000) theories. He defines **holism** as an eternal dynamic interaction between four "spheres": the mechanical (external) individual sphere; the mechanical (external) collective sphere; the internal collective sphere (common values), the internal individual sphere (emotions and consciousness). Clearly, in reductionist and rational approaches, the external individual sphere receives all the attention. "Classical" ecologic scientific movements are especially interested in the collective, but always external, sphere. More recent scientific interests attempt to go beyond that by including more values and emotions (that is to say consciousness). Holism, as defined by Wilber, is evidently founded on a **constructivist** approach. This is discussed in more detail in the next chapter.

- The proposed ontology fits clearly the reality of the **sciences of complexity** in Prigogine's definition of them as the study of dynamic non-linear systems. In particular, he was always very interested in two important aspects: the role of time and behavior far from equilibrium. He illustrated the constructive role of time, as expressed in the principle of the irreversibility of time, in complex processes. This principle states that an important consequence is that in complex systems it is not possible to extrapolate the future from the past. Complex systems are extremely sensitive to the initial conditions. Minimal changes in these conditions can have major influences on the further development of the process. Finally, Prigogine identifies the most productive state of a (complex) system as one that is far away from equilibrium: "order at the edge of chaos".

- John Holland, a pioneer in artificial life and agent systems, has developed a complex adaptive approach (CAS) called **agent based simulations**. This approach simulates the interaction between different agents and, consequently, simulates **emergent behavior** in those kinds of systems. An agent, according to Holland, is a mini software program. Each agent has characteristics. It is necessary to define the field of action (the limits of the system) and to identify a minimum of interaction rules (and exchange rules). Then, it is necessary to make the system iterate and simulate the dynamic interaction of those agents. The agents meet each other, interact, exchange (and so learn) and, step by step, form a global behavior with qualities that emerge from the interaction itself.

- **Synchronicity,** according to Pauli, appears in all the sciences and the techniques in which simultaneity plays a role. It is necessary to take into account that this is not to speak about a causal coherence (from cause to effect), but about **coincidence** (as occurring together in time). This has to be considered as potentially useful, even if we cannot explain the more profound cause of the simultaneity. We must remember that we always speak of synchronicity if the events concerned happen in the same period of time. The relationships therefore, to use Jung's words, become **a-causal**.

- The implication of these observations is that the phenomenon of **"entanglement"** (**non-locality**), including a real activity at a distance, is not simply epistemological. It is, in effect, ontological by nature (Polkinghorne) and can be called **"a quantum interpretation"**.

- Sheldrake and Bohm (1982) broached the subject of **"implicit order"** as something like a ground underneath time, a totality, from which each movement is projected in explicit order. For everything seen, there is something in implicit order at the origin of this projection. If there are a many repetitions of an event, then behind it, there is a built constant component. A sort of (fixed) link is born. Via this process, the forms from the past can continue to live in the present. This is more or less what Sheldrake calls **morphogenetic fields**, created by **morphogenetic resonance**.

- Ayurveda considers the human being as a self-organizing system composed of a many simple elements which are, when taken independently, very simple (unintelligent), but which together form a formidable **distributed intelligence**. In parallel, a company can be considered as a network of "simple" elements where each "know" what they must know to be able to form effective networks with others.
- The ontological nature of this quantum structure forces us to look again at our approach to innovation and, on a wider scale, at our economic theory. **The understanding of innovation must therefore be based on the "carrying along" of quantum structures, synchronicity, morphogenetic fields and individual space for self-organization.**
- In their recent work, the Bogdanovs, in search of what they define as the Bogdanov Singularity, suggest the existence of a fifth dimension. This dimension would be a **fourth dimension of space, expressed in imaginary time**. This theoretical development suggests a formal system in which time and space indeed get closer to each other; in fact, they share a dimension. Their proposed theoretical framework could be the beginning of an explanation of most of the concepts illuminated here.

Quantum economics or the quantum interpretation of management

Classical business economics in the light of a quantum interpretation

It is clear that what we know as business economics, the theory that forms the basis of our managerial thinking, can no longer hold within a quantum interpretation of the world, other than as an exception to, or a specific case of, a more general rule. In this section, I explore the framework of a new kind of economic thinking that fits the quantum interpretation and that allows us to get a deeper insight into business practice.

Standard business economics is based on four main assumptions. The first one assumes that all economic agents show rational behavior. Though this is certainly partly true, it is obvious that, for instance, in buying behavior there is not always a lot of rationality. Worse, marketing, in fact, aims to influence so called rational behavior, with mostly emotional elements. The acceptance of marketing as a valid activity and even a managerial discipline fundamentally contradicts this assumption. As argued in this book, no observation, no measurement and even more so, no interpretation can be objective, therefore the assumption of full rationality cannot hold in reality.

The second assumption states that the different economic players are fully informed (a necessity in order to be able to act rationally). Specifically in this internet era, this assumption seems highly theoretical. Not only is it virtually impossible to have all information, but even more so the interpretation of all available information brings us again to the non-rationality of information. Indeed, information can only be transformed into knowledge by individuals; knowledge that allows the user to enact behavior (action and shaping). Being fully informed, independent of the knowing subject, is not reasonable.

The next assumption is the alternative use of resources. In practice, this means that once a resource is used in one product, it cannot be used in another product any more. This is a clear industrial point of view in which we mainly produce material products. In the knowledge economy, this is different. Information and knowledge are perpetually usable and what's more, the more it is shared, the more its value increases. As argued earlier, that is what causes the law of increasing returns (see Brian Arthur earlier). The law of diminishing returns, a basic one in the classical economy, doesn't hold in the knowledge economy and doesn't hold in the "today" economy.

The fourth assumption, which is a convenience one and one that probably causes less harm, is that there are a limited number of goods and services. It is clear that, certainly in the knowledge economy, services are often used for different purposes. Any service defined might therefore become a set of different services, according to the use that the clients imagine.

Mandelbrot, particularly in respect to financial markets, finds a similar set of assumptions that modern financial theory makes in order to justify their financial models. In his latest book, Mandelbrot illustrates the catastrophic consequences of those assumptions on day to day financial portfolio management, destroying both the theoretical concept of those models and their financial performance. The assumptions he identifies behind classical financial theory are:

- People are rational and only aim to get rich;
- All investors are alike;
- Price change is practically continuous;
- Price changes follow a Brownian motion (independent of consecutive observations; statistical stagnation of price changes; the normality (Bell shape curve) of changes).

In general, the strong assumption behind most financial processes, but equally behind many managerial processes, is the normality of phenomena (99% of the observations fall between the mean, plus or minus 3 times its standard deviation). Observational reality certainly does not conform to this assumption in most volatile markets.

Clearly, these assumptions all fit into a reductionist framework, limiting reality to a theoretically viable environment. But the consequence is that observations in such a limited framework do not allow extrapolation into a real world that does not obey the assumptions. The Economist (April 17th, 1999) described it in "Quarks and coaches" as follows: "The one group of people to whom most businessmen rarely turn is economists. Big firms ask economists to predict the ups and downs of national economies, but when it comes to finding ways to run their own company better, many managers would sooner consult an astrologer".

Furthermore, there are a number of concepts defined that don't really matter, that are acceptable but not really relevant, or do not add any value to the understanding of a particular problem. An example of such a concept is "the circular flows of income and spending between business and households", where banks and governments play the role of "multiplier" or "catalyst". Both multiplier and catalyst are concepts based on different assumptions. Multipliers indeed fit equations and causal relationships. A catalyst accelerates a situation without always knowing precisely where it will move to. The use of the word "catalyst" in fact suggests a different kind of reaction where, what is meant when analyzed in more depth, is really a multiplier. Reality has shown that tax policy, possibly based on these theories, does not always seem to work. In fact, it became a political debate and hence a political choice, whether one *believes* in a more important role for the government (always via taxes) or not. Independent of whether economic theory would work, tax policies are political choices, where all different parties assume or invent possible side effects that would make all the difference.

The claimed aims of macroeconomic policy, again a set of political choices, are full employment, stable prices, economic growth and balance of payments equilibrium. So called macroeconomic models prove unable to catch the dynamics of those markets, and therefore become highly irrelevant if a country comes into a highly dynamic environment (hyperinflation, political treaties, threat of a revolution, etc.). In case of a stable situation, of course, those models would work, but aren't necessary in that case, since behavior is stable.

The essence of monetary theory is based on the equation MV = PQ (quantity of money x velocity = price x quantity). Neither untrue, nor wrong, but it is not particularly helpful for the manager.

And that summarizes the essential "axioms" of business economics.

Next, I would like to summarize what is known as business economics by briefly going over the structure of a standard business economics textbook. A textbook would start describing the "international economic environment" concentrating on high level aggregations like: average wage level, labor cost per unit, trading price, competitiveness and efficiency that would *not* be discounted in any other variable. Such a chapter would finish up with the role governments play in business practice, referring to legislation, taxes, trade zones, etc. This kind of chapter is an example of what we argued earlier, that economics, in general, reasons on an entirely too high level of aggregation in order to be able to find any useful relationship at all (apart from a causal one).

Most textbooks contain a chapter on macroeconomics; that is interesting but not really part of business economics. In a chapter on the organization of firms and markets, where we expect to see some organizing principles, mechanism on how processes emerge, etc. we mainly find legal issues: a summary of a business law course.

The chapter on business objectives is the one that builds foremost on the assumptions and axioms (stated or hidden) of business economics and mentioned earlier in this chapter. The chapter starts with a discussion about mission statements, carefully avoiding identifying whether we talk about a goal or a path. The earlier chapters of this book have made this difference clear, as well as its consequences. Referring to the "rational behavior" assumption, a company is claimed to pursue the profit maximization principle. This maximization is based on a number of equally impossible assumptions that in fact limit reality to an artificial (unrealistic), but above all, linear and stable situation. Those assumptions are:

- No division between ownership and control (which in practice is, of course, years out of date for any larger company. The ownership – the shareholder-ship – is represented in a general assembly of shareholders, but the daily management – the control – is done by professional managers). An interesting discussion here is whether we observe a different kind of management in SMEs (where ownership and control are often either in the same hands or close to each other) and larger companies. Most research indeed suggests a difference.
- Full knowledge of costs and revenues (referring to the full information general assumptions) which is often neither reached nor reachable. An additional problem is that even if we can identify a fully correct picture at any moment, this would deny the dynamics of this process (certainly on the revenue side).
- No problems with fixed cost allocation (since there is theoretically only one product). In most companies, this is far from reality.

- Rational behavior and only one objective, which are weak assumptions as already argued.

The difference between ownership and control (not to mention other stakeholders who are dramatically ignored in business economics) also opens the debate between sales revenue optimization, growth maximization or sustainable development. Simon (1996) talks in this context about "satisfiers" instead of maximizers.

The classical mistake, or should I say weakness, resides in the process description of how to get to the corporate goal due to oversimplified assumptions **and** presumed static, linear behavior. Business economics focuses on fixing the path, instead of explaining the emergence in networked systems. Next, the fixed path is realized and management reduces itself to the control mechanism of the realization of the path (not even always of the goals anymore). The law of increasing returns (described earlier) in a knowledge economy, is only one of the examples of how disastrous the classical law of diminishing returns is when discussing the knowledge economy. The illustration of this type of mistake can be found in the classical aspects of business economics: demand analysis; cost theory; pricing theory.

Demand analysis is often done using linear regressions (in best cases, as described in textbooks), denying dynamic behavior of markets. Apart from the basic assumptions already mentioned, a number of technical assumptions (often hidden) need to be fulfilled in order to be able to apply linear regression. Homoscedasticity (normal distribution of the error term) and the absence of multicollinearity (collinearity between explanatory variables) are only two of them. Non fulfillment of these assumptions causes numerical deficiency on the results that cannot be observed in the classical statistics of the regression analysis. *In quasi stable, quasi linear markets, all those models work which only illustrates that this situation is a special case (a simplified form) of a more generally valid quantum interpretation.* In fact, the regular business economics theory is a special case of the more general quantum economics theory, only applicable to quasi stable and quasi linear situations.

The fixed and variable cost theory, based on oversimplified assumptions of no cross relationships and full information, is again a special case of a more general cost behavior structure. Once we accept cross relationships between products (services) and human production actions, we automatically fall into the network paradigm.

Other than in oligopolistic markets, which are again a special case of fully interacting markets, pricing in non-linear dynamic markets becomes a question of strategizing. The best example of strategizing games can indeed be found in game theory. The best known case is no doubt the prisoner's dilemma, in which two "players" play against each other, each having two possible strategies. (Reality, of course, is infinitely more complicated, with a huge number of possible strategies for each player.) The unknown in the game is that each of the players ignores what the other plays. Game theory knows zero-sum games or non-zero-sum games. Game theory has been used to illustrate pricing games. As the law of increasing returns suggests, strategizing of prices goes much further. According to Arthur's theory the aim is to get a snowball effect going, at the right moment. If a company strategizes a market correctly, it should be able not only to price correctly, but to do so at the correct moment. That kicks off the dynamic process of market penetration, often leading to important market shares. A wrong strategy (price or timing) causes the product to die out. The law of increasing returns explains why demand analysis and pricing cannot be considered differently. In dynamic situations (knowledge markets), market behavior and price interact in continuous feedback loops and can therefore only be studied jointly. It is clear that this market behavior, incorporating pricing issues, will become the backbone of the quantum interpretation of business economics.

Most classical textbooks have two more chapters. A chapter on investment analysis, concentrating on investment appraisal that is highly dependent on a lucrative anticipation of the expected future returns. A final chapter needs to discuss corporate strategy formulation, discussing goals, but most often fixing paths. Porter's chain of value analysis, and/or his five forces model has survived the major quantum revolution. It still identifies a number of generic strategies: cost leadership, differentiation and focus, that, if all assumptions indeed worked, would lead automatically to a fully transparent market with all players having all the information. This would reduce strategy to the one and only really plausible strategy in such a situation of fully informed markets and players, which is a pricing strategy (hopefully based on a cost leadership). In case, once again, the assumptions were true, and the model would work, it would push the remaining players to minimal profits and eventually into losses, which we can indeed observe in certain markets. The airline market is just one illustrative example. As much as markets are emergent and pricing is one of the many loop variables in such markets, strategy cannot be identified, but equally emerges out of the interaction of market players.

In this chapter we would like to propose a new approach to business economics (in practice) which I would like to call a quantum interpretation of business economics. It is clear that stable and linear markets are a special case of this quantum interpretation, as simulations could easily visualize. The laws on which this economic interpretation is based are the ones described in this book.

The basic idea of the quantum interpretation and its visualization tools

Describing companies and markets, we indeed describe the continuous non-linear and dynamic interaction of agents, with their feelings, within a holistic concept. Business behavior is the outcome of such interaction. Business economics is the theory describing the reasons why this quantum interpretation should work, but equally *how* it works, as is done in the principal chapters of this book. The issue now becomes to find a correct visualization tool.

Values are the vision of the company. They are situated on the quantum level, smaller and more subtle than the molecular or atomic level. They are situated in the area of emotions and feelings, the area where sub-atomic particles and forces all seem to flow together (in the unification theory). Eventually, as argued, it all starts in the unified field, the field where we expect consciousness to reside. Thoughts and feelings are already a form of aggregation in that general consciousness. Those values, feelings and emotions are on the level where we are all much more unified than we ever can be on an atomic level. On this level, it makes sense to talk about interacting networks of autonomous agents. But again, to start with, we have to consider the values as drivers and feeders of this quantum reality.

The quantum interpretation of business economics has three complementary emphases: one on the environment, one on the company itself and one on people's interaction. Put another way and in order to label them closer to current business practice we could say: market behavior, management learning and human interaction.

Market behavior describes the environment of the company, the context, the interaction that takes place in what we call markets. Markets are not necessarily physical markets. Even what we call physical markets is really composed of a lot of so called virtual components. All players and influences are of course never physically present on such a market. Policy is made and has an impact, without always really being very explicit. In fact, under market behavior we talk about market and pricing interactions out of which strategies emerge.

Management learning considers the company in its most essential processes (as described in this book): innovation and knowledge considered as learning processes. Instead of a control oriented model, we need to develop and apply a learning oriented process in particular around innovation and knowledge. Both are essential for the longer term development of the company. Both innovation and knowledge management may need some supporting technical tools (like financial reporting, logistics, etc.). However, the latter are necessary but not sufficient elements of management. Those elements are easy to copy, can be described and easily optimized, and can therefore never become a real source of sustainable (profitable) development. It does not make them useless, but just as with the architect's profession, it isn't the tools that the architect uses that make the difference.

Human interaction of people (inside and outside the company) is probably the one complex resource that needs to be understood and carefully monitored. Human interaction needs to be understood as the potentiality of the interaction of people (agents) producing either individuals who co-create out of emergence (on the one extreme) or agents who cause a real disastrous conflict (on the other extreme). The situation obtained is not what is important, but rather the process of potentiality and its evolution. Human interaction, just like management learning, might need some supporting techniques that are, however, never of a nature to replace the necessity to understand the interaction itself.

Up until now there have been few publications about the process of business economics as a learning and emergent concept. Likewise, neither have there been many publications about emergent behavior and the methods of studying it. However, three exceptions have greatly inspired me with agent simulations and neural networks with, to my way of thinking, satisfactory results.

Epstein and Axtell describe in their book "Growing Artificial Societies" how artificial societies can emerge, how they self-organize, how they grow, how they learn and even how they enter into conflict (and how they resolve these conflicts). The book comes with a CD with simulations where one can clearly see what is described in the book. This book is absolutely recommended as a first initiation into the domain of emergent behavior. In different steps, the "societies" learn things which are always more difficult. The purpose of the book is not specifically to show that simulations will effectively be a copy of the reality. It shows that agent simulations can be a path for visualizing emergent behavior. In addition, the book shows that we can obtain a form of "self-organization" in these learning "societies". The book creates a sort of learning laboratory for those who are interested in the emergence of artificial social systems. This book was certainly, for me, a motivation to work on research on agent-based simulations. It visualizes the types of processes on which I wish to obtain more depth.

Another remarkable book is Wolfram's "A new kind of science". This thick and impressive book gives very detailed (perhaps too detailed) examples of emerging behavior, in the sense of an organization suddenly finding itself in disorder. It is a hugely detailed research towards a scientific approach which is constructivist: which builds from very minuscule particles.

The book compares simulation diagrams in search of structure, similarity, order and chaos. It is a plea for a new scientific approach. In light of the large quantity of evidence in the book, it seems to me difficult to still seriously doubt the feasibility of agent simulations after reading this book. The book supports very clearly the scientific concept according to which multiple different elements, each very simple in itself, by following simple rules of interaction, can create complex behavior. This approach entirely fits the theoretical framework which is developed here. It supplies the fundamental empirical dreams for a lot of theoretical concepts which are commented on here.

Mandelbrot has developed what is known as fractal algebra. Fractal algebra is based on the concept of self-similarity: a combined repetition of simple structures can give a complex form and therefore a complex form can be easily approximated by an iterative combination of such simple structures. The basic figure of such structure is a fractal. Artificial life research is in fact based on a similar kind of assumption. In line with Wolfram's study, Mandelbrot creates complex geometric figures that seem to approximate (financial) market behavior rather adequately. Wolfram's and Mandelbrot's proposals are pure geometric approximations of the same kind of reality that I attempt to approximate in this book using either neural networks or agent simulations. The advantage of the latter, for use in management and business, is that the structure of interacting agents (or interacting knots) comes closer to a corporate reality and it is easier to identify within a social reality. Mandelbrot's books, however, illustrate that his fractal geometric approach has huge potential for understanding market behavior in particular and most probably management issues more generally.

Some questions to reflect on

Buckingham and Coffman's studies of organizational effectiveness came up with an interesting checklist. According to them, exceptional managers, what I would call values-based managers/leaders, create a workplace in which employees emphatically answered 'yes' to the following questions:

1. Do I know what is expected of me at work?
2. Do I have the materials and equipment I need to do my work right?
3. At work, do I have the opportunity to do what I do best every day?
4. In the last seven days, have I received recognition or praise for doing good work?
5. Does my supervisor, or someone at work, seem to care about me as a person?
6. Is there someone at work who encourages my development?
7. At work, do my opinions seem to count?
8. Does the mission/purpose of my company make me feel my job is important?
9. Are my co-workers committed to doing high-quality work?
10. Do I have a best friend at work?
11. In the last six months, has someone at work talked to me about my progress?
12. This last year, have I had opportunities at work to learn and grow?

It would appear strong if you would indeed answer yes on all those questions. If you are able to answer yes, could you give examples? If you were unable to answer yes, how would you describe your reality in this respect, and what should change for you?

Bibliography and further literature

Arthur B (1998), 'The end of certainty in economics', in Aerts D, Broekaert J and Mathijs E (eds), *Einstein meets Margritte*, Kluwer Academic, 1998

Baets W (2005), *Knowledge Management and Management Learning: Extending the Horizons of Knowledge-Based Management*, Springer

Baets W (2006a), *Complexity, Learning and Organisations: A Quantum Interpretation of Business*, Routledge

Baets W (2006b), 'Complexity theory: dynamics and non-linearity are the only reason for knowledge management to exist' in Boughzala I, Ermine, J-L, (eds) (2006) *Trends in applied knowledge management*, Edition Hermes Penton Science

Bogdanov I and Bogdanov G (2004), *Avant le Big Bang*, Editions Grasset & Fasquelle

Caro M and Murphy J (eds) (2002), *The world of quantum culture*, Greenwood Press

Chopra D (1990), *Quantum Healing: Exploring the Frontiers of Mind Body Medecine*, Bantam Books

Clauser JF and Shimony A (1978), 'Bell's Theorem: Experimental Tests and Implications', in *Reports on Progress in Physics*, 41

Cushing J (1998), *Philosophical concepts in physics*, Cambridge University Press

Dalla Chiara ML and Giuntini R (1999), 'Quantum Logical Semantics, Historical Truths and Interpretations in Art', in Aerts D and Pykacz J (eds) (1999), *Quantum structures and the nature of reality*, Kluwer Academic

De Meijgaard H, (2002), *Wolfgang Pauli Centennial 1900-2000*, PhD Thesis TU Twente

Dirac P (1958), *The principles of Quantum Mechanics*, 4th Ed, Oxford University Press

Einstein A, Podolsky B, and Rosen N (1935), 'Can Quantum-Mechanical Description of Physical Reality Be Considered Complete?', in *Physical Review*, 47, reprinted in Wheeler JA and Zurek WD (eds), *Quantum Theory and Measurement*, Princeton University Press

Heisenberg W (1927), 'Uber den anschaulichen Inhalt der quantentheoretischen Kinematik und Mechanik', *Zeitschrift für Physik*, 43 In English translation: Wheeler JA and Zurek WD (eds) (1983), 'The Physical Content of Quantum Kinematics and Mechanistics', in Wheeler JA and Zurek WD (eds), *Quantum Theory and Measurement*, Princeton University Press

Klein MJ (1964), 'Einstein and the Wave-Particle Duality', in Geherson DE and Greensberg DA (eds), *The Natural Philosopher*

Mitchell E and Williams D (1996), *The Way of the Explorer: An Apollo Astronaut's Journey Through the Material and Mystical World*, Putman's Sons

Pauli G and Jung H (1955), *The Interpretation of Nature and Psyche*, translated from German, Routledge & K Paul

Schrödinger E (1935), 'Die Gegenwartige Situation in der Quantummechanik', *Die Naturwissenschaften*, 23 English translation as Wheeler JA and Zurek WD (eds) (1983), 'The Present Situation in Quantum Mechanics', *Quantum Theory and Measurement*, Princeton University Press

Sheldrake R (1995), *The presence of the past*, Park Street Press

Sheldrake R and Bohm (1982), 'Morphogenetic fields and the implicate order', *ReVision*, 5:41–48

Simon HA (1996), The Sciences of the Artificial

Varela F (1979), *Principles of Biological Autonomy*, Elsevier-North Holland

Wilber K (2000), *A Brief History of Everything*, Gateway

5 Inclusive Business (Holism)

Sustainability

Instead of following many other authors in discussing the true nature of sustainable development, our approach aims, ultimately, to transform the drive for sustainable development into a concept of sustainable performance. Brundtland (1987) in what was, if not the first then certainly the most influential definition, set out sustainable development as: **development seeking to meet the needs of the present generation without compromising the ability of future generations to meet their own needs.** This Brundtland definition introduces at least three dimensions: the economy, the ecology and the society, and it suggests that they are interconnected. It furthermore introduces a time and a space dimension, and it raises a governing issue. By introducing space and time as variables in the equation, Brundtland has introduced a paradox in managerial thinking. The classical Newtonian view on management cannot cope with a moving and integrated space-time concept. From that perspective, as long as the society and the economy move slowly, one can make a fixed time-space approximation. That era is over. The complexity of the world (its non-linear and dynamic character) combined with the speed of change, no longer allows for non-linear static approximations. Classical metrics fail and the thermometer becomes the disease itself.

The Brundtland definition introduces the paradox of the short term versus the long term. Short term efficiency is required in order to remain attractive to shareholders; at the same time a longer term sustainability orientation is needed in order to be attractive to the stakeholders. Paradoxes enforce choices; choices and balances between different and sometimes orthogonal interests. Another paradox that Brundtland reinforces and which is not new is the paradox between reductionism and holism. Classical managerial approaches mainly, if not exclusively, focus on financial performance: the so-called "bottom-line". With the Brundtland definition's introduction of extra dimensions – for example, societal, ecological, temporal and spatial – no reductionist approach is up to the task of helping a manager answer the issues raised by the massively increased complexity.

Nevertheless, attempts have been made. One example was to introduce the concept of corporate social responsibility and then request reports on the company's responsibility. Companies have also been required to report on their ecological footprint and, ultimately, may be held responsible for being ecologically neutral, and may even have to "pay" for their carbon emission rights. This again turns responsibility (a value) into an economic good that can be traded as an emotionless economic good. It doesn't matter if a company pollutes, as long as they pay for it. That opens the way for countries who are willing to sell their "non-production" of carbon emission, to get some money for their economic development, just as there is a market for healthy third world body parts, such as kidneys, for wealthy recipients in richer economies. From a holistic perspective, needless to stress, this only shuffles the problems around and, as usual, it ends up in the laps of the powerless. A reductionist approach to sustainability, responsibility, and even ethics, will only lead to displacements, not to solutions.

Participants in the Global Compact Summit can sell off the carbon emission that they cause in the process of flying to the summit. When are we going to use video conferencing and, in so doing, open up such a summit to all those that are economically unable to attend? Why do we still organize higher education at certain localities for the happy few that can make it and afford it, and leave out millions of people who are struggling to get education and, through education, development and growth? The technology is available; it is an issue of choice. Within a reductionist frame, a reductionist answer is offered: make "misbehavior" an economic good. On the assumption that everything can be reduced, assume that everything is an economic good and therefore anything can be commercialized. But can responsibility simply be diminished to the status of an economic good?

Global Compact principles

The Global Compact is a program started by the former Secretary General of the UN, Kofi Annan, at the Davos Summit in 1999. It is (in the words of the Global Compact program itself) a framework for businesses that are committed to aligning their operations and strategies with ten universally accepted principles in the areas of human rights, labour, the environment and anti-corruption.

As the world's largest global corporate citizenship initiative, the Global Compact is first and foremost concerned with exhibiting and building the social legitimacy of business and markets. The program accepts that business, trade and investment are essential pillars for prosperity and peace. But in many areas, business is too often linked with serious dilemmas – for example, exploitative practices, different forms of corruption, income equality, and barriers that discourage innovation and entrepreneurship. On the other hand, responsible business practices could, in many ways, build trust and social capital, and contribute to broad-based development and sustainable markets.

The ten principles of Global Compact are the following ones:

Human Rights

- **Principle 1:** Businesses should support and respect the protection of internationally proclaimed human rights;
- **Principle 2:** make sure that they are not complicit in human rights abuses.

Labour Standards

- **Principle 3:** Businesses should uphold the freedom of association and the effective recognition of the right to collective bargaining;
- **Principle 4:** the elimination of all forms of forced and compulsory labour;
- **Principle 5:** the effective abolition of child labour;
- **Principle 6:** the elimination of discrimination in respect of employment and occupation.

Environment

- **Principle 7:** Businesses should support a precautionary approach to environmental challenges;
- **Principle 8:** undertake initiatives to promote greater environmental responsibility;
- **Principle 9:** encourage the development and diffusion of environmentally friendly technologies.

Anti-Corruption

- **Principle 10:** Businesses should work against corruption in all its forms, including extortion and bribery.

The Global Compact is a purely voluntary initiative with two objectives:

- Mainstream the ten principles in business activities around the world
- Catalyze actions in support of UN goals

To achieve these objectives, the Global Compact offers facilitation and engagement through several mechanisms: Policy Dialogues, Learning, Country/Regional Networks, and Partnership Projects.

The Global Compact is not a regulatory instrument – it does not "police", enforce or measure the behavior or actions of companies. Rather, the Global Compact relies on public accountability, transparency and the enlightened self-interest of companies, labour and civil society to initiate and share substantive action in pursuing the principles upon which the Global Compact is based.

The Global Compact is probably the one initiative of the UN oriented towards companies. It cooperates closely with the office of the High Commissioner for Human Rights, the United Nations Environment Program, the International Labour Organization, the United Nations Development Program, the United Nations Industrial Development Organization, and the United Nations Office on Drugs and Crime.

The Global Compact claims to offer its participants the following benefits:

- Demonstrating leadership by advancing responsible corporate citizenship.
- Producing practical solutions to contemporary problems related to globalization, sustainable development and corporate responsibility in a multi-stakeholder context.
- Managing risks by taking a proactive stance on critical issues.
- Leveraging the UN's global reach and convening power with governments, business, civil society and other stakeholders.
- Sharing good practices and learnings.
- Accessing the UN's broad knowledge in development issues.
- Improving corporate/brand management, employee morale and productivity, and operational efficiencies.

Many companies have subscribed to the Global Compact and that in itself is encouraging. But even the voluntary support of a community program doesn't necessary change a lot if the pressure for ruthless growth – with an adequately increased bottom line – remains the corporate credo.

As much as it is not difficult to grow if one doesn't want to be sustainable, at the same time, it is not difficult to be sustainable without growth. The question, hence, becomes how to rethink growth. Growth in itself is not a problem. It should not be forgotten that entire regions and populations make legitimate claims for a decent development that in one way or another will include a certain type of growth. Such responsible growth will need a managerial approach of sustainable performance.

Inclusive business

The imperatives today, however, are further advanced and more so in emerging economies than in more mature markets. Porter and Kramer (2011) discuss the reinvention of capitalism in the Harvard Business Review: Times Have Changed. For them the bigger part of the problem lies with companies that still interpret value creation as optimizing short-term financial performance. This view overlooks the well-being of the customers, the viability of key suppliers and the economic distress of communities. They argue that business has to take the initiative to bring business and society together again. For them this is different from social responsibility, philanthropy or even sustainability; it is rather a new way of achieving economic success. They, however, still remain within the classical managerial paradigm, where there is little space for innovation around values, and bringing in wider societal needs. Within that paradigm, companies should focus on creating "shared value", and not just profit. We argue in this book that this definitely needs another paradigm if it wants to go beyond the (rather conventional) self-interest of the company in all this. For them, the agenda remains company specific with a clear corporate (only) focus.

EABIS (European Academy of Business in Society) recently devoted a conference to "From Corporate Responsibility to Sustainable Business". Perhaps we need to go beyond the concept of Sustainable Business and talk about "Inclusive Business" – business with a wider positive impact for all. Inclusive business can most likely only be values-based and values-driven. But in order to talk seriously about inclusive business, we have to touch on the prevailing paradigm. As someone said: *we have squeezed out of the Anglo Saxon paradigm on responsibility what it has and it was not enough.* Are we, business schools and business people, willing to explore a more inclusive paradigm?

When talking about inclusive business, consider some of the following situations. How can we organize supply chains in such a way that local (small) suppliers can play a role? Why do we still transport fresh food, fruit and vegetables from miles away where we most likely have local growers? This supply chain issue is of course true for any economic activity. Do we feel as a company a responsibility towards the development of local or small business? Another example is the concept of Sustainable Mining, whereby a mining house does not limit its activity and responsibility to the exploitation of the mine, but also contributes equally to the development of the entire community around the mine. This should allow, with possible mine closure, that the community around the mine can continue its economic development. Can we consider that the mining house's responsibility is not limited to the results of the mining operations, but equally to the economic development of the community? Concerning the bottom of the pyramid, is it the idea that companies try to sell products to the bottom of the pyramid that are not made for that bottom, are entirely too expensive and not of real value added? Are companies taking responsibility for designing for the bottom of the pyramid and inventing franchising systems that fit the bottom of the pyramid?

As an aside, I feel that businesses have taken over from the business schools in this matter. Business schools no longer have the prerogative to create knowledge in this field. That is not bad per se, but it reinforces the necessity for much stronger cooperation between business schools and companies. The World Business Council for Sustainable Development (WBCSD) is just one example of this thought leadership.

As usual, the discussion at the **EABIS** conference focused on profit. But profit is not the issue. The problem is that business often is not inclusive. The driver is the inclusiveness, the values-based focus, and not the profit. But profit is what we need. And that brings us to the discussion about capitalism. Many would like to add something positive to capitalism (responsible capitalism, social capitalism, or whatever). For me, capitalism has everything to do with the ownership question and then we should not even talk about capitalism anymore, as Mintzberg says, "beyond Smith and Marx". The discussion about capitalism is an historic one. Today, it is about the development of more innovative forms of inclusive business, like cooperatives (just to name one already very old form), community owned businesses and employee owned businesses.

Who is in charge? We are. We, business schools and businesses alike, should innovate our thinking in order to create social innovation and to eradicate poverty, inequality and exclusivity. A breakdown in the "social ecology" would be really dangerous, and the tremendous inequalities in the world are a potential time bomb.

Dipak Jain, the dean of INSEAD, feels that the real danger today is inequality. We need to try and come up with a plan that benefits all. That focus forces us to train our students differently. We should pay attention to "Reflection" (where am I, what am I doing, where is my contribution), "Renewal" (how can I grow beyond myself) and "Responsibility" (on an individual level, and what leadership is all about).

Management students should know that they are a happy few in the world and by having this opportunity to study they take on a responsibility that goes beyond themselves. "To whom much was entrusted, of him more will be asked" (Luke 12:48 – The Bible).

In the shadow of the UN Summit on Sustainability, PRME (the Principles of Responsible Management Education, part of the UN Global Compact program) held its third academic summit in Rio in June 2012. An Inspirational Guide was launched where Business Schools that would like to engage with PRME can receive guidance and examples. It was encouraging to see that a growing community of Business Schools has become interested.

However, at the same time, the ever returning fundamental question remains: is it the individual who behaves unethically and should it be individuals taking up their individual responsibility? Or are there other reasons to consider? If we can limit the misbehavior of individuals then Business Schools are not to blame and companies (or should I say "corporations") are not to blame. We have saved the system and we do not have to ask some fundamental questions. We can add more courses on Ethics in Business or Sustainable Management Practice, but the rest is in the hands of individuals.

But is it realistic to think that an individual would not be part of a wider whole, a company for instance, or an economy, and that an individual, to a certain degree, is only part of a wider set of assumptions, indeed a paradigm? I feel that this is the correct discussion. What are our assumptions? What is the purpose of business? Are we interested in creating added value, other than what we return to shareholders? What is growth worth, if it would not be inclusive?

Denying the reality that people fit organizations liberates us from many interesting questions. It liberates us from being critical about what we teach, and it allows us to continue teaching tools and techniques instead of supporting the development of the "being" of the potential manager. It liberates us from challenging our linear, non-systemic assumptions about the economy. It liberates us from the discussion that we train for individual performance, and not for "us", for cooperation, for inclusion. The student cohort present at the conference felt that they entered a business school with the best of intentions but were "brainwashed" (the word they used) for individual performance.

Isn't it about culture, about tradition, about comfort and about the very fundamental paradigm of business that we have been supporting and teaching for the last few decades? Changing this will take time and effort, but do we have much choice? Can we continue the development of economies and emerging economies in the first place, based on a growing inequality between poor and rich, between unemployed and employed, between individuals and collective needs? It is not about us and them; it is about all of us being in the same boat. And we do not need great declarations of our governments or international bodies. What prevents us from starting tomorrow, in whatever jobs we have?

The lively debate between some politicians and the mining industry about the advantages and disadvantages of nationalization, as is currently raging in South Africa, is really 30 years outdated. It is not wrong, nor it is not completely without meaning. It is just outdated. The world has changed. We are in 2013 and business as usual is just not good enough anymore.

The story is known for as long as I have been alive. Socialist oriented politicians (by the way this is not a South African issue only) believe that important industries need to be controlled by the "public" (which often means the cast of the politicians). Sounds fair: strategic importance, contribution to all, business has short term targets, etc. (By the way, most politicians have short term targets also, i.e. being re-elected in the coming few years). Anyway, we easily mix "public" with "politics" and the "greater good". But history has not proven that these links exist. An alternative to nationalization, along the same lines of thinking, is a super-tax. The response from industry is the need for cash in order to invest (not sure this always happens by the way), but the track record of industry is not always one to encourage us to trust them to take care of the long term perspective, let alone the "greater good". This debate can go on for decades (as it has), but it is a war on principles, nothing more.

We know from experience that nationalization seldom works and if there is still doubt just look at Zimbabwe. But more profoundly, there is not really something like a "public" company or a "private" company. There are companies, that all follow the same basic logic of the working capital cycle (for each movement you should get out more cash than what you invested or eventually you will go bankrupt). The ownership might be different, but the purpose should be the same: create added value, deliver something that society needs, and contribute to the development of the economy and its people. Some companies could target more economic value, some would target more social value, and some more societal value. Indeed, all companies should be value driven. This is not a new concept, but it has often been forgotten during the same 30 years of debate on nationalization.

And in classical (macro) economic theory, once wealth is created the government is there to take care of the fair distribution of that wealth, mainly by taxing and subsidizing. More mature economies (like Europe) show us every day where that can lead.

If we bring value, purpose, meaning, contribution and the like into the realm of the company (where it theoretically should be anyway) then the issue of distribution is no longer a macro-economic issue, but it becomes a micro-economic one and indeed, we do not have the theories to deal with that. That is why academics need to develop fresh ideas around values-based leadership, social innovation, inclusive business, etc.

This is where inclusive business becomes center stage. If a company would indeed take its responsibility seriously, and would take care of community development (say around a mining site), develop youth (discover and develop leadership capacity in those communities), contribute to the creation of social businesses and work with local SME suppliers, provide healthcare for the workers, we would not need to discuss nationalization. The greater good would be taken care of.

A number of years ago I held the Philips Chair in Information and Communication Technologies at Nyenrode University in the Netherlands. An annual budget of a company like Philips is bigger than the budget of most of the African states together. Who do you talk to if you would like to have a fairer world? If Philips would build, with each plant they create, a school and a hospital, wouldn't most of the problems be solved? And isn't it the corporation's responsibility to take care of the people working in and around the plant? Aren't they the main stakeholders?

Companies should not replace governments, and governments are still there to take care of those that are not really able to take part in the economic process (due to lack of education, health issues, social issues, etc.). For government, taking care means education, housing, social services and so forth. But companies should develop inclusive business, targeting the greater good of the communities within which they are installed and work with. The driver of business cannot only be value to shareholders. It should be contribution to the community and again, academics might contribute some thinking about how to measure that and how to manage that.

We can no longer hold on to "them-and-me" business thinking. The world has become complex and uncertain, and still, certainly in Africa, has an unacceptably high degree of inequality. We are all in the same boat and other than changing our management paradigm into one of inclusive business, we might need to forge more public-private initiatives. Not to forget the potential for social entrepreneurship. Instead of continuing to pay 80,000 ZAR (US $10,000) for a house in a settlement, what prevents us from organizing a contest for the design of a 10,000 ZAR house (US $1,200)? Design for affordability, not for the ones that don't need it. We still design 80% of our products for 10% of the people. When are we going to design 80% of the products for 80% of the people, affordable and responding to a real need? That would be interesting "Bottom of the Pyramid" thinking, instead of thinking how to market products to more people that don't need it, and can't afford it.

It is not about them and me, it is about us and about value creation.

Inclusive business calls for a much more holistic understanding of business.

A holistic model

Holism is a term that is loosely defined and interpreted by many people in different ways. Is there a common notion of holism? Is there somebody who one day tried to compile all the theories? Perhaps it is evident that one should have all sorts of critiques here.

This chapter builds on one of Ken Wilber's concepts. Wilber visualizes something that could be called different dimensions of the image of the holistic world. It is summarized in the following figure.

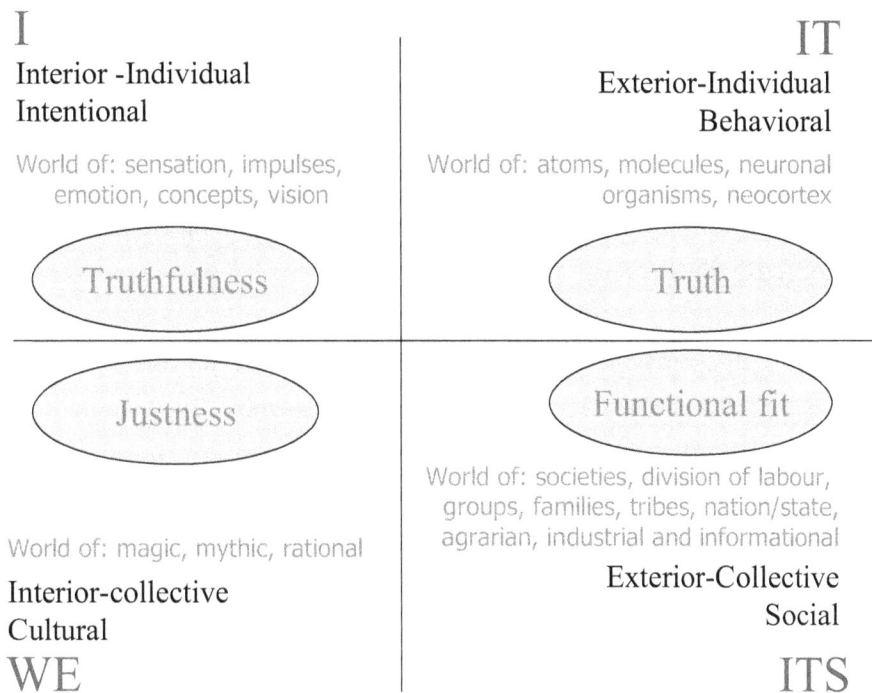

```
        I                                              IT
Interior -Individual                          Exterior-Individual
Intentional                                        Behavioral

World of: sensation, impulses,          World of: atoms, molecules, neuronal
   emotion, concepts, vision                   organisms, neocortex

      Truthfulness                                 Truth


        Justness                             Functional fit

                                        World of: societies, division of labour,
                                        groups, families, tribes, nation/state,
                                        agrarian, industrial and informational
World of: magic, mythic, rational
Interior-collective                           Exterior-Collective
Cultural                                           Social
WE                                                 ITS
```

The figure is developed around two dichotomies: external-internal and individual-networked (collective). The top two quadrants make reference to the individual level. The bottom two quadrants refer to the collective level. The quadrants on the left have to do with the internalization of Man (or processes, or things), while the quadrants on the right examine, let us say, the mechanical part (the external). A holistic image is obtained, according to Wilber, if all the quadrants receive sufficient attention. He labels these quadrants the 'I' quadrant, the 'We' quadrant, the 'It' quadrant, the 'Its' quadrant. All the quadrants matter in order to achieve a life, an observation, a research, and a holistic interpretation.

In the top right quadrant, we study the external phenomena, for example, how the brain functions and so, naturally, reduce it to very specific parts such as atoms; classical reductionism. However, understanding the functioning of a specific atom does not necessarily allow us to understand the functioning of the whole (the consciousness of the human).

What we call, at the heart of science, a global approach, is found in the lower right quadrant. However that is only one of the four dimensions of holism. Here, one can consider the systemic approaches (still mainly mechanical) of ecological concepts, sustainable development, etc.

To really understand what the brain produces, requires attention to the left part of the diagram. In humans the brain causes: the emotions, feelings, concepts, etc. which are used in daily life.

No matter how detailed the understanding of the right part, it still says nothing about what a human thinks or feels. To get to the dimensions on the left, the classical approaches are insufficient. Communication is the only means to try to understand how people feel and what emotions they experience.

In the left part there is also a collective dimension: one could label it "culture". That is related to what are accepted as groups, norms, and values. So a holistic understanding cannot bypass these internal individual and collective dimensions.

Classical science goes completely in search of the 'truth' (identified top right). More and more global approaches of the systemic in science appear as the functional whole. The true notion of Man and his emotions which we call, a little paradoxically, a "flesh and blood" man, does not give a real understanding of truth and fairness. That requires attention to the three other quadrants in order to provide a more complete understanding than the dominant thinking western culture allows. This book aims for a more holistic approach in management research and in the understanding of phenomena.

At the heart of each of the four quadrants we find a natural evolution from physics, via biology, psychology and theology, towards mysticism. Translated into the fundamentals, this goes from matter, via life, thinking, and the soul, towards the spirit. This demands a lot more explanation for which Wilber's book is essential. In a crude summary, holism can be said to consist of an ensemble of 'I', 'We', 'It' and 'Its'. This is quickly recognized in certain metaphors of holism, such as 'Art meets science and spirituality', the "I", "We" and "It" of Wilber, or his ideas, could be expressed as saying that the hands, head and heart lead to holism.

A holistic model for business

Applying this holistic model of Wilber to management, describing companies and markets, within the context of the paradigm developed earlier in this book, we indeed describe the continuous non-linear and dynamic interaction of agents within a holistic concept. Business behavior is the outcome of such interaction. Business economics is the theory describing the reasons why this quantum interpretation should work, but equally *how* it works (see Baets, 2006).

The quantum interpretation of business economics has three complementary foci: on the environment; on the company itself; and on people's interaction. Translated to current business practice, they could be called: market behavior, management learning, and human interaction.

Market behavior describes the environment of the company, the context, the interaction that takes place in what we call markets. Markets are not necessarily physical markets. Even what are called physical markets consist, in part, of so-called virtual components. All players and influences are of course never physically present in such a market. Policy is made and has an impact, without always being very explicit. In fact, market behavior involves talk about market and pricing interactions, out of which strategies emerge.

Management learning considers the company in its most essential processes (Baets, 2006): innovation and knowledge considered as learning processes. The move is from a control-oriented model, to developing and applying a learning-oriented process, especially around innovation and knowledge. Both are essential for the longer term development of the company. Both innovation and knowledge management may need some supporting technical tools (like financial reporting, logistics, etc.). However, the latter are necessary, but not sufficient, elements of management. Those elements are easy to copy, can be described and easily optimized, and can therefore never become a real source of sustainable (profitable) development. It does not make them useless, but just as with the architect's profession, it is not the tools that the architect uses that make the difference.

Human interaction of people (inside and outside your company) is probably the one complex resource that needs to be understood and carefully monitored. Human interaction needs to be understood as the potentiality of the interaction of people (agents) producing either individuals who co-create out of emergence (on the one extreme) or agents who cause a disastrous conflict (on the other extreme). The situation obtained is not what is important, but rather the process of potentiality and its evolution. Human interaction, just like management learning, might need some supporting techniques that are, however, never of a nature to replace the necessity to understand the interaction itself.

Up until now there have been few publications about the process of business economics as a learning and emergent concept. Likewise, there have not been many publications about emergent behavior and the methods of studying it either.

Previous work (Baets, 2006) reported on a number of real life projects, researched in existing companies and markets that formed a first layer of experimental evidence for the quantum interpretation. At this stage, the aim is to reach a diagnostic that allows a manager to consider this company and himself as a leader, according to those three complementary foci: on the environment; on the company itself; and on people's interaction.

Applied to management: A holistic management interpretation

Of course it is clear that the Anglo-Saxon model has brought insight into the functioning of markets and companies and therefore it is extremely important to clearly understand this model. But there is more. While the Anglo-Saxon model implicitly wants to wash away diversity as a disturbing factor, it becomes clear in the wave of mergers and acquisitions currently happening around the world, that diversity can be a creative force. Therefore, a creative use of diversity becomes important in order to tackle the corporate world in the coming years. Openness to diversity and the understanding of different world – and economic – views will enrich future managers considerably. This can be conveyed through the metaphor of the mosaic. If the world consists of different bright colors, then either the colors can be melted together in order to make it one color, or instead, can be combined to create a mosaic, which preserves the original range of colors, and networks them to form an aesthetic arrangement. Besides considering management as a science, management can also be understood as an art. A holistic management approach clearly aims to enrich the prevailing Anglo-Saxon one.

Therefore, in some ways, the proposed vision on management is one of diversity, sustainable development and network structures. Study of the evolution of contemporary companies illustrates that even the larger corporations are in fact a highly dense network of business units, outside providers, individuals, clients, etc. In fact, these combine to form a number of often flexible, overlapping and dynamic networks that cut across the company, instead of just one simple, tidy organization with clear boundaries.

A more holistic management approach cannot focus exclusively on the search for truth, and not only because absolute truth doesn't exist. Despite the difficulty of measuring the internal quadrants of Wilber's model, it is clear that it is rather those internal quadrants that will make the difference. The values, the culture, and personalities of people, be they managers or employees, are going to become the intrinsic cause of the emergence of a responsible management approach.

The Wilber model illustrates the different dimensions of holism in human action based on a framework of two axes. The two axes oppose, on the one hand, individual to networked (collective) and, on the other hand, internalized to externalized. Developing a complete, broad and integrated picture of a person (a manager or a human activity, such as management), one should study the four quadrants formed in this picture to form a systemic view.

The individual-network dichotomy illustrates that in all human activity, although the individual is crucial, there is always a collective dimension. That collective dimension of interacting individuals in companies, markets and societies is increasingly one that is networked (as opposed to a strict hierarchical organization common during the last decade). The internalized-externalized dichotomy is one that illustrates that most knowledge is experience-based, and acquired by experimentation in order to become actionable knowledge via internalization (concepts very popular in knowledge management theory). Nevertheless there is an important aspect of externalized, transferable information that is the visual part of what people read, share, should know, etc.

This diagram can be used to define a vision for any management development activity (or organization). Values and culture belong in the bottom left quadrant, in between internalized and networked. Some the contemporary choices explored and accepted in this book are a choice for diversity as a constructive power. The long term perspective has an inherent dimension of social responsibility, humanism and relativism. These are some examples of shared values and cultural dimension that eventually are going to form the basis of all corporate drive. This left part of the figure is much more concerned with how people (students, future managers, managers, clients) experience culture and common values, how they co-create and co-construct them, and how they are shared.

Such a vision can only be translated into action by people (students, future managers, managers) who have the personality to take on this challenge, and who have the qualities and the motivation to make a real difference in the world. Not only does this necessitate a strong focus on personal development as a backbone for all managerial approaches, but it also highlights the need for companies to organize around lifelong learning and career development for their employees. A key element of management becomes the management of human resources, which translates into managerial competency inventories (assessment centers), personal development programs (coaching, etc.), to create a much greater learner-centered approach.

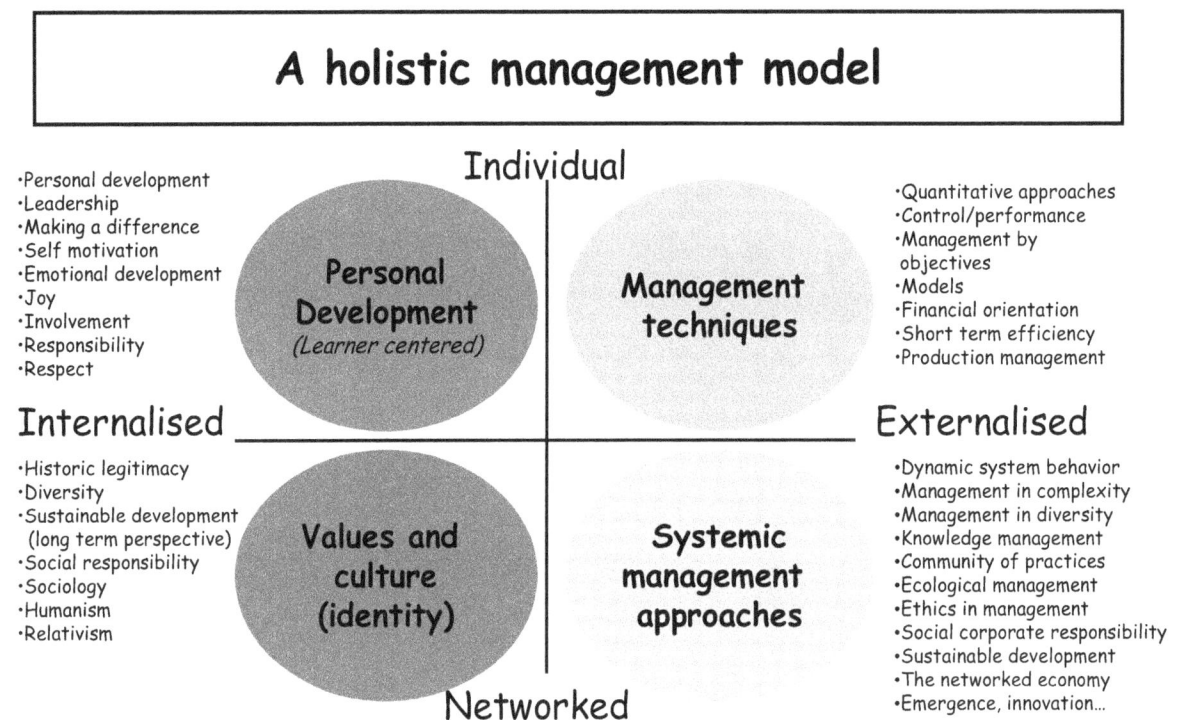

A holistic management model

Individual

·Personal development
·Leadership
·Making a difference
·Self motivation
·Emotional development
·Joy
·Involvement
·Responsibility
·Respect

Personal Development *(Learner centered)*

Management techniques

·Quantitative approaches
·Control/performance
·Management by objectives
·Models
·Financial orientation
·Short term efficiency
·Production management

Internalised — — — — — — — — — — Externalised

·Historic legitimacy
·Diversity
·Sustainable development (long term perspective)
·Social responsibility
·Sociology
·Humanism
·Relativism

Values and culture (identity)

Systemic management approaches

·Dynamic system behavior
·Management in complexity
·Management in diversity
·Knowledge management
·Community of practices
·Ecological management
·Ethics in management
·Social corporate responsibility
·Sustainable development
·The networked economy
·Emergence, innovation...

Networked

These value choices and this focus on personal development, enable innovation and improvement in management techniques. The top right quadrant has a more Anglo-Saxon management approach (or we could label it a more mechanistic approach): a minimum condition to be a successful manager. Its characteristics would include: quantitative approaches, control oriented procedures, performance management, models, financial focus and short term efficiencies. Effectiveness and efficiency are, and remain, important tools for becoming a sustainable company. They are necessary conditions, but, in no way are they sufficient any longer.

The bottom right quadrant complements this model with systemic management approaches. Systems, in this sense, are interacting elements that create a logic of their own that surpass the simple addition of the composing elements. This quadrant contains the more ecological approaches to management: network theories and applications, sustainable development models, complexity theory and concepts around diversity as a constructive force, etc.

A holistic management approach is the "interweaving" of these four quadrants. It is based on a clear vision and values that make a choice for personal development as the backbone of corporate activities. The choice allows people to innovate and optimize their management techniques and to enrich them with a more systemic management practice. Only by pulling the elements of the four quadrants together can the individual develop into a responsible manager who is able to pilot a company for sustainable performance. A manager, just as any other employee, becomes the entrepreneur of his or her own development, within a dense and intensive network of peers. In contrast, the Anglo-Saxon model is focused mainly in the right-upper corner and, therefore, although companies might pay some attention to culture or personal development, the focus remains firmly on the realization of financial results.

Now some questions to consider

- Does your company value unconditional responsibility?
- Is your company interested in the integrity of people?
- Is it appreciated in your company that all people are equal in their being? Or are there differences based on income, background, etc.? Does the company operate from the acceptance that, fundamentally, we are all equal?
- Is it appreciated in your company than people behave consciously?
- Is your company honest and straightforward in its communication? Are people expected to communicate authentically?
- Are negotiations in the company based on a constructive attitude, or are negotiations rather done in a fighting mode?
- Is coordination in the company valued, and is it expected that people coordinate their activities and actions precisely?
- Are conscious responses valued, rather than giving the desired responses?

- Is emotional mastery valued in your company? Is the emotional development of people considered crucial?
- Are projects evaluated on all their merits, not just on financial factors?
- Are processes in the company very rigid? Do people have the opportunity to correct processes if necessary?
- Is harmony between people considered crucial? Is interaction between people appreciated?
- Are confidence and control in your company both part of daily management practice? Are they considered to be mutually exclusive or rather two necessary extremes of the same continuum?
- Are confidence and motivation created in order to improve the knowledge-sharing inside the company?
- Is confidence-building, on all levels, a continuous effort in the company?
- Does the company pay attention to knowledge-sharing in order to improve corporate learning?
- Does the company pay attention to confidence-building and motivation in order to improve corporate learning?
- Is there a strong sense of motivation in the company, since it is believed that motivation is a key condition for a good organization?
- Confidence cannot be built without a continuous sense of interaction. Does the company pay attention to this interaction?

- Is every employee part of the corporate learning effort? Is strong support given to each individual to take part in that corporate learning?

6   Values

As argued before, a systemic view on the company starts with a thorough reflection on values. In this chapter we aim to broaden the scope to management by values. Management by values will be the focus for managing for sustainable performance. Indeed, sustainable performance is exclusively based on the realization of socially or societally relevant values. It concentrates on the realization of real value added for the customer, the citizen, the stakeholder, and it does not limit its focus to the shareholder only.

In the first part of the previous century, Management by Instructions (MBI) was what was then called the scientific way of management. Since that time, the evolution of the behavior of markets, and also of our understanding of this evolution – especially in terms of an increasing complexity, uncertainty and rapidity of changes – has fuelled further evolution in our managerial thinking. The 1960s, for example, gave rise to the still popular Management by Objectives (MBO). MBO arose alongside ideas on the role of the group and of group thinking: the idea of matrix organizations, project groups, sales teams etc. This understanding of organizations and their accompanying management style, sometimes guerilla-like, has contributed to economic success over the last few decades. More recent has been the emergence of Management by Values which continues to have a slow uptake. Nevertheless, as this book illustrates, there is a growing demand for more human, purposeful and meaningful orientation of business. What does it all lead to?

Dolan et al. (2006) suggest that the following four interconnected trends are heightening organizational complexity and uncertainty, and contributing to situations where the MBO approach reaches its limits:

1. The need for quality and customer orientation
2. The need for professional autonomy and responsibility
3. The need for 'bosses' to evolve into leaders/facilitators
4. The need for 'flatter' and more agile organizational structures.

Quality and customer orientation are confronted with the issue that in today's markets, value added becomes an issue for continuation – or call it survival. A highly developed customer expectation can only be met either by a value-adding product or service (something which competitors do not offer) or by a price challenging offering (which of course, in the long run, is not viable for the company). Consider the simple question that in practice does not seem to be that simple to answer: what is the value added of your company? What are the market, the economy and the society missing if your product or service would no longer be there (e.g. if it went bankrupt)? Are companies able to state their value added to society and if they would not be able to state it, how could they manage the company to realize those values? If they do not have them, why do they exist at all from an economics point of view (other than for making an individual profit)? Maybe there was no answer since they were all looking for the perfect answer. Further in the book, we will illustrate at least one tool that is able to help you in this discovery.

The need for professional autonomy and responsibility is one that has to do with the re-focusing of the human skills on the human – and the mechanistic skills on the machine. The more technology progresses, the greater the need for humans to take decisions and to use technology to best realize their potential. Successful companies today seem to clearly understand the need for the human dimension in management. In a networked structure, whether a company or an economy, the intense interaction of individuals can only produce emergence if those individuals have autonomy, are responsible and have the necessary professional skills. A soccer team will only function if all players are professionals (they are skilled in playing soccer), they have their autonomy on the field and they are willing to take on their responsibility in the game. There is no other way to manage a soccer team, nor is there any different basis for a company.

Success needs to be based on 'bosses' that evolve into leaders and/or facilitators. The chapter on leadership develops this a bit further. Leadership is related to communication and as Dolan et al suggest, instructions are the management tools of 'bosses', objectives are those of administrators and values are the tools of leaders.

Though many are convinced of the need for flatter organizations, very many traditional organizations are oriented towards hierarchical control with:

- Those who direct and think (or are supposed to);
- Those who control the ones who produce;
- Those who produce.

Some 'bosses', but only a few first-class ones, continue to be necessary, but not as controllers of irresponsible operatives. Rather, in line with Dolan et al's research, their role should be to transmit values, facilitate work processes and allocate and co-ordinate resources.

The scenery of values

As already illustrated in previous chapters "shareholder value only" belongs to the mainstream managerial paradigm that is increasingly called into question. With less and less time to lose, people cannot afford the luxury of continuing to think in a paradigm that hardly questions the "negative" side effect of its own ontology, let alone its impact on all living species, including ourselves and nature. The framework of a short term business view, ignoring the devastating impact of our consumerism on our own environment and our own wellbeing, is no longer tenable.

The discussion on values is sometimes made somewhat artificially complicated. And I will add some of that complexity later in this chapter. There is a very simple way to define what is good and bad, and what are values and what aren't. "Good" is what you happily and proudly talk about to your children and grandchildren. "Bad" is what you rather prefer not to talk about to your children and grandchildren. It can almost be that simple. And indeed, what you do in your job is what you should be able to talk about around the family dinner table. If not, that might indicate some lack of values in your actions and performance.

As stated previously, we sometimes see a strange separation between private life and business environment and Kofman (2006) clearly states that this separation is the cause of much "unethical" or "non-responsible" management behavior. The manager can be at the same time a parent or grandparent and they will talk honestly and discuss with their children and grandchildren the importance of honesty, integrity, and ethics. At the same time they do not hesitate to shirk responsibility for the disasters created in the organization they help to manage and lead. Some go so far as to say that today's managers do not incur any risk any more: at their recruitment they negotiate a golden handshake for the moment the company wants to get rid of them. Poor results or not, substantial bonuses are paid out every year. Where is the link to the risk that such so-called managers run? What would justify their extremely high salaries in the absence of any risk?

Arguably large sums of money are unfairly "earned" through non equitable trade, child labor, unsafe working conditions, unfair legislation and regulation, unfair competition, and fraud in the construction sector which seems to take place in most countries. It is almost place and culture independent; but it is paradigm dependent. Changing this attitude therefore needs an evolved managerial paradigm.

Europe and the US have had some interesting cases. Well known and respected managers of large multinationals were accused of insider trading, which is illegal in many countries. The challenge is to find evidence for insider trading. In respected financial institutions, trading by employees is not permitted. But how can one exclude insider trading by a family member or friends of managers who have key positions in those financial institutions. They can easily share their knowledge in a (also for them) very profitable way. Despite the strict laws and regulations in this matter, it is the fundamental paradigm that governs "management" (and its supporting ideology) that makes this un-ethical use possible and even underpins it. Banking became, like many other industries, a self-referential system. Inside the system it works highly efficiently by using a "jargon" that only the insiders understand. The outsiders do not understand what happens in the system and are therefore excluded from the supreme insider possibilities. Insider trading need not be deliberately unethical behavior. It can be nothing more than a logical consequence of the self-referential system of contemporary banking.

Running a small, sometimes family-owned, business often shows another set of values. Such an "owner" of an organization knows all the people she works with. She knows that she needs the ideas and creativity of all the other people in the company. She feels responsible, not only for all her family members, but also for the people she works with. She considers them as an extended family. She has a vision. She would be able to answer the question of the value add that her organization brings to society. She is committed to the organization and the people she works with (see chapter 8 on leadership). She does not hide behind hierarchy, protocols and the like. She is her company.

The present shareholders of an organization are not the "owner-managers" of the organization any more. There are now shareholders on the one hand and managers on the other. They have different goals, intentions and ideas. Shareholders do not necessary need a vision or a mission. They keep a distance from the organization and the people that work in and for the organization. They are much more interested in managing figures with obvious emphasis on certain figures that interest them most: share value, dividends, etc. If they believe that the organization will do worse in the future, they will leave "the sinking ship" without hesitation, and often long before the water becomes visible to others. Some would call this recklessness that gives no thought to the impact on other stakeholders of the company. A number of acquisitions offer dreadful examples of this, such as the recent breakdown and takeover of ABN-AMRO Bank.

It seems that feelings of empathy are minimal. Currently empathy, respect, a peaceful mind, and love seem to be separated from what we consider business to be. Talking about peace and love is in many parts of the world something you do in private and not in public, especially not in the world of business. In business, the prevailing belief seems to be that the analytical, isolated mind is superior and separates us from our hearts, since minds are much more effective and efficient. But what do we call effective and efficient? Shareholder value only? Return on investment only? Short term (financial) results? Continuous competition?

But what if, as argued in earlier chapters, it is not possible to separate mind and thoughts from the rest of the body? What are the consequences of false hypotheses and assumptions? What price might be paid for these (wrong) mindsets? What about poverty, starvation, humiliation, aggression, child labor, abuse, and other cruelties? It could be that our reason can deal with all of these, but what about feelings and health? Could this be why people in many organizations and corporations avoid talking about love, compassion, empathy, and peace? Could it be that the decisions made by the so called corporations could be completely different if they would not exclude compassion? Is this what people fear most in business? And what is the cause of the many burnouts?

To recap what I said in the introduction, the separation of the owner-manager into an owner (as shareholder) and a manager not only changed the purpose and the method for the shareholder, it also changed them for the manager. As Whittington wrote in his award-winning 1993 book "What is strategy and does it matter?" managers have invented a new type of skill in order to justify the role of the manager. In the era of the owner-manager, the role of that owner manager was clear: it was the leader who committed to the vision of the company, who committed first and who functioned in a co-creating mode. In the absence of that commitment and given that the manager takes a technocrat's role (i.e. managing on behalf of someone else), a new skill was necessary to justify the role and position of the manager: that became **strategy**. Gradually, strategy disconnected from purpose, meaning, commitment, and involvement. A manager is hired, negotiates his golden handshake upfront, has a high salary with a multitude of bonuses and runs no risk. The risk-return logic of entrepreneurship has become one of "administration" (we indeed train managers to become masters in business "administration"). The answer of Whittington is devastating: after having explained what strategy is, it appears to him not to matter.

Everyone is interrelated and we do not want to judge people for what we could call a short term vision. Nevertheless this short term vision causes many problems. Enormous amounts of money are invested in advertising and marketing campaigns to make sure that as many people as possible consume products and use services that are not only unnecessary, but which may even have negative side effects (such as health-related issues with certain types of food, drinks or other legal drugs). In many European countries, Christmas sales are seen as the most important instrument to measure the confidence of the buyers in the national economy. Will we ever be able and courageous enough to re-think growth? We hope that in a new paradigm this might be possible.

Some principles

Before talking about values per se, it is important to spend some time on principles that allow and support management by values. Values in themselves can easily be identified, but if a manager wants to start managing by values, she will see the difficulty of starting the process. Values need a context, and without that context, values are little more than wishful thinking, existing in abstract.

At the core of its vision, the Alliance recognizes the unity of all life and a wholehearted adherence to the noblest aspirations of humankind (as proclaimed in all spiritual and humanist traditions that call for compassion and the celebration of life). The values and principles of the emerging movement for a new humanity (and of the Alliance, which is trying to serve it), are based upon the support of policies, causes and actions that favor respect for life, human dignity, freedom, ecological sustainability, and peace.

The basic tenet of this approach is a consciousness based on the inseparability of all life (i.e. that everything is connected and that therefore our wellbeing is the wellbeing of everyone). This consciousness, I believe, cannot be just passive, otherwise it would remain irrelevant. Instead, it has to be expressed for the benefit of all through service that improves life for all mankind. Love and action essentially need to go together, as Hafsat Abiola suggests while saying that action without love is meaningless and love without action irrelevant.

Sustainability, according to Ben-Eli, calls for deep transformation in all aspects of human activity including our worldview, our values, our technology, our governance and more.

A growing number of people need little convincing that establishing the concept of sustainability as the organizing principle on our planet, will foster a well-balanced alignment between individuals, society, the economy, and the regenerative capacity of Earth's life-supporting ecosystems. It is a challenge unprecedented in scope and urgency in our time. It requires a fundamental shift in consciousness as well as in action. It calls for a deep and simultaneous transformation in all aspects of human activity including worldview, values, technology, current patterns of consumption, production, investment, governance, trade and more.

The concept of 'sustainable development' as coined by the World Commission on Environment and Development and, with it, the term 'sustainability' itself, have been gaining increasing recognition around the world in recent years. Wide-spread use has been followed by growing ambiguity. As a result, both terms are employed within a very broad spectrum of meaning, often to the point of trivialization. Expressions such as 'sustainable loans' or 'sustainable projects', for example, are often used in international agencies which provide financing for development. The terminology relates to questions of whether loans are likely to be repaid, or if projects are likely to be self-supporting beyond the term of initial backing. It has become completely divorced from the deeper and more important questions regarding the very nature of development and its ultimate impact on humans as well as the environment.

To be serious about ensuring a sustainable future, however, will mean being guided by more rigorous concepts and principles that could provide clear blueprints for the required change.

Nothing could offer a better perspective on the deeper meaning of the concept of sustainability than the direct experience of aboriginal peoples and the way their lives have always been intimately linked to their environment. In a documentary film on New Guinea made some years ago, the film makers interviewed a local tribesman. He was a hunter of birds of paradise, a revered profession for generations, passed on from father to son. The birds' feathers are prized for ornamental decorations in sacred rituals. He related the story of how he was doing well, had a good wife and owned two pigs. Then one day he was able to acquire a hunting rifle. Overnight his harvest of birds exploded. With every shot, birds were virtually falling into his hands. He grew rich, obtained a new, younger wife and many more pigs but suddenly, and to his bewilderment, there were no more birds left to hunt.

In a moment of lucid insight, he understood that a 'profit' gained today at the expense of tomorrow cannot be considered real wealth. He also saw how the new miracle tool which brought him such swift abundance, turned into a dark curse, destroying the very resource upon which his livelihood depended. In the 'old days', birds were hunted with blow arrows, a much more demanding practice than spraying lead pellets around. It yielded fewer birds with each hunt, but also left the total stock basically intact. Moreover, in a technique perfected through generations, arrow tips were wrapped with a leather bulb. On impact, a bird would fall to the ground, knocked momentarily unconscious. The few desired feathers would be plucked and the bird, after gaining its composure, would fly away able to grow a new crop of feathers in time.

In his simple observations, this native hunter was able to strike at the core meaning of sustainability. His story brought to the fore two crucial aspects: that ultimately, the concept relates to a particular type of balance in the interaction between people and the carrying capacity of their environment, and that in achieving such a balance some form of self-restraint must be involved. It is this specific kind of balance which must be the focus of a meaningful definition of sustainability, applicable to any population and its related environment: amoebas in a Petri dish, algae in a lake, or humans on the planet.

The current prevailing definition of sustainability emphasizes cross-generational equity, clearly an all-important concept for any society that wishes to endure, but one that is operationally insufficient. Since specific wishes of future generations are not easy to ascertain, it often fails to provide unequivocal guidance when specific policy decisions are debated. Anchoring an alternative definition directly to the relationship between a population and the carrying capacity of its environment, offers a more advantageous approach. It assumes a number of key variables, for example, population numbers, a measure of wellbeing, total inventory and rate of consumption of resources, the impact of by-products generated by human activity on the absorption capacity of the environment, the impact of new technologies in opening or hindering new evolutionary possibilities, and the like, that are all potentially measurable. Hence, the following definition (Ben-Eli):

Sustainability: A dynamic equilibrium in the processes of interaction between a population and the carrying capacity of an environment, such that the population develops to express its full potential without adversely and irreversibly affecting the carrying capacity of the environment upon which it depends.

This definition points to the dynamic nature of sustainability as a state; a state that has to be calibrated with time, again and again, as changes occur in population numbers, or in the resources available for supporting all humans at a desired level of wellbeing. It does not seek to define specifically what such a level is, nor to limit yet unimaginable possibilities for social evolution. It recognizes, however, boundaries and limits that must be maintained by stone-age tribes and industrial societies alike. As long as the underlying conditions for equilibrium are maintained, the wellbeing of future generations is assured.

The set of sustainability principles which follows is grounded in Ben-Eli's definition. The principles are articulated in broad terms but can receive a specific operational meaning in relation to particular sectors of the economy, development issues, business strategies, investment guidelines, or initiatives taken by individuals. We express them in relation to the following five fundamental domains (all representing essential aspects in the interaction of human populations and the environment):

1. *The Spiritual Domain:* Which identifies the necessary attitudinal orientation and provides the basis for ethical conduct.
2. *The Domain of Life:* Which provides the basis for appropriate behavior in the biosphere with respect to other species.
3. *The Social Domain:* Which provides the basis for social interactions.
4. *The Economic Domain:* Which provides a guiding framework for creating and managing wealth.
5. *The Material Domain:* Which constitutes the basis for regulating the flow of materials and energy that underlie existence.

The result is a set of five core principles, each with its own derived policy and operational implications. The set is fundamentally systemic in nature, meaning that each domain affects all the others, and is affected by each in return. Rather than a list, the set should be approached and understood as a coherent whole. The framework of these principles enables a nurturing context for discussing values.

The **first** principle relates to the spiritual domain, to the basic assumptions we hold about the very nature of reality and the values we hold. It calls for recognizing the fundamental mystery that underlies all existence and the seamless continuum that links humans and our technology with the rest of the biosphere, and with the outermost reaches of the cosmos. This principle means honoring the earth with its intricate ecology, fostering compassion and an ethical perspective in all human affairs, reintroducing a sense of sacredness and reverence to all interactions, linking inner transformation of individuals to transformation in the social collective, and fostering the emergence of a genuine, wise, planetary civilization.

The **second** principle, relates to the domain of life. It recognizes that the lasting viability of all complex, self-organizing systems – rainforests, coral reef populations and industrial economies alike – depends on their very complexity. It is their internal variety that allows for the emergence and re-emergence of different configurations in response to change. This principle calls for ensuring that the essential variety of all forms of life in the biosphere is maintained. It means assuming a responsible relationship with all species and ecosystems, conserving the variety of existing gene pools, harvesting other species only within their regeneration capacity, limiting human encroachment on other life forms, and enhancing biological diversity even in areas of human habitat.

The **third** principle, relates to the social domain. It recognizes the need for a new agenda for society based on human dignity, open processes, responsive structures, plurality of expression, social justice and global solidarity. This principle calls for maximizing degrees of freedom and potential self-realization of all humans without any individual or group adversely affecting others. It means fostering respect for cultural diversity as the cornerstone for social interactions, establishing universal rights and responsibilities for all individuals and communities, ensuring inclusion in governance and equitable access to natural resources, strengthening cooperation as a basis for managing global affairs, and rejecting war as a method of resolving disputes.

The **fourth** principle, which relates to the economic domain, recognizes that the accounting system used at present to guide the economy grossly distorts values. It does so by pricing environmental services practically at zero, by repeatedly counting consumption as if it were income and by ignoring important cost components, 'externalities' such as impacts of depletion, pollution and waste. The fourth principle calls for the adoption of an appropriate accounting system, fully aligned with the planet's geological, ecological and societal processes. It means employing a comprehensive concept of wealth involving the simultaneous enhancement of all key forms of capital; incorporating critical externalities in all cost accounting; recognizing a measure of wellbeing and human development in economic calculations; ensuring that taxation and regulation policies are designed to accentuate desirable outcomes and optimize for the whole; and finding ways for calibrating market mechanisms to reflect the true value of the global commons.

The **fifth** principle, relates to the material domain. It emphasizes the idea that the limits on possibilities in physical systems and thus on the productive potentials in the use of resources, is ultimately prescribed by the primary laws of physics. The principle calls for using superior design to ensure that the flow of resources, through and within the economy, is as close to non-declining as permitted by natural laws. This means using resources consciously and creatively, eliminating waste, recycling each molecule and employing new knowledge in order to increase performance with each cycle of use. It also means avoiding depletion of capital resources and increasingly using sources of income instead.

Ultimately, any serious reflection on the concept of sustainability and the five core principles that together prescribe it, reveals that the spiritual principle is essential for the possibility of attaining sustainability as an enduring state. It alone underscores the difference between a greedy, egocentric, predatory orientation and a nurturing, self-restrained approach to the world. The spiritual principle drives, integrates and centers the other four principles. It provides the attitudinal orientation that is absolutely essential as a basis of change and, to quote Satish Kumar: "*The moment our attitude changes, everything will start to change.*" Or in Gandhi's words: "*We must be the change we want to see in the world*".

As Jack Welch (former CEO and Chairman of GE) wrote in a letter to shareholders: '*In the old culture, managers got their power from secret knowledge: profit margins, market share, and all that... In the new culture, the role of the leader is to express a vision, get buy-in, and implement it. That calls for open, caring relations with every employee, and face-to-face communication. People who can't convincingly articulate a vision won't be successful.*'

New leaders should be able to have firm dialogues on values. Ethics should be defined and explained in their companies. The organization should be completely transparent and it should be possible for people to analyze the values that drive the organization.

It is important to have internal dialogues in organizations about these values. We are convinced that this can be organized and a profitable situation retained by living according to these values.

During one of our classes we had a debate on responsible management. The question was whether the government and the society should be responsible for sustainable development and performance more than organizations. We personally think that business cannot be separate from society. The businessman and businesswoman are part of society both as individuals and as managers simultaneously. Companies are more often more responsible for pollution and the use of (natural) resources. The impact of the biggest organizations is the least impressive. Some of them have more money and more power than average developing countries in the world (as mentioned before, Philips, as only one example, has a budget larger than certain regions in the world). **It is their responsibility, isn't it?** They invest their money in election campaigns with the hope of obtaining favorable treatment. They can make a decision overnight to delocalize their companies and production processes. Instead of preaching within their families about honesty and integrity, they need to act with those virtues in their businesses.

Does it mean that an individual would not have an impact? We believe that individuals do have an impact. Paraphrasing Steve Jobs: *"It is the people that are crazy enough to think that they can change the world, that are the ones that eventually will do so."*

Another burning question is whether it is possible to do something for the environment and nature without knowing what nature needs? We felt that this question is based on the idea of separation – the disconnection between the observer and the subject. In a new paradigm the observer is connected to the subject. The observer is part of the subject. According to a quantum interpretation, the observer creates the observation while observing. The least we can therefore say is that we are nature ourselves. Nature is not something out there, separate from us.

This only takes a shift in perception and a small change in consciousness. In our business school environments we aim to stop teaching in the traditional sense and rather try to create an environment in which learning can take place. This follows our belief that we are all connected, we believe in unlimited possibilities and that we are able to create something for the better of all living beings. In certain cultures, if one talks about spirituality and business in a new paradigm, it happens that the word "sect" is used. That kind of old thinking avoids giving the opportunity to young people to take responsibility for their own future, and denies them the right to live in peaceful and natural surroundings. It is each individual's choice and freedom to try and make this world a better place, or alternatively, not to bother about it, as Jane Goodall suggested. According to Chopra, change cannot start on the surface. It can only be generated from consciousness, and translated into management terminology, that is where we get to management by values.

What are values?

Without too much effort, it is possible to come up with a whole list of possible corporate values: liability, availability of information, involvement, reliability, conflict solution, consensus, creativity, democratic process, sustainability, ecological awareness, honesty, ethics, organization as a family, decency, shared identity, shared vision, shared values, equal chances, community services, harmony, humor/ pleasure, innovation, integrity, quality of life, long term perspective, emphasis on global thinking, nature conservation, humility, mutual support, openness, training possibilities, optimism, personal growth, personal satisfaction, personal freedom, political involvement/activism, recreation possibilities, respect, respect for the law, risk mindedness, social justice, social cohesion, social responsibility, social security, solidarity, spirituality, strategic alliances, strict moral/religious rules, tolerance, transparency, responsibility, diversity, to make a difference, faith, public health and security, prosperity, continuing improvement, peaceful cooperation, friendship, freedom of expression of opinion, conscience of values, world peace, employment and many other values.

Dolan et al (2006) propose a tri-axial model of organizational values: economic-pragmatic values; ethical-social values; emotional-developmental values.

Economic-pragmatic values:

- Efficiency
- Performance standards
- Discipline

Ethical-social values

- Honesty
- Congruence
- Respect
- Loyalty

Emotional-developmental values (related to trust, freedom and happiness)

- Creativity/ideation
- Life/self-actualization
- Self-assertion/directedness

Adaptability/flexibility The single most critical success factor for Management by Values (MBV) is congruence between what corporate leaders say they believe and what their actions and decisions communicate they believe, in both the short and long term. One should not only preach the gospel. A first step to be taken in management by values aims to achieve high performance in day-to-day work by making it more meaningful.

But what are values?

Dolan et al claim that values are more than just words. Values guide and direct our behavior and affect our daily experiences. Espoused values represent a mismatch between what we say and what we do. Values that are demonstrated through consistent and enduring behavior are lived values. So far, for the ethical-social dimensions they are what they call preferential choices. From an economic perspective, value is also the measure of the significance or importance of something. And gradually, Dolan et al glide away to what are classically called values – the economic value of something (that in theory is expressed by its price).

They even refer to Porter's (1985) value chain, saying that this chain would be a reflection of the shared values of the people that constitute the company. Concerning the emotional-developmental dimension, they identify 'final' values and 'instrumental' values and they suggest that the number of final values a person habitually holds would be less than a dozen. Instrumental values would be much more. The latter can be subdivided into personal values (what is important in life), ethical-social values (what you want to do for the world), ethical-moral values (how you think you should behave) and values of competition (what is necessary to compete in life).

A few examples of each can clarify this subdivision:

- Personal values: happiness, health, salvation, family, personal success, recognition, status, material goods, friendship, love, etc.
- Ethical-social values: peace, planet ecology, social justice, etc.
- Ethical-moral values: honesty, sincerity, responsibility, loyalty, solidarity, mutual confidence, respect for human rights, etc.
- Values of competition: culture, money, imagination, logic, beauty, intelligence, positive thinking, flexibility, sympathy, courage, etc.

Companies and people move from beliefs to behavior via values. Beliefs and values are indeed closely related. Personally we would like to go a bit deeper into our understanding of values, though the classification of Dolan et al gives due attention to human developmental issues. Exploring the book further, however, does bring the Management by Values approach back, at least partially, to the realm of efficiency and management for (financial) result. We think beliefs and values need to be brought closer to each other. At this stage we therefore define a managerial value as ***a measurable belief of value added that leads to action*** and later we will illustrate how to operationalize it as a workable concept.

A step by step process

Dolan et al define Management by Values as a major change process in the company. Accordingly, based on change management theory, they suggest the following step-by-step plan for putting MBV into practice.

It starts with a pre-change phase in which the company asks itself whether they are serious about a culture change? Are they in for the long term and how do you define the long term? Do they have the right type of leadership to initiate and sustain the process? Do they have the necessary resources?

Next, they propose that the company should distil shared essential values. Currently, corporate strategic plans are notoriously confusing in their use of terms like vision, mission statement, strategic purpose, objectives, behavior guides, values and goals. In this phase the company is expected to collectively visualize the kind of future desired, which will lead to the final values that should be integrated in the organization's mission and vision. The current set of values should be analyzed and compared to the desired one (a SWOT on values). Finally, a consensus on the change path should be built. All this is designed to happen in dialogue with all the stakeholders.

Once agreement is reached on the change path, the project teams will commence their work. Their purpose is basically to convert the essential values into objectives for action. These include the design of a set of new practices and policies, especially a human resources policy based on the values. This relates to recruitment and selection by values, training and development by values and performance evaluation, and recognition of effort according to compliance with values. Finally, they propose that the realization of operational values should be monitored via culture audits.

In Dolan et al's processes, there is a high risk that through those very processes, management by values will gradually revert back to management by financial values (economic values). Such processes are familiar, are measureable, are simple to visualize as progress, and can easily be understood in terms of (financial) appreciation. Ultimately, they are very reassuringly close to business as usual. The planned process described by Dolan et al is interesting, but it carries the potential to confirm inertia, and needs strong and visionary leadership to maintain momentum and reach the desired end.

Conscious business: another starting point

Would it help to start even a little more a-centric? Would the culture shock be made bigger by limiting the values to consciousness-related values in line with Kofman's (2006) view that conscious business means finding your passion and expressing your essential values through your work? A conscious business seeks to promote the intelligent pursuit of happiness in all its stakeholders. It aims to produce sustainable, exceptional performance through the solidarity of its community and the dignity of each member.

Ken Wilber (in Kofman, 2006) talking about Kofman's book 'Conscious Business: How to Build Value through Values' says that integral mastery begins with mastery of self, at an emotional level, a mental-ethical level and a spiritual level. Anything more than that is not needed; anything less than that is disastrous, according to him. Peter Senge (in Kofman), on the same book, yet highlights another important issue. The key to organizational excellence lies in transforming our practices of unilateral control into cultures of mutual learning. When people continually challenge and improve the data and assumptions upon which their map of reality is grounded, as opposed to treating their perspectives as **the** truth, tremendous productive energy is released.

Collins (2001) studies what drives average companies to take a quantum leap and become extraordinary. He concludes that a crucial component of greatness is a group of leaders with a paradoxical blend of personal humility and professional will. These leaders, whom Collins calls 'level 5', channel their ego ambition away from themselves into the larger goal of building a great company. Conscious employees are an organization's most important asset; unconscious employees are its most dangerous liability. So what are conscious employees?

Kofman uses seven qualities to distinguish conscious from unconscious employees. The first three are character attributes: unconditional responsibility, essential integrity, and ontological humility. The next three are interpersonal skills: authentic communication, constructive negotiation, and impeccable coordination. The seventh quality is an enabling condition for the previous six: emotional mastery. Conscious employees take responsibility for their lives. They don't compromise human values for material success. They speak their truth and listen to others' truths with honesty and respect. They look for creative solutions to disagreements and honour their commitments impeccably. They are in touch with their emotions and express them productively.

Kofman proposes a systemic organizational map that comes very close to our own development that is laid out in later chapters. In line with Wilber's proposal, he offers a matrix consisting of the columns 'I', 'We', and 'It' and adds three rows (in each column): Product/Result oriented (Have); Process/Behavior oriented (Do); and Platform/Structure oriented (Be). However, most importantly, they are systemic and the purpose is to manage those as a holistic system.

Kofman illustrates the difference between unconscious and conscious attitudes through the following table.

Unconscious attitudes	Conscious attitudes
Unconditional Blame	Unconditional Responsibility
Essential Selfishness	Essential Integrity
Ontological Arrogance	Ontological Humility
Unconscious Behaviors	Conscious Behaviors
Manipulative Communication	Authentic Communication
Narcissistic Negotiation	Constructive Negotiation
Negligent Coordination	Impeccable Coordination
Unconscious Reactions	Conscious Responses
Emotional Incompetence	Emotional Mastery

A big, tough samurai once went to see a little monk. "Monk", he barked, in a voice accustomed to instant obedience, "teach me about heaven and hell!"

The monk looked up at the mighty warrior and replied with utter disdain, "Teach you about heaven and hell? I couldn't teach you about anything. You're dumb. You're dirty. You're a disgrace, an embarrassment to the samurai class. Get out of my sight. I can't stand you."

The samurai got furious. He shook, red in the face, speechless with rage. He pulled out his sword, and prepared to slay the monk.

Looking straight into the samurai's eyes, the monk said softly, "That's hell."

The samurai froze, realizing the compassion of the monk who had risked his life to show him hell! He put down his sword and fell to his knees, filled with gratitude.

The monk said softly, "And that's heaven."

Zen parable

This book attempts to integrate management by values into the larger context of a holistic management view, illustrating the role of the values-based leader. We have developed (and will describe further) a diagnostic for sustainable performance. Once it is used to make the diagnosis, that diagnosis can serve as a guiding principle (see last chapter). As argued in this chapter, management by values is primarily a spiritual choice, but within a context of principles that operate within a systemic approach. In the rest of the book we further develop such a context, its diagnostics and a methodology for practice.

Some questions for reflection:

Could you, as an employee of your company, evaluate yourself on the following qualities/values:

- Unconditional responsibility
- Essential integrity
- Ontological humility
- Authentic communication
- Constructive negotiation
- Impeccable coordination
- Emotional mastery

Once comfortable with the fact that employees/managers would be conscious (and therefore are able to contribute to the realization of values), the next step is to consider the supportiveness of the environment for enabling that realization.

Buckingham and Coffman's studies of organizational effectiveness came up with an interesting checklist (as mentioned previously). According to them, exceptional managers create a workplace in which employees emphatically answered 'yes' to the following questions:

1. Do I know what is expected of me at work?
2. Do I have the materials and equipment I need to do my work right?
3. At work, do I have the opportunity to do what I do best every day?
4. In the last seven days, have I received recognition or praise for doing good work?
5. Does my supervisor, or someone at work, seem to care about me as a person?
6. Is there someone at work who encourages my development?
7. At work, do my opinions seem to count?
8. Does the mission/purpose of my company make me feel my job is important?
9. Are my co-workers committed to doing high-quality work?
10. Do I have a best friend at work?
11. In the last six months, has someone at work talked to me about my progress?
12. This last year, have I had opportunities at work to learn and grow?

Could you draft your situation based on your answers to the above?

7 Personal development and leadership (you and the values)

A new paradigm needs an adapted set of competencies for managers who want to manage within it. Management **in** complexity (not **of** complexity), management **in** diversity, management **in** respect for multiple solutions and multiple truths, and management **in** paradoxes: these are the necessary skills of the manager of today. "Wave or particle?" it only makes a difference in the eye of the observer, the manager. Machines cannot realize values and cannot make intuitive choices. Machines cannot choose between multiple possible truths; managers who behave and think as machines cannot either. In this chapter we explore personal development in order to eventually come to a conversation about leadership.

We could write a little or a lot on this topic, but ultimately every individual will have to take responsibility for their own personal development. It is all related to personal activities and experiences and therefore not easy to write about, and even harder to explain how somebody should go about doing it. Despite the fact that many books have been written on the subject it is not easy to capture all the aspects and dynamics in a book. Having said that, what we can offer are some ideas, some suggestions, which might help you as individual to start your exploration. These suggestions can never be complete solutions. No instrument, independent of how good it is, is able to replace the necessary experimentation and change process a human has to go through. As I mentioned before, one eventually has to lay down the path simply by walking it; that is always the case. Keep that in mind while reading this chapter. What is described here is only the intermediate part of the process to reach the goal, i.e. becoming a learning individual, not clinging to a fixed formula. While learning, the human advances in personal development.

In many dictionaries a "person" is often described in her relationship with theatre and the person is then a role that is played. Only in second-order does the "individual", the personality comes across. It is good to remember Varela here when he defines "enacted cognition". Enaction is typically what a good theatre player does; she does not play the act, she becomes the identity, the personality of the person, the role she plays. Development is often interpreted as "giving growth, bringing to its full potential". Educating and transferring knowledge are other ideas related to development that can be found in a dictionary. The duality between the individual and the "role" that the same individual plays in the network of people surrounding him proves to be very important and will be discussed further. Working at personal change, processes will always have to take place within the given framework of reality and within the existing human network. A person is only the personality he is within his context.

If we continue with the theatre metaphor, we could translate personal development as follows:

> *Developing and bringing to full potential the roles that the player plays (or could play) in the big theatre play (drama or comedy) that is called life.*

However, in a theatrical play we can anticipate with some certainty how it evolves. The set does not change all the time and the different roles are distributed and do not often change during the play either. During the rehearsals the roles and the interaction of the players are fine-tuned and, in general, we expect actors to stick to their respective roles. The play itself and the ending are known by the actors and directors upfront. At least, that is the case in most plays. The ambiance can be different, players can act better or worse, but we don't expect actors to suddenly start doing different things from what is expected. A theatrical play takes place within the scripted framework and structure. Such a play is not really a complex system. The play of life, on the contrary, is a complex system, an ever-changing, dynamic and non-linear system.

One could consider the life in which we are all actors as a big play. But a theatrical play can be interrupted at any time, during the rehearsals and the actual performance. We could rearrange the set, or even slightly adapt the roles and, after repeated rehearsals, we are going to achieve the desired results.

Why this theatre metaphor as an introduction to personal development? Since both the set (the context) and actor are important, but even more so, the interaction between the different actors within the dynamics of the "playing field", and all this within the given limits of the play chosen. In real life, the play is not written yet.

The individual will have to explore and become aware of the possibilities and limitations of the play in which he performs, before being able to play a really active role and a role that is possibly ever-changing. Without new insights, personal development doesn't really take place. I will highlight that when I talk about a possible learning structure for supporting personal development. The combination of new insights on the one hand, and the experience of a different learning approach, internally oriented (reflexive) instead of externally (transfer oriented) on the other hand, are key to personal development. The insight element (the externally oriented, the transfer oriented) refers to the right-hand side part of Ken Wilber's holistic figure. The focus on internally-oriented learning has everything to do with the left-hand side of the same figure, i.e. the interpersonal as experienced by the individual and the highly subjective enaction of the "I".

If we want to do something with the ideas of this book, we have to start searching for a more holistic understanding of different learning situations. As already suggested, we can only give sketches of possible actions, but keep in mind that life and in particular corporate life, offers many possibilities for such experiences on a daily basis. Instead of creating them artificially we could also use reality as a large field of experimentation. To start off with, some personal coaching and acquainting yourself with some self-coaching techniques are very useful. This support could be organized and formal, for instance within the framework of a workshop if the aim is to create a more learning-focused team, or in a more individual setting of personal coaching if the aim is more a trajectory of personal development.

In order to keep it accessible, we cluster the possible actions that you can take in three segments, but they are ideally parallel programs. Since it is you as an individual reading this book we start with the focus on the individual. Next we consider some potentialities of the individual within his network and, in practice, the organization or the company in which the individual is active. But even the organization or company cannot avoid the logic of complexity that is omnipresent. A learning individual within a non-learning organization only leads to frustration. Therefore it is necessary to touch upon some aspects that have to do with the organization or the company: we refer here to some fundamental choices that need to be made.

Focus on the individual

The prevailing paradigm, fitting a reductionist rational view of reality but one which we want to eliminate, is the following: One invents a learning path (or a learning plan) with fixed learning goals that use well defined means in order to reach the set goals in a set time after which we expect the learner to have become measurably smarter or better. Similar to the case of the theatrical play, we presume that we can anticipate the final result from the very beginning and that the roles are fixed. In doing so, we try to arrest our way of thinking as much as possible and the conception of our learning, and we keep it as confined as possible; that is what we often call personal development or renewal. We teach the individual to keep as closely as possible to the predefined play within its given set.

A more holistic approach, however, starts directly with the learner being able and willing to identify learning goals, and wants to maintain the freedom to continuously adapt those goals and in doing so, maintains the possibility to continually learn. The deepest inner emotion of the individual then becomes the driver for possible change. A person takes responsibility for his own learning. There is no stagecoach driver sitting upfront on the box; every individual chooses his or her own path.

That also implies that if a person (or manager) is not able to access his inner emotions – which unfortunately often happens in the western world – the starting position is from the outset very difficult. The design of one's own learning goals cannot be dictated by the world, the environment or what the company would like you to learn – the imagined wished-for behavior or the desired competencies that somebody should possess.

We cannot presume that somebody will walk the path that we have imagined for them, supported by those means that we have identified to be helpful and important and that will lead to better results. Even the goal that we have for another person is often clearer to us than to the individual.

We should not underestimate how extremely implicitly this process becomes internalized. As already discussed, we collectively keep such a system alive and under continuous reinforcement. Schools, youth clubs, social meeting places, TV programs, newspapers and radio flood our daily environment with messages that are consciously and unconsciously stored and metabolized in our bodies and these are many expressions of the culture in which we live. We seem to live in full freedom without realizing that this is only a "dependent" freedom, a relative freedom. Philosophically we could question whether we are at all able to think out of our box. But in that case, all potential for continuously adapted learning, what I would like to call the *real* learning, would become obsolete.

The learning human, therefore, needs to return first to their own inner feelings and sensation. In the western world this is close to a kind of mission impossible, since we strongly underestimate the potential of the embodied mind (as described earlier), a mind/body driving energy. In our world, we often mix the power of thought with an extreme application of the analytical brain function.

Our actions (or our non-actions) are very much driven by our thoughts. Those thoughts are much more consistent than we often think. We are continuously searching for arguments to reinforce our thoughts and give them a higher level of truth. In doing so, we create our own world of thoughts and we keep it alive as much as possible. Our assumptions drive our thought, and eventually drive our action.

If we think that the world will collapse as some religious groups do, then we will see conflict and problems, violence, disasters, etc. everywhere. On the other hand, if we think and observe in term of progress (growth) and if we define progress from a purely economic and technical viewpoint, we start considering countries as developed and less- or even under-developed countries. If we pay more attention in our actions and thinking to the rational side of our consciousness, we will observe the world in a more reductionist manner. If we prefer objectivism to subjectivism we again choose another angle. In doing so, at least I presume, there is something akin to dualism and that dualism would mean a difference between two things or viewpoints.

In Eastern cultures people pay more attention to personal experience (to the subject), since the objective side just exists and is factually the same for everybody. The individual's interpretation is what makes the difference. That personal sensation gets more attention and therefore there is less of a difference between the inner and the outer world.

No doubt, it will be difficult for the learning manager to get close (enough) to their own inner feelings. Indeed, (guided) meditation is a possible way to get in touch with and re-discover the inner self. Experience has shown that it is extremely difficult to take the first steps on this learning path. Not only do we not have much experience with exercises like meditation (though ritual prayer is not necessarily that different), but unfortunately there is also a lot of esoteric movement around techniques like these that do not always pay it proper service. In our world, the search for the inner self is highly discredited – we pay a high price for this. Do not forget, however, that thought invariably leads to action. If you want to become a learning individual, you will have to start with focusing on your own learning goals.

> *You are where your thoughts are*
> *Assure yourself that your thoughts are there*
> *Where you would like them to be*

Once this first obstacle is overcome, one cannot understand personal development independent of the culture or environment in which someone emerges. Personal development has to do with how someone considers their culture or environment. These thoughts give security and structure to our existence, but at the same time they limit our learning and/or they can make someone a prisoner of his own life. The "we" experience of culture refers to the left lower quadrant in Wilber's holistic picture.

The personal learning aims are still central, but now we consider them within the network in which a person operates (very often the company). For simplicity, we can call that the external sensation of personal learning, but also then explore the fact that this part can be "shared". What is learned, and how individuals experience that learning, remains highly personal. But part of the learning goals and part of what has been learned can now be shared. There is a common context.

In order to support this process, we have developed a methodology and have made it available via electronic media, for example through electronic learning platforms or corporate intranets. Particularly for companies and larger groups this latter variant is interesting and allows working on a somewhat larger scale while keeping the required flexibility.

The aim is to allow participants (managers, learning individuals) to realize their individual learning goals – walking the path to find the path – based on a personal responsibility. The anticipated result is that managers are able to manage their personal development plan better than before (beyond this organized course). The methodology consists of a number of steps and though we briefly describe them here, this description is in no way the methodology itself. Neither does this give real insight into the experience that the learner gets when applying this method.

At the start of the learning trajectory, there is an intake interview that roughly deals with the following questions, with the aim that participants explore their own current feelings:

- Who am I?
- What do I want to attain or what do I want to learn?
- What do I need in order to do that?
- How do I anticipate achieving that?
- By when do I want to have accomplished this?

The aim is to translate in a very detailed yet simple way, a number of individual wishes, intentions and expectations. Based on the results a personal learning coach could be sought. Next, participants start working on the more content-focused parts of the course, always using a learning-by-doing approach (in fact many other courses could fulfill this need, though some are better adapted for the purpose than others). A course in this context can never be a traditional knowledge transfer, teacher driven course. As already indicated, personal development can only flourish when learners are confronted with new insights, preferably insights that challenge the individual. Within the right circumstances the combination of new insights and personal development will continue. The trio of insight, form and meaningfulness (science, art and spirituality) that we identified earlier is the guiding principle for the entire methodology and course. This "course" could just be daily practice, which brings personal development squarely back into workplace learning.

One could use competency criteria and behavioral criteria, in order to facilitate the desired learning (see questions at the end of this chapter). The knowledge and innovation approach advocated in this book is clearly and exclusively one based on competency development. Competencies of possible interest to a manager that could be explored are: courage, initiative, independence, the capacity to deal with stress, capacity to convince, organizational sensitivity, ability to cooperate, flexibility, ambition, energy, etc. Of course, these criteria need to be adapted to suit different companies or organizations and to what each individual wishes to learn.

The role of the leader is hopefully clear now: to stimulate, to activate, to motivate, to inspire and to increase enthusiasm. However, the success factor that underpins this approach remains the responsibility of the learner for their own personal learning. The learner decides where to go, firmly gripping the steering wheel. The learner reacts on what is offered, but also creates. The learner respects others' opinions and listens to others. The learner contributes to the learning processes of all other participants, but also respects the privacy of others. In practice this list is longer but this offers some insight into the basic rules of the game.

This rather external approach to personal learning and development can only succeed if we do not ignore the emotional component in this learning and developmental process. Learning without emotions is like training a monkey for the circus.

Focus on the network

While we have paid much attention to the person (let us say the personality of the manager), personal development cannot be seen independently from the structures in which the individual operates. This book has highlighted these concepts a number of times. What can a manager do in order to become a learning individual within a non-learning environment? How can a manager create a learning environment? A few ideas could help give orientation in line with the paradigm developed in this book. We look at it as the person (manager) participating in the game called the company.

We generally observe that people leap quickly to potential solutions without really listening to the problem and without using the power and insights of others. The manager is often immediately ready with his answer, his solution. There are many procedures in place to solve problems and even emergency procedures in case the first ones did not work. Depending on the target decided, an optimal path is automatically deduced. And the target itself is almost automatically generated by the question or the problem. Indeed a rather mechanistic way of organizing, but observing managerial practice, this seems to be the practice of the day. Add to this the hierarchical organizational form and we are faced with static, non-learning organizations. In even the best cases, the improvement of a procedure will often only lead to a marginal increase in efficiency. In the worst case it is completely counterproductive with no result. What can be done in such a case?

First of all, we have to observe that given the rather strict mechanistic basis of western management thinking, it is extremely difficult to change that radically. Therefore, and certainly in the initial phases, some coaching, training or education will be necessary and will yield results. There are multiple possible ways of dealing with this and these should be considered case by case. Again this will depend on the people involved and the context within which they work.

What should be acquired first are the rules of the game of the network. In the previous chapter we elaborated in some detail on these rules of the game, but we will summarize them here. In order to allow a network to achieve autopoiesis, a number of conditions should be met. The network should be ring-fenced in order to (technically) avoid deviation from the path and having elements of the process fall away. Returning to the analogy of playing soccer, it means that we should first define the soccer field and rules in order to avoid deviating into playing another game (remember that the field is an integral part of the game). The boundaries do not necessarily have to be too restrictive and therefore confine the playing area, but it has to be clear for all players. For soccer players it is clear that soccer is played within the lines of the field. If we move the boundary (and make the field larger for instance), we would not have exactly the same game on a larger field, but would instead create a different game altogether. The larger and more diverse the field, the more possibilities exist and the more potential the game has. Hence, the first task of the manager is to define the boundaries and size of the field.

Next, all players have to attempt to optimize and maximize their own interest. It is the role of the manager to bring together the players who contribute to a larger common purpose, yet still enhancing their respective interests. That common purpose is not easy to determine and it is also not the path to be followed. We will return to this later. Since each individual optimizes their own behavior, it is not required of the manager to give too much direction or exercise a lot of control. This is easier said than done.

Finally, participants should agree on a minimum set of rules of interaction and communication. In soccer the rules of the game are essentially that players should not touch the ball with their hands, should not kick and shove each other, etc. In business, rules would be mutual respect, clear, sufficient and continuous communication (and here knowledge management could again play a role), etc. It is the role of the manager to co-create these rules in consultation and cooperation with players but, above all, to facilitate adherence to, and recognition of, the rules. In optimal conditions this communication should be easy and productive. As discussed in detail in some of my other books, this leads us rapidly into knowledge management as a facilitator for continuous learning.

In summary, the manager has three main tasks:

- Define boundaries and make sure that everybody knows and understands what they are;
- Motivate everybody to optimize their personal interest as much as possible while supporting individuals to contribute the best of themselves;
- Identify clear and simple communication rules with the aim of aiding effective communication.

In practice one could work at this in different work forms, though workshops have proven to be the most straightforward.

However, there is a small "but". We should all know where we would like to go. When Alice in Wonderland asks the cat which path she should take, the cat's question in turn was where Alice wanted to go. Since she did not know, the path didn't matter much. If one doesn't know where to go, every path is an equally good one. That does not mean that a predetermined target absolutely has to be reached. But without a goal we cannot make any initial choices. If, when arriving at a fork in the road, you don't know where you want to go, you cannot make a definite choice and you remain at this fork (or place in your career).

The human in his world

The goal has everything to do with the aim of the company. In many cases, a company does not really have a vision. Most company "vision statements" are the same: service to clients, growth, quality, etc. They are almost interchangeable. And from that "vision", managers automatically attempt to plot a path: which steps should be taken in order to realize the vision?

However, there is frequently a step before that which is concerned with paradoxes and often mutually exclusive choices: what is the value that the company is contributing to society? Next we should consider how the network could be organized (the minimal network requirements) to realize the choices made. That is what I would like to call a "business architecture" – it is the first sketch of the network organization that we want to grow, to cultivate.

This can clearly only be achieved by gathering people around a table. In order to avoid immediately falling back into attempts at defining the path, external facilitation is highly desirable. Some examples of fundamental choices that should be addressed in such workshops are:

- Short term orientation (shareholder value) versus longer term vision (sustainability)
- Are we in search of "simplicity" (limiting and controlling the complexity and hence the possibilities) or rather complexity (creative potential)
- Is the management approach one of control (spreadsheet management) or rather one of stimulating initiative
- Do we consider diversity as a creative force or rather as a disturbing factor

Concerning the design of a business architecture, different methods exist, though most of them are not based on the self-creating and self-organizing power of a network. When choosing a methodology it seems important to us that it should be based on a well thought-out paradigm, in line with the identified aims. And let us keep in mind that here too, order will lead to chaos.

Leadership: the driving force for realizing values

To accept a holistic management approach is to accept that responsible management goes far beyond the traditional, mechanistic and control-driven view. It even goes beyond the desire to create an interrelated economy because that interrelatedness (right lower quadrant in our holistic model) is only a consequence. The basis and drivers are values, purpose and meaning. It is a management style that is value-driven and that gives true meaning and space to everyone's need for personal development, improvement, and ultimately learning. It further considers that the personal development of each employee provides the driving force and the energy for the success of the company. In other words, leadership becomes central in management.

Much academic research has been devoted to leadership, leadership styles and leadership training. Instead of replicating that here, this section develops a metaphor around the orchestra and its conductor, to generate a checklist for sustainable leadership. It is based on a 1999 BBC recording made in cooperation with the conductor Nierenberg and the BBC orchestra. The analysis of this metaphor will produce a leadership checklist – a set of questions to help evaluate existing leadership quality, and will also provide a learning path for creating more inspirational leaders. Nierenberg had placed a number of managers (as he calls it – people that occupy the podium) inside the orchestra, in order to be able to make different types of observations. He then undertook a number of experiments with the orchestra during which he asked the managers to observe and reflect. Retrospectively this emerges as a superb course in leadership via experimentation. The main lessons learned from this powerful metaphor can be identified as follows:

First, accept for a moment that the orchestra is the company, with its multiple divisions, geographical locations, middle managers, etc. The purpose of the orchestra is to deliver a service (to create an emotional sensation with the audience – any sensation of joy, grief, danger, despair, etc. – whatever the score and composer chose it to convey). There is some hardware involved (musical instruments), there is a common process (the score), but all that is only in support of a service to be delivered in real time to a client. That is not so different from what most of the companies claim to do in Europe and the US. The conductor is the CEO. The conductor is not the best "first violin" that is afterwards promoted to conductor. If an orchestra were to do that, they would lose twice: first, they lose their best first violin, and second they risk appointing a conductor who's not necessarily the best person for the job. Being a conductor is a profession that, of course, needs a more than average knowledge of music, playing instruments, harmony, etc. but that, above all, is a profession of leadership in its own right. A conductor is indeed a leader, a visionary, an inspirer.

Management often promotes the successful marketing manager or financial manager to CEO. And, if he or she is indeed a successful marketing or financial manager, the company loses the successful manager but it has no guarantee that it would have a good CEO, and unfortunately the promoted manager will most probably continue to have a functional focus. Like the orchestra's conductor, being a manager is a profession in its own right, requiring good technical and functional knowledge, but most importantly he or she needs to be a leader that is able to keep the holistic view of the orchestra and, simultaneously, the service to be delivered to the audience. A conductor is not the one who plays the music. He or she has another role to fulfill – the role of the visionary leader, the motivator, the coordinator, the one that sets out the vision and takes the responsibility of the podium. In this way, a really good CEO is no different from a really good conductor.

Playing music involves many, many decisions to be taken, all individually and most very small, but taken together the interaction of multiple individual decisions makes or breaks the success of the music performance. Each musician has the capacity of balance between activity and restraint. Both are equally important, both for playing the instrument and for coordinating with the others. Each and every individual should be able to perform his or her task. These are the essential cornerstones of the service eventually delivered. The instrument (the hardware) really becomes part of the body. It appears that the violin (for example) is nothing more than an extension of the body. And ultimately the body plays the music, not the violin. The violin is only the sensory connection with the external world. Two musicians playing the same score on the same instrument can create a different sound and a different sensation. While playing, all the senses are engaged, senses that go far beyond analytical or technical skills. Delivering a service has to do with all the senses, with emotions, with connectedness with the client. Playing music is, for each musician, an incredible act of coordination. They need basic technical skills, but the value added is created in the coordination, both inside themselves and within the orchestra. Each musician has to have the ability to work together in a team.

The teamwork creates the sensation and, if a musician fails in that teamwork, the dissonance could become disturbing to the orchestra's performance. Other team members cannot necessarily make up for the failing musician. This coordination, this teamwork, needs a constant sense of awareness, of presence, of being in the "here and now". The conductor, and each musician, all need this sense of awareness. Being at work, and really creating value, needs a sense of awareness and presence. Therefore it is an illusion to be able to separate private from professional life. Being aware and present is something that is done with the entire body, the senses and the emotions – it is a holistic presence in the way described above.

An organization, just as the orchestra is made up of "positions", has geographical positions. In the orchestra, the violins are in the front, the percussion is at the back. Each position, however, goes with a different level of information. It is clear that the violin player in the front will hear more of what the other members of the orchestra play, than the percussionist at the back. They all do not need to have the same information. The conductor, however, needs to be aware that they all have different levels of information. Information management, information flow, and communication inside a company are therefore of outmost importance. We do not need to know everything, but information needs to be clear, transparent and adequate.

Coordination stimulates communication and given the crucial role of that coordination, communication does need a lot of attention – the quantity, the quality and the tone. Only the leader has the global view. It is precisely this global view that gives the leader the responsibility of the podium. Managers like to take the podium, but they do not always assume the responsibility that goes along with that podium. A true leader always assumes his or her responsibility, afforded by the podium. Today we see too many shareholders and managers alike that do not feel responsible for the company, the people (the musicians) and the clients (the audience). Connected with the eagerness to get the advantages of the podium (the salary, the status, etc.) it explains some malaise in today's management practice. Essential to success on the podium is the responsibility that goes with it.

An orchestra does not need a conductor, if it were only to play music. In the absence of a conductor, the orchestra can be remarkably self-organized – they get started, play, and just coordinate more. Obviously, that is not where the leader's role is. A leader is not there to organize the others. They can do that perfectly well themselves. Do not forget that each and every individual is perfectly capable of doing his or her job. In the absence of a formal organizer (which is not the same as a formal organization) the network of communication that the company essentially is, only becomes more intense. What then, is the role of the conductor? The conductor sends signals to the orchestra and gets feedback. It is the conductor's role to send and receive (and listen to that reception). What the conductor precisely sends – see below – is something very important (we would almost say something very sacred).

Ultimately, the energy that the audience feels while the orchestra plays the music comes from the composer and the many musicians that have already played that music (in line with the morphogenetic fields of Sheldrake). But in the concert hall, the energy comes from the people and from the purpose. It is the combination of musician and purpose that delivers to the audience that immensely satisfying, intense feeling of music (if it is well played; the "flamencos" call that "duende" – the indescribable feeling of being together and interconnected that brings the musicians and the audience into a more trance-like state). It is this combination of musician and purpose that creates the energy that the audience feels. It is the same combination of employee and purpose that the customer would be able to feel. That is what creates the energy necessary to deliver the service. Within this realm, the leader creates the space for the others in order to co-create that experience.

What is the message that the conductor sends out? The conductor (and hence the leader) always says what has to be done. He or she projects a vision. A conductor should never correct a musician (anyway, the music would have to stop to allow it). That doesn't mean that at the next rehearsal one cannot debrief the performance, learn from the errors and decide on corrective (learning) actions. Learning is, in fact, the essential component of observation and debriefing. How many times in our managerial practice do we "correct" people? How many times do we, hence, stop the music? And how many times do we lose the opportunity to learn from experiences instead of correcting them?

However, once a message is sent out, it takes time for the organization to respond. In the situation of the orchestra the response time is very short. In almost all other organizations the response time is much longer. This is a difficult moment. Once the vision is sent out, one has to wait until a response comes. The more the vision is supported and believed, the easier that period of waiting will be. If, on the other hand, there is no vision, or the vision is merely a window dressing act, the risk is high that the manager is going to adapt and/or correct the signals sent out rapidly, or even send out new (and different) signals, for fear of not getting any response. This results in unclear communication, and unclear communication makes it extremely difficult for the musicians to perform well. The leader has a vision and he or she sends out that vision. Then the leader waits for response, trusting the musicians.

Leadership is about committing to what has not yet happened. Leadership deals with creation, innovation and new directions (not copying what others have already done). It is the leader who commits first and if the leader would not be able or capable of committing, then the musicians cannot follow. The role of a leader is important; the one of a manager much less so. With some creativity, management can be seen as rigid leadership. The conductor's experience with rigid leadership is however discouraging. If the conductor attempts to conduct (to lead, to manage) the orchestra rigidly, it seems to create confusion amongst the musicians. They do not know what the conductor wants to send out precisely. They don't feel confident and at the end, rigid leadership slips off the line, the purpose – that for which we ultimately act. Just as rigid leadership creates confusion, so too does unnecessary movement. The latter creates un-clarity and that, in turn, creates tension with the musicians and eventually leads to under-performance, or worse. As with micro-management, rigid leadership, overly controlled leadership, unnecessary movement and messages, and bad communication all lead to tension, loss of purpose and under-performance. At the end of the day, the controlling leader gets precisely the opposite of what he or she aims for.

In the TV program that Nierenberg presented he does a final experiment. He asks his orchestra to do two very comparable acts. Twice the musicians are asked to play for a particular person (a client). In the first experiment they have to play technically as correctly as possible. The violins, for instance, have to move their bows exactly in the same place and in the same manner as the first violin. In other words, though they will all play technically as correctly as possible, they are not really playing for the client, but they are primarily internally oriented. Their focus is on doing it the way they should do it. In the second experiment each and every musician should play in such a way as to try to give the person (client) that great feeling of despair and salvation that (in the example) Brahms intended to provoke with his music. They play technically as they feel they should (since they are all capable of performing what they are expected to), but their focus, of course, becomes outward bound. Their focus is really towards the client. In the first experiment, and now applied to business, most companies will consider this experiment as client focused. For Nierenberg, this is not the case. Not surprisingly, the music sounds very different and much more convincing in the second experiment as compared to the first. It is not enough to know that there is a client. It is not enough to say that we are client-oriented. We should all play as if we are playing for that one and only client. Without delivering that client-orientedness, the playing is bound to be technical, without a vision, and without that, the message rarely comes across. It is this external focus that gives meaning to our work.

The leadership's checklist

Based on the previous section, we have drafted a so-called "leadership checklist". It is just a checklist that helps to identify how close one is to becoming a real leader, instead of just a manager. Part of this checklist will be used in the overall holistic diagnostic tool, Cassandra, which will be developed further. An honest and detailed reflection on this checklist allows the reader to progress on the journey to sustainable leadership.

- Are we able to take many 'decisions' in parallel?
- Are we able to balance between activity and restraint; or are we capable of 'slow' (well considered and thought through) management?
- Do we base our leadership on the belief in each individual's ability to perform his task?
- Do we consider any 'instrument' we use as an extension of our enacted leadership?
- Do we engage all our senses?
- Do we see management as an incredible act of coordination (and not control)?
- Are we really able to work together in a team?
- Do we have a constant sense of awareness?
- Are we aware that organizations are made of 'positions', and that there is a different level of information related to each position?
- Are we aware that only the leader has the global view and do we act accordingly?
- Are we assuming the responsibility of the 'podium'?
- Are we aware that the orchestra doesn't really need the conductor?

- Do we accept the self-organizational capacity of the organization?
- Do we see the company as an intense network of communication?
- Do we behave as the conductor who sends signals and receives signals back; are we open to receiving these signals back?
- The energy that makes the company turn, ultimately comes from its purpose: do we have a purpose and do we manage that related energy?
- The energy, created by the purpose, is carried and transmitted via the people: do we manage people accordingly?
- Do we, as managers, create space for the others?
- As managers, do we say what *should* be done (rather than what should *not* be done)?
- As managers, do we project a vision; or do we rather correct people's behavior?
- Are we aware that power always goes with responsibility and do we take the responsibility of our power?
- Are we able to perform 'slow' management, knowing that there is a response time?
- Leadership is committing to what has not yet happened; is that our daily practice?
- The leader should commit first. Do we do that?
- Rigid leadership creates confusion. Are we flexible enough in our leadership style?
- Rigid leadership chops off the line (the purpose). Can we identify when we chop off the line?
- Unnecessary movements (unnecessary activity and change) create confusion. Do we actively limit confusing messages and actions?
- Un-clarity causes tension and under-performance with the people. Are we always crystal clear in our communications?
- Are we aware in what we are oriented to the technicality of processes? Do we see where this limits our client focus?
- Are we sufficiently externally focused? Are we aware that it is the external focus (the desire to serve a client that is waiting and paying for your service) that gives meaning to our work?

Some managerial competencies

In certain cases companies have identified the managerial competencies their managers require. In other cases, those competencies need to be defined. However, monitoring the process of the learning coach/manager will need a kind of tool, some identifiable goals, and competencies that the learner aims to develop. The following offers an example of a list of managerial competencies appropriate for developing a manager with the ambition to be able to manage within a more systemic context (the list is not exhaustive). Could you score yourself on this list?

- **Analytical skills**
- **Problem solving skills**
  - Identification of variables and constraints
  - Identification of information sources
  - Information management
  - Creation of solutions and their prioritization

- **Project management skills**
  - Scenario building
  - Identification of multidimensional solution spaces
  - Risk management
  - Structuring and controlling

- **Vision development**
  - Understanding the economic context
  - Anticipation of competitive evolution
  - Imagination and creation of innovative actions
  - Production of coherence/holism

- **Managing performance**
  - Management of indicators
  - Translation of ideas into actions that create value
  - Management of information, and IS (information systems)

- **Client orientation**
  - Don't produce for yourself
  - Master and develop quality
  - Satisfy customers (internal and external)

- **Accepting diversity as a creative power**
  - Stop ethnocentric thinking
  - Make use of cultural diversity
  - Use diversity as a constructive principle
  - Learn about diversity (cultural, religious)
  - Facilitate networking

- **Decision making skills**
  - Operationalizing
  - Installation of a Management Information System
  - Anticipation, correction, and analysis
  - Propose actions

- **Communication skills**
  - Management of communication supports
  - Organization of communication flows
  - Anticipation of communication needs

- **Groupworking**
  - Mastery of team oriented parameters and attitudes
  - Understanding and identification of each other's role
  - Enrich roles
  - Anticipate hurdles
  - Share knowledge and experience
  - Flexibility
  - Adaptability

- **Leadership/Motivation**
  - Propose and assume responsibility
  - Create synergy
  - Listen
  - Construct
  - Convince
  - Motivate
  - Support and back-up your co-workers

- **Coaching**
  - Evaluate
  - Inform
  - Organize and support workplace learning

- **Respect for the human being**
  - Cultivate an open mind
  - Be aware of and accept differences
  - Be tolerant and show humility
  - Be sensitive to context

- **Self-motivation**
  - Be able to motivate yourself in all circumstances
  - Be involved, more and more

- **Creativity/Innovation**
  - Be open for and apply change
  - Dare to innovate
  - Embrace complexity and variety (don't limit)
  - Be a continuous "learner"
  - Allow and support others to learn continuously

- **Entrepreneurship**
  - Be an entrepreneur
  - Be an actor in development

- **Management learning**
  - Progress your own "knowing"
  - Learn from your errors
  - Incorporate continuous learning

- **Personal mission**
- **Stress Management**
  - Time management
  - Conflict management
  - Prioritization of difficulties and opportunities

- **Social responsibility and sustainable orientation**
  - Take societal responsibility for your actions
  - Societal/environmental engagement

- **Ethical mission**

8 Innovative leadership (values in management practice)

The essence of innovation

The essence of innovation starts with critical thinking. In the first place, one has to get comfortable with the knowledge that we do not always have the right answer. In fact, in situations where we don't have the answer, we have an ideal situation for creative innovation. We have to feel comfortable in the gap between what we know and what we don't know in order to shift into innovation successfully. This refers to a mind-set, as well as a paradigm, as argued earlier. This mind-set is the starting point in our approach to innovation.

We have to investigate what our assumptions are. What we do, what we think, what we dream and ultimately are able to do, is based on a whole set of assumptions. These include, for example, the functioning of reality, the client, the market, the product, and the role and purpose of innovation. There are no right answers in innovation and there are no right answers in our assumptions. It becomes a practice of asking questions. Crucially, the right question is more important than the right answer.

At the very beginning of any creativity process or any innovation process one has to start dreaming. The essence of innovation is to be able to discover what does not yet exist and what would contribute a certain value to society. If one does not want to be limited by any earthly limitation, we can only conceive such an innovation in a dream world. Very often, the limitations of innovations, or the fact that innovations eventually do not appear to be very innovative, start already in the face of dreaming. One has to dream big. Limitations can come later. But dreaming as big as possible is the correct start for any innovation. In order to go from dream to reality there are many different routes. Some of the most common are: deduction, causation, induction and analogical reasoning.

Next we are invited to think in "full color". Thinking in full color means to see into the issue from different angles, different perspectives, and different possibilities. One should learn to work around decisions from multiple and very often conflicting perspectives. An innovative leader needs to learn to build his or her judgment in paradoxes. The issue is not to solve paradoxes; the issue is to accept them and to live comfortably within the paradoxes. We need to accept these paradoxes in order to be able to move the company into a higher level of integration, a higher level of awareness, a higher level of consciousness, as discussed earlier.

What does it mean to think creatively and innovatively? In many cases, we have to start by analyzing large volumes of ambiguous data. If we want to be in the innovation space we do not have clear, correct and interpretation-free data. Correct and relevant information does not always exist within the innovation space where we wish to work. We are referring to real innovation, meaning "what is not yet there", and hence the data cannot be there yet either. The next step would be to frame the problem. In the face of dreaming and dreaming big, we have to keep possibilities open as far as we can. However, and there are techniques for doing this, at a certain point in time we will have to frame problems. One cannot innovate within an infinite space of opportunities.

Ultimately, we have to create infectious action, and that infectious action should be based on design principles. A few headlines of design principles are the following: Where possible, we should try and use teams that are as diverse as possible. The easiest and best way to use design principles is to work on well-defined projects. We have to acquire an approach of emerging problem solving. During the process of design we should have a number of cycles of doing, debriefing and learning. Innovation means trying to fail as rapidly as is feasible, learning and correcting the failure. But trying to fail fast, of course, goes against the idea of failure avoidance which we all naturally prefer to do. We would have to be brave and make a mental shift towards accepting failure as a learning tool and not a measurement of competency. Any prototype should be tested vigorously. The entire process should also be run and managed correctly. Too many innovation projects fail due to poor project management.

The innovative individual

Now, based on current research findings, let us investigate a few of the qualities of the innovative individual. The innovative individual is relentlessly curious. Curiosity is the basis of most innovation. Being an individual that is curious is of course something which is more of a quality, a mind-set, than something that can be trained. An innovative individual equally needs to be passionate and enthusiastic. The road to innovation is not always an easy one and therefore a great deal of energy, enthusiasm and perseverance is crucial to succeed on the path towards innovation. Furthermore, if one is not passionate about the concept, or the project, or the dream we'd like to realize, the chances of realizing that dream are limited. The individual who wishes to become a great innovator has to be tenacious. Innovation takes time, effort and energy, and it will not always be an easy road. An innovative leader, of course, equally needs to be a very creative person. That creativity might show up very often as a capacity for visualization. Training in visualization is therefore indispensable to support innovation. When talking about creative potential, we therefore could include a capacity of visualization into the creative arts, but that is not essential.

An innovator also needs to be interested in the ability to discover which, amongst others, is linked with the capacity to associate. We have to be able to collect ideas and, in particular, to look elsewhere for those ideas. Many of the most useful new ideas will not be found in the immediate vicinity of the problem. One has to question and observe and have an attitude of questioning everything. Inventions like the Apple Mac are based on questioning the need for a fan in a PC, which at the time were big and noisy. Simple but profound questioning can lead to breakthrough inventions. An interesting tool for doing so could be the use of metaphors. Metaphors allow speaking without getting caught up in the details of the operations.

Simple, but profound questions might also help. What is…? What caused…? Why and why not…? What if…? Those questions might lead us to look for better ways of doing what we think should be done.

A difficult yet crucial activity is to become as intimate as possible with the client. In the section on techniques we will deal with some techniques for doing this. Only if we get a clear and "intimate" understanding of the needs of the client, can we use innovation to fulfill those needs. A starting point might be to look for anomalies. Whilst looking into what is taking place, pay attention to observing with all the senses. Be aware and develop a deep awareness.

Do all this within a network of people. Surrounded by people you might get bright ideas from those that are with you on the journey. For the same reason, use outside experts.

Finally, experiment. Cross physical boundaries and cross intellectual boundaries. Innovations will probably be found where others have not yet been looking.

The Innovative team

When discussing the innovative team we consider people (the innovative leader, the innovative team members), processes – which we will address later – and a philosophy. In order to establish innovation I would like to suggest the following philosophy: Innovation is the job of everyone in the company, not just of those earmarked to take responsibility for innovation. Disruptive innovation is an equal part of our innovation portfolio. Not all innovation should be disruptive, but it is an important part of the overall portfolio and should receive adequate attention. I believe that an innovative approach that has the most chance for success is one where we deploy multiple small, properly organized and agile innovation project teams. Those teams should take smart risks. Without taking risks innovation will most likely not happen. However, risks should be seriously considered with a deep knowledge of, and intimacy with the customer.

Teams should ideally be practically diverse. Some degrees of diversity might, indeed at first, appear to be counterproductive, but overall it appears that high degrees of diversity pay off in creativity and innovation. Last but not least, an important credo for such teams is to have fun together. Innovation is not only hard work. It should be properly organized, teams should make sense, and the project management should be effective, but it is the fun, the playfulness and the creativity that will be important drivers for innovation.

From a process point of view, a number of processes have proven successful in the past. Further in this chapter, we are going to mention a few techniques, and at the end of the chapter we are going to suggest a specific approach: the Innovation Road Book culminating further in the Cassandra tool.

Innovative leadership

Innovative leadership has a lot to do with leadership per se, and therefore we refer to the previous chapter, dealing with leadership within this inclusive paradigm. Bringing this closer to innovation, innovative leadership will equally need a vision. We need to agree on where we would like to go. Without a vision it is very difficult to take any relevant decision. Without a vision, any decision is a good one. Referring back to Alice in Wonderland, I would like to paraphrase the cat. When Alice asks the cat which road to take, the cat asks Alice in turn where she would like to go. When Alice replies that she doesn't really know, the cat appropriately replies that if you don't know where you would like to go, then any road is a good road. This may be fine if you're Alice in Wonderland but it could be problematic when there is more at stake? In other words, it may not be that important to have a vision in order to work towards real innovation, but in the absence of a vision, it is impossible to take an informed decision right now.

An innovative leader should not be fearful of failure. Failure is an important part of innovation. Without failure, not much learning takes place. Learning is indeed easier in the case of failure. One should not promote failure, but accept it and gain learning from it. An innovative leader should equally be able to manage conflict. Teams, and specifically diverse teams, might have high degrees of opposite views, crucial for evolution, but not always easy to manage. In line with this, the innovative leader should also be able to manage diverse agendas. Innovation is not only limited to brand new products or developments. It is equally a dynamic process of improvements fitting current corporate or departmental agendas.

At a certain point in time, a leader needs to commit resources at the right time, the right amount and for the right purpose. Innovation does need investment and it is always a visionary decision to match the need to the possibility.

Last but not least, innovative leaders are certainly not process optimizers. Though project management should be done correctly, an innovative leader has a different focus, capacity and drive.

Innovation techniques

A number of innovation techniques are available, and have been applied with more or less success. We would like to run through a few of them here.

The first one, that I will describe further, is an extended version of what is known as the Blue Ocean Strategy. The Blue Ocean Strategy has been a successful book, suggesting a framework in order to be able to identify Blue Oceans for a company (as opposed to Red Oceans of competition), where a company should be able to thrive. Though in the short term, this no doubt makes sense, in the longer term there is no reason why a Blue Ocean would not become a Red one of competition. However, the model used for the analysis is an interesting one, particularly in order to analyze what to do in order to go from the current to a desired state. Whenever this situation presents itself, this model could be used (see further under the Innovation Road Book).

- Another interesting and useful model is the "Business Model Canvas" of Osterwalder and Pigneur (Wiley, 2010). This model helps us with business model generation. It requires detailed thought for a number of relevant elements of a business model. The model questions areKey partners to the innovation (or the company or project)
- Key activities (the transformation that is taking place)
- Key resources (what is necessary)
- Value proposition (what value is created and where does this value go)
- Customer relationship (relates to the intimacy discussed earlier)
- Channels (of distribution)
- Customer segments (some creativity is required here)
- Cost structures
- Revenue streams

Particularly in respect to customer intimacy, the authors propose a few questions, which they label as "The Empathy Map". The questions raised are, in respect to the customer:

- What does she think and feel? What really counts for her? What are her major preoccupations? What are her worries and aspirations?
- What does she see (senses)? Who are her friends? What is her environment? What does she see (sensorial intake) that the market offers?
- What does she say and do? What is her attitude in public, her appearance, her behaviour towards others?
- What does she hear? What do her friends say, and what does her boss say? What do other influencers say? And who are those influencers?
- What pain does she have? What fears, what frustrations and what obstacles does she see?
- What gains can she see? What are her wants, her needs, and how does she measure her success?

Again, to help with the transition from the current to the new, you could either use the Extended Blue Ocean Model or more profoundly, the Cassandra tool described in the next chapter.

We have a long list of techniques and approaches that might be useful in innovation thinking, creativity sessions and brainstorming sessions of different kinds. We will list the best known, but it is clear that in order to really make sense out of them, some practice will be necessary. Some of those tools (like Soft Systems Methodology) are very rich and powerful, but not that easy to apply. It would need a bit of interest and training to get started with them. Most of the techniques will speak for themselves.

Some of these techniques are:

- Soft Systems Methodology (a methodology designed by Checkland, very popular in IS design and political consensus building, focusing on meaning and shared understanding)
- Rapid prototyping
- Reversal techniques. In order to see the consumer as a consumer, could you for a moment assume she would become a producer? The French energy company has successfully introduced solar panels on roofs for individuals to produce their own electricity, but also to sell the overproduction back to the energy company. By doing so, the energy company has been able to, with lots of small investments, rapidly build a high performing solar network, which they would never have been able to do, on their own.
- Lateral thinking
- Rotating attention. Leave your frame of reference and understanding behind and move into a space of deeper understanding.
- Techniques of direct analogy
- Bisociation (compared to the wider association)
- Subtraction. Take something out of your reasoning that seems crucial: can you imagine a restaurant without food?
- Design for extreme affordability. Can you imagine a (child) incubator without electricity? Can you imagine a refrigerator without electricity?
- Tell a story to "blind" people, and look for their perspective
- Ideation. Come up with a funnel of ideas: the normal ones, the crazy ones, the impossible ones, etc.
- Visual thinking (using visual techniques)
- Story telling
- Scenario building

All of those have successfully been applied in isolation and in a broader methodology (like the Innovation Road Book).

An experience-based methodology for innovative leadership: The Innovation Road Book

In this section of the chapter we suggest a possible approach, a methodology, to take on, and execute leadership in innovation. Obviously the method suggested fits the paradigm shift proposed in this book, and it equally incorporates a number of questions and questionnaires that have been introduced earlier in the book. The ultimate tool – Cassandra – a tool with somewhat broader application than a purely innovation perspective, will be detailed further in the last chapter of the book. Cassandra is an audit and management tool that allows the manager to audit and analyze a company or a situation from a systemic point of view. It allows for the design of a change agenda, both on a personal level (the personal version) and on corporate level. More interesting, though, is to have both levels together, based on the same tool, within the same innovative paradigm.

The Innovation Road Book is focused on innovation per se, and could be used with or without Cassandra as a final overall systemic change management analysis, leading into a particular change agenda.

This section proposes how to operationalize some concepts developed in the book, in particular related to the innovation part of it. It offers a set of checklists and questionnaires – discussed in earlier chapters – which, together, act as a roadmap to innovation leadership. This roadmap is available for use, either as a step plan for implementing innovation, or alternatively for benchmarking one's own potential in comparison with other companies. However, in order to use it to its full potential, either training or tutoring might be necessary. The checklists indeed fit a wider concept (as the book argues in depth) and, without a thorough understanding of this concept, the checklists themselves will be less effective and have less impact.

> Wanderer, your footprints are
> the path, and nothing more;
> Wanderer, there is no path,
> it is created as you walk.
> By walking,
> you make the path before you,
> and when you look behind
> you see the path which after you
> will not be trod again.
> Wanderer, there is no path,
> but the ripples on the waters.
>
> Antonio Machado

These methodologies form a continuous loop of evaluation, designing, laying down the path by walking (Machado), learning, re-evaluation, re-designing, etc. The remainder of this appendix will mainly focus on assembling a number of checklists and tools that together make up the roadmap.

The values and the vision: what is the contribution of the company?

Values-based innovation starts in the right lower quadrant of Wilber's systemic model, i.e. with the identification of the (shared) values. Since they very often remain hidden or unknown, and since they are the drivers of the sustainable performance process, the first step involves making them explicit and discussing how far they are shared. Why try to answer the question of what the values of the company are and/or what it contributes to society? If the company would no longer exist, what would society miss? If the creation of employment would be a value for a company, then bankruptcy would certainly cause a loss of value. However, this would imply that the creation of jobs would be a core value of the company (and not a necessary resource constraint). Values-based leadership will be driven by those shared values.

The first stage might start from a very exhaustive list of possible values purely to make it easy for people to start choosing. In the second stage, those values will be negotiated in order to find out what the shared values are. Once these are agreed upon, they can be translated into personal development issues like leadership and learning.

Though this is the first crucial step in the Innovation Road Book approach, we are not going to re-discuss this here. We refer to the chapter on values and the checklists in order to facilitate this important first step.

As discussed earlier, Buckingham and Coffman's studies of organizational effectiveness produced the following interesting checklist. Exceptional leaders need to create exceptional workplaces where innovation can really foster. According to them, exceptional managers create a workplace in which employees emphatically answered 'yes' to the following questions (and relate them to the innovation climate and approach in the company):

13. Do I know what is expected of me at work?
14. Do I have the materials and equipment I need to do my work right?
15. At work, do I have the opportunity to do what I do best every day?
16. In the last seven days, have I received recognition or praise for doing good work?
17. Does my supervisor, or someone at work, seem to care about me as a person?
18. Is there someone at work who encourages my development?
19. At work, do my opinions seem to count?
20. Does the mission/purpose of my company make me feel my job is important?
21. Are my co-workers committed to doing high-quality work?
22. Do I have a best friend at work?
23. In the last six months, has someone at work talked to me about my progress?
24. This last year, have I had opportunities at work to learn and grow?

And again, the number of "yes" responses gives you an idea of the organizational effectiveness, or the degree in which employees and managers feel supported by the company in their endeavour to realise an innovation culture.

Benchmarking: from dream to reality (do we make a difference?)

Imagine an organization that has been able to identify values or the anticipated value-add of its existence or activity. The next step in our continuing journey is to establish some kind of benchmark. Compared to other companies, activities or industries, does the organization deliver something that is not yet delivered elsewhere? Can a number of elements, which would give a certain concrete idea of the direction to follow, be identified? Would they really be different and capable of forming the industry standard? This kind of benchmarking is not for competitive reasons, not for finding blue ocean strategies (as in Kim and Mauborgne, 2005), but for helping to identify the things that make a real difference, both in a detailed and simple fashion. It is this analysis that will help enable our marketing support, our commercial argumentation, our commercial message, etc. It is going to help to translate values, mission and value-added into communication (internal, as well as external).

In a two step procedure, the first makes a rather classical benchmark analysis. The second attempts to evaluate the innovative potential. Is it possible to ensure that what is offered is a real innovation (rather than just a copy of an existing product or service)? Does the proposal have the potential to innovate the market, the industry and to make a social difference? In aspiring to this new development what resources are needed?

For the first step, we base our analysis on an extended version of Kim and Mauborgne's (2005) blue ocean concept. For the second step we use part of an innovation roadmap methodology (designed earlier within the innovative learning-by-doing platform, for practising managers to learn about management while creating and managing; captured under the framework called Free For All). The roadmap itself contains more steps than the ones used here, but these are restricted to the most essential ones that fit the methodology proposed in this chapter.

The **first step** is based on the following figure that is itself based on the blue ocean concept. The blue ocean strategy invites a company to develop products and services that tap into a blue ocean (an ocean without fierce competition, compared to a red ocean of "bloody" competition). The approach proposes to ask the following four questions:

1. Which factors that the industry takes for granted should be eliminated?
2. Which factors should be raised well above the industry's standard?
3. Which factors should be reduced well below the industry's standard?
4. Which factors should be created that the industry did not previously offer?

The answers to those questions give an idea of how the company, new product or whatever else positions itself in the market. Equally, the answers, especially to the fourth question, give an initial indication of the innovative potential of the company, service, etc. Though these factors can be identified individually, this is typically an exercise done in an animated workshop, since some of the questions might be rather challenging.

Extended from "Blue Ocean Strategy" by Kim and Mauborgne

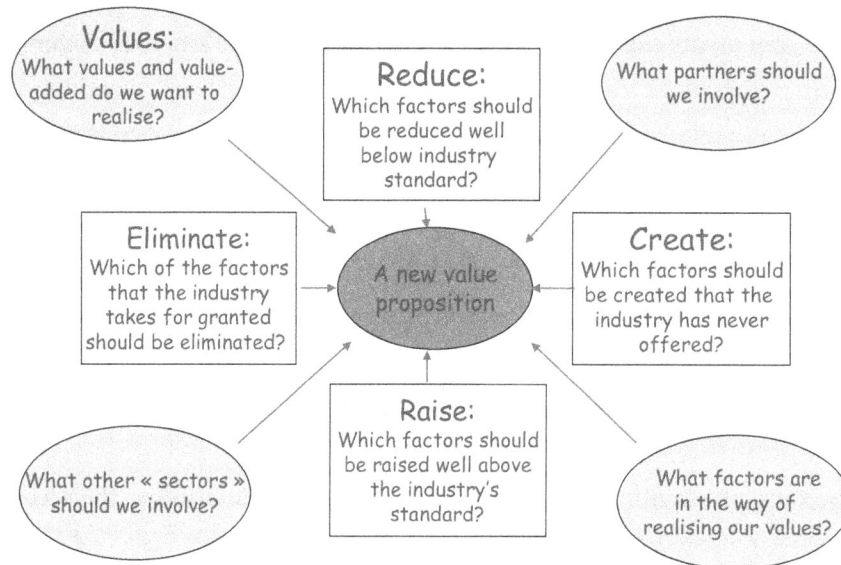

Values:
What values and value-added do we want to realise?

Reduce:
Which factors should be reduced well below industry standard?

What partners should we involve?

Eliminate:
Which of the factors that the industry takes for granted should be eliminated?

A new value proposition

Create:
Which factors should be created that the industry has never offered?

What other « sectors » should we involve?

Raise:
Which factors should be raised well above the industry's standard?

What factors are in the way of realising our values?

But we want to expand the blue ocean approach with an additional four questions that position the company (or its new product or service) within a broader network (of partners), related to the specific purpose of realizing values, and demand a more intense and varied innovation focus:

- What values and valued added do we want to realise, compared to what exists (at this time)?
- What factors are in the way of realizing those values?
- What partners (companies, organizations) should we involve?
- What other "sectors" should we involve in our activities?

It is worth recalling that one of the remarkable observations in social entrepreneurship is that companies and services are often not limited to one specific sector or industry. The (social) business model innovation advocated here, aims to realize the same openness to others and to enrol solutions into a holistic focus on the value-added of the company (that will be reinforced by the use of Cassandra later on).

The road book approach

In the overall innovation literature, a rather clear distinction is made between the phase of creativity and the follow-up phase that is commonly addressed as the innovation phase, the phase of creation (detailed planning and production). The first phase receives low priority in innovation literature, though most literature also agrees that success and failure of new product development is often already 'genetically imprinted' at the start of the so called innovation process, based on the quality of the creativity phase. A second, well identified reason for failure can be found in the process of the creation phase. What we call an innovative project in our Masters in Business Innovation and Intrapreneurship (MBI&I) clearly contain both aspects. Where we certainly stress the importance in time and effort spent on the first creativity phase, we do require at least an inventory of the resources and limitations to overcome, for the creation phase.

Based on what common theories suggest, an innovation process, the way we have described it, contains roughly 5 different phases:

- Idea generation
- From idea to real world (how to translate an idea into a concept that can be communicated)
- Assessment of the innovative potential (annex the commercial feasibility) of the project
- Inventory of the internal capacities and constraints in order to assess technical feasibility
- The economic (and mainly financial) feasibility: the business plan

Though a certain progression in time seems logical, certainly in the first three phases some feedback loops will prove to be necessary and extremely beneficial in adding value. However, at a certain point in time and after a number of feedback loops, one should continue into the development phase and the economic viability study. The following diagram illustrates the process which we will detail with the help of some checklists and relevant issues/questions further on in this document.

Frequently a difficult step is to translate ideas into the real world. The idea is clear in the mind of the idea-owner(s), but then needs to be translated into a form that can be communicated to a wider audience. That is not a typical problem for the innovation process, but successfully overcoming it is of paramount importance and key for further successful development. In order to support you in this key step, we offer some ideas of soft systems methodology (SSM) which is a methodology designed to transform ideas into the real world, with the aim is to eventually design Information Systems. In the MBI&I program, a workshop on SSM and action learning is scheduled, but the main concepts can already be practiced here.

Once the idea is translated from the owner's mind into a form that can be communicated (with sentences, activities, to-do lists), it is useful to assess its innovative potential. It is difficult to evaluate the innovative potential of an idea if it is not, to some extent, expressed on paper. Therefore, this step can only be undertaken after the 'translation from idea into activities'.

The logical consequence from idea generation, via translation into a communicative action description in order to evaluate its innovative potential, is a cycle that does not necessarily immediately generate the eye-catching new product or service. Here a likely feedback-loop probably brings you back to the phase of idea generation. Creativity and innovation is very often a process of incremental steps, rather than earth-shattering breakthrough ideas. It might be possible that this feedback-loop needs to be taken a number of times. That cycle of three phases is the backbone of the creativity process.

Once a 'go' decision is taken, we arrive at the following phase, which is one of researching the internal capacities and constraints that are key to a future successful implementation. In this phase an inventory is made of resources and constraints and, in the event that constraints could be hindering, possible solutions are to be considered. It is possible, though not indicated on the figure, to have additional feedback-loops, bringing you back from the inventory phase again into the idea generation and its following steps. The more the innovation process can be kept dynamic, the higher the chances for innovative products. Don't forget, though, that at a certain point in time you will have to go on to the more procedural part.

The last step, then, is the economic and financial feasibility study that translates ideas, capacities and constraints into a business plan. The business plan is very often the communication tool for going on the market in order to find support, finance, etc. for your proposal; and should be considered as that. It is also a communication tool and should accordingly be made clear and attractive. Though the business plan deals with the economics and financials of the project, most of those are already identified earlier in the process. When you have assessed the innovative power of the project (in an earlier stage), it would have been key to have a good and clear idea of the markets and potential customers. Some other indicators that are mandatory for the business plan are already considered in earlier stages. Therefore we say that the business plan is more about financial feasibility and justification, than about economic viability (that implicitly has already played a role much earlier in the process), and therefore, it is rather an outcome than an input. But keep in mind its important role as communication tool in the process from development to real market. Technical and commercial viability is translated in this phase into a plan that helps you to finalize the funding issues.

In some respect, the innovation approach proposed here can be compared with the knowledge creation cycle of Nonaka and Takeuchi. They also identify a number of steps that start from an individual's knowledge creativity and leads via communication and socialization to a wider supported shared vision. In order to give you further insight and possible cross-reference to the knowledge management literature, I summarize the knowledge creation cycle here.

- Knowledge creation starts with the individual

- However, knowledge needs to be shared. Knowledge sharing takes place in different, often consecutive steps:
- Socialization, that often starts with the formation of a team
- Externalization is e.g. taken up with conversations, using metaphors and analogues
- Combination is supported if the team's proposal contains clear specifications, recognizable also to the others (outside the team)
- Internalization occurs when the new knowledge extends the individual mental models

- Knowledge creation is a group activity, but the organization needs to support and facilitate

- The 5 conditions for launching the knowledge spiral:
- Intention
- Independence
- Fluctuation
- Creative chaos
- Redundancy
- Diversity

- Knowledge creation is non-linear and interactive:
- Exchange of individualized knowledge
- Development of a concept
- Verification of the concept
- Construction of an archetype
- Level exchange of the knowledge

- Middle-up-down management, instead of top-down or bottom-up
- A hypertext-organization in which people are linked to each other, based on the interest and need of that particular moment. Hypertext-linked organizations are very flexible and have different groupings, based on different commonalities at the same moment. Some of these groupings might be overlapping. Neither the formal hierarchy, nor the flexible task groups are organizational structures that are knowledge-creation friendly.

The following sections give detailed elements, issues, questions and checklists that will help you through each phase. Though they need not be followed up in extensive detail, they are the commonly accepted questions that can help you in your realization, as well as in the development of your own approach. In any case, answers to most of the mentioned issues/questions should be dealt with in the project report. And don't forget: your final report is a logbook of your process, not just a description of the result. Your road book/logbook is a learning device for yourself, but also serves to support you in your learning and when performing your evaluation.

For ease of use, the road book is organized in bullet points, and can be seen as either suggested questions or possible actions. Some of the ideas are grouped in so called methods, approaches or methodologies. Others are only a single issue or question. Use this road book creatively and it will support your learning.

The idea generation (phase 1)

A few ways that one can generate new ideas:

- Organize brainstorm sessions
- Talk to outsiders, eventually ask outsiders as mediators for brainstorms
- Organize focus groups
- Seek interaction between yourself and an audience (like in a theater setting)
- Write (archetypal) stories

- Dream your dream, or a customer's dream
- Take a brilliant existing product/service; transform it to your market
- Imagine a breakthrough product/service; map it onto your business
- Inter-company innovation has specifically high potential; think about interesting companies

The Balint method is a group method used in diagnostic situations (e.g. medical; intervision and coaching). It can also be used (with some creativity) for an idea-generating session. It contains a number of successive steps with some built-in loops:

- Problem inventory (idea listing)
- Choose a problem (idea)
- Organize information sessions by questioning (by others) the problem (idea) chosen (the problem owner or idea owner is the one questioned)
- Try to invent a solution (try to invent a valuable idea/product/service)
- Members of the group give feedback to the problem or idea owner
- Evaluate the process together

Another (individual) method, particularly designed for idea generation, is the one named after de Bono and consists of 7 steps:

- Decide what you really want (to do)
- Check whether the realization of it would be good for you
- Create the context or the fantasy that you are going to build
- Now start thinking in your dream; think about a specific action; fantasize that you are executing that action
- Generate the feeling of satisfaction or joy that you would experience if your dream would come true
- Now, let your fantasy go (also for possible bad feelings)
- Put it aside, and let the process work for itself

Key to a successful creative spiral is the power of both fantasy and being oneself – it is very much about the positive thinking to be undertaken. In the intial phase, wishes, imagination and belief play an important role. The innovator should give free rein to those feelings. In the second phase, the innovator should start talking about his ideas to others and start to investigate its degree of reality (see next section). In this phase willpower is important.

Some final ideas

- Give time for reflection and 'incubation'
- Everything is "out there"; it all has to do with managing one's attention

- Creativity requires time
- 'Encourage' results, inputs or ideas of any kind

From idea to reality (phase 2)

Once we feel certain that we have formulated our initial idea, the next step is to translate this into a concept that can be communicated to others, whether inside or outside the team. The aim of this phase is largely to clarify the mental picture behind the idea, not only for personal clarity, but also to make it easier to communicate. A well-known method for supporting this transformation is called soft systems methodology (SSM) and it is successfully used in the pre-phase of Information System (IS) design. A workshop in the MBI&I will give particular attention to this approach, but this project is a perfect opportunity to test things. The basic idea behind SSM is one of systems thinking *about* the real world.

What SSM aims to do is translate perceived problems, ideas, issues, etc. into actions than can be dealt with easier, that are more grounded within the real (corporate) world. It uses activity systems in which actors, aims, activities, transformations, etc. are identified. Therefore the method has not only been used for preparing IS development projects, but also in situations where clarification of vaguely felt issues was difficult, but important. That is what we propose to use SSM here for.

The following diagram visualizes the SSM process consisting of three steps. The first step, which might already have been taken in the brainstorm phase, is the drawing of what is called **'rich pictures'**. These are drawings that illustrate the idea and some of the actions that form part of it. It can be compared with simple maps of ideas (like mindmaps). A certain SSM 'code' should be followed in order to make these rich pictures. Here are some examples to illustrate.

Examples: 2. Rich pictures

Extract 1 – Pears soap

Pears transparent soap, which is expensive, is made by dissolving soap in alcohol and allowing the alcohol to evaporate slowly. This is done in moulds that are the shape of the soap bars: the natural shape achieved when the solvent evaporates is the oval with the characteristic depression in it. The economics of the process depend entirely on recovery of the solvent for recycling. At least 98% has to be recovered if the process, which is in any case slow, is to be made economic: hence alcohol recovery has to be carefully monitored.

The picture corresponding to this extract is given in Figure 2. The picture is essentially in two parts. The extract describes a 'process' and the upper part of the picture is a process description. We are also told something about the process and so the lower part of the picture identifies the three features as the process characteristics. The above extract is a fictitious example used to provide a simple illustration. A more complex example is given in the second extract and this is also fictitious.

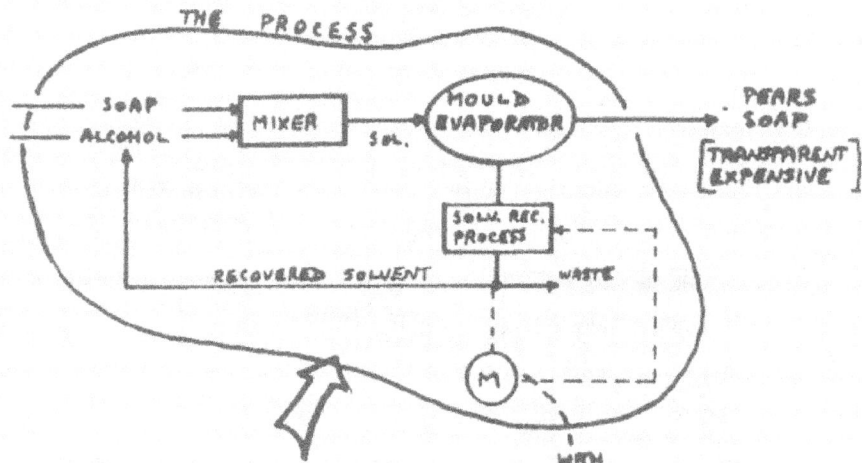

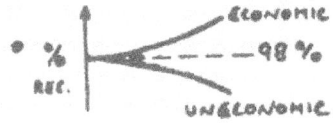

Figure 2: Rich picture for Pears soap

Extract 2 – Slimline shoes

'Slimline', a manufacturer of women's shoes, are hoping to improve their performance with a new range called 'Carefree'. (From a peak return on capital of 22% three years ago it first fell to 15% then 11%.) The Managing Director discovers that the Production Department has introduced a new type of glue to attach the soles to the uppers. This eliminates a previously used sole-roughening process which enabled them to achieve an 8% reduction in production cost. The MD, however, when investigating a Marketing Department complaint that for the last two weeks they have been down 20% on the supplies of shoes from production, finds that the glue is in short supply. It seems that the Purchasing Section of the Production Department has cancelled an arrangement by which they receive a 35% discount on bulk supplies of the original glue (this discount could now not be reinstated) and are buying the new glue ('STIX'), at the same price as the old glue, from a different supplier, who has failed to meet delivery promises.

Figure 3 is the rich picture corresponding to this extract.

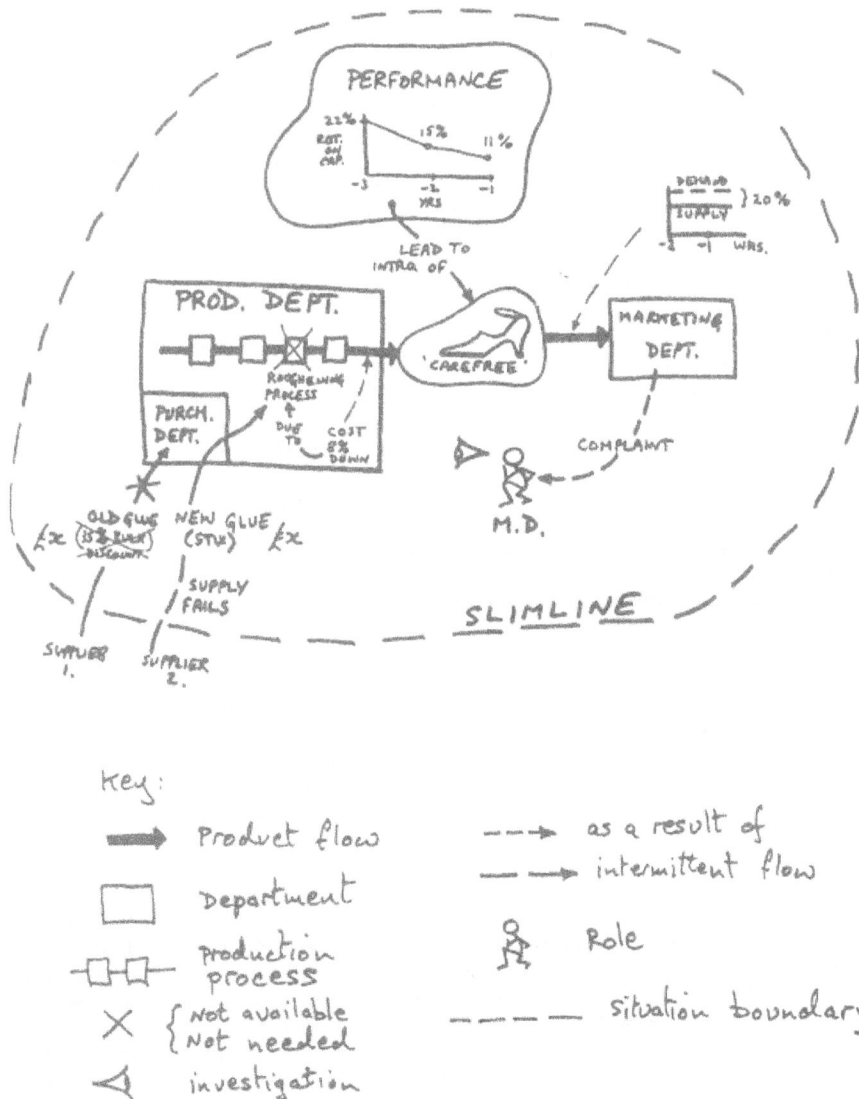

Figure 3: Rich picture for Slimline shoes

The final example is represented by an actual extract from a national newspaper.

Extract 3 – Meccano

The workers at the Edge Hill (Liverpool) factory of Airfix Industries are currently staging a 'work-in'. This particular factory produces Meccano, the traditional construction toy, and Dinky Toys, which range from model cars through all varieties of vehicles to agricultural implements. The situation has arisen because Airfix have stated their intention to close the factory, making some 940 workers redundant. Very little investment in new machinery has taken place over the last 50 years, resulting in production methods which are antiquated. The workers claim that they have a viable product and, given the opportunity, they intend running the factory as a workers' cooperative. This would require financial support from the government and a meeting has been arranged between local union officials and representatives of the Department of Industry to discuss the situation.

Meccano, which has been a household name in toys for most of this century, was invented by J.F. Hornby, a Liverpool businessman in 1893. As the business developed he added model trains and Dinky toys, all three products being highly successful. After the last war they suffered fierce competition from other manufacturers such as Lego, Triang, and Matchbox toys, resulting in the decline of the Meccano share of the market. Fifteen years ago, Hornby Trains Ltd. was bought out by Triang, leaving the two product lines currently produced at Edge Hill.

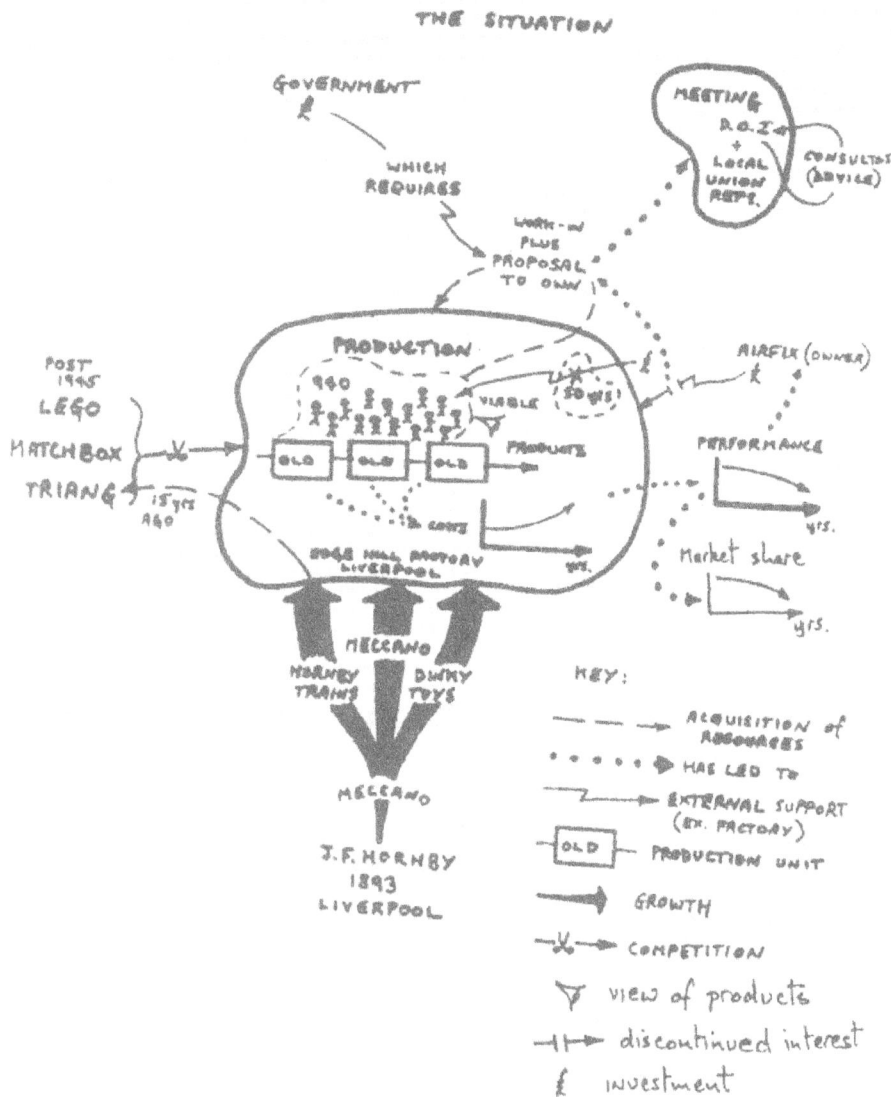

Figure 4: Rich picture for Meccano

The picture in Figure 4 focuses on the factory of Edge Hill in Liverpool. This represents the current state of affairs following growth and diversification since 1893. A number of arrows of different kinds are used and the meaning is explained in the key. This example is intended to illustrate the need to use different type of arrows to cope with the variety of meaning.

Although the extract makes no mention of a consultant, one has been included to make the point that, if we are being asked to interact in some way with an organization, we should include ourselves in the picture. We are part of the situation and our relationship to it is important. This illustrates that the consultant has been brought in by the Department of Industry (DOI) with the terms of reference: to provide advice to the meeting. Thus including the consultant (or ourselves, as consultant) we make clear who the client is and their expectations of us.

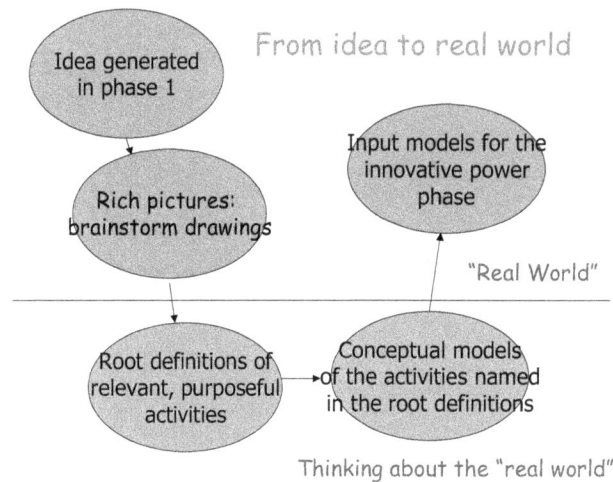

Figure 5: From idea to real world

In the next step we start considering the real world, using a structured approach. The Rich Pictures are translated into **Root Definitions** (RD) that describe the essence of the purpose to be served. Each root definition is one sentence, in which the verb conveys the transformation. A root definition consists of six elements that form the acronym CATWOE.

C: Customer (the recipient of the output of the transformation, the victim, the beneficiary)

A: Actors (individuals that would *do* the activities in the resultant conceptual model)

T: Transformation process (input-output conversion)

W: Weltanschauung – world view or wider world perception (statement of belief about the purpose, aim, wider good, the world)

O: Owner (wider-system decision maker with authority over the system defined)

E: Environmental constraints (external to the system defined)

CATWOE is defined within a framework of (corporate and/or IS) development. Therefore some of the elements of CATWOE might at first seem odd. However, in order to translate an idea into a real world situation one should also think about the actors that eventually will execute things, and the owners (the Management Team or an outside entity) that should support the development and make the 'go' decision. There is no need to stick that closely to the given labels. There is, however, a need to identify all the elements and bring them together into an activity.

Here are some examples of root definitions:

Examples: 2. CATWOE and root definitions

Many examples exist in the literature related to SSM (soft system methodology) which illustrate the incorrect usage of CATWOE. A few are used here to illustrate various aspects of the relationship of CATWOE to a root definition (RD) taken mainly from student practice. The example is given followed by a brief description of the faults.

Example 1 – Related to an RD representing a manufacturing company

RD   A system to manufacture and sell a specific range of products at minimum cost in order to make a profit.

C   The market

A   Production Department and Marketing Personnel

T   manufacture for sale

W   MD

O   not specified

E   profit

This example is probably the result of the casual application of the CATWOE test. The RD (root definition) is sparse but is still a legitimate definition. It is initially poorly structured since the use of the word 'and' between 'manufacture' and 'sell' means that there are in fact two transformation processes.

Thus, logic would require the resultant model to contain activities to do with both manufacturing *and* selling. The transformation process identified within CATWOE, i.e. 'manufacture for sale', only leads to manufacturing activities.

The actors are specified as 'Production Department and Marketing personnel'. This may well be a reasonable choice of actors but they do not appear in the RD. The RD would have to read:

A system, operated by Production Department and Marketing personnel, to...

The customer is also not specified within the RD although 'the market' appears within CATWOE. These errors arise because the student was still thinking about the real world to which the RD was seen to be relevant, rather than concentrating on the intellectual process itself.

The existence of two transformation processes makes the specification of customers difficult. The recipient of the output from 'manufacture' could well be the Sales Department whereas the recipient of the output from 'sell' would be an actual customer (within the market).

Although 'profit' is stated as a requirement within the RD it is not an externally imposed constraint. 'Minimum cost', however, is. The controller of the system can decide how much profit to make but cost *must* be minimal.

The fact that Owner is not specified within the RD illustrates the proper use of this CATWOE element. The student could now have decided whether or not it would be useful to include an 'Owner' and who the 'Owner' might usefully be. The iteration may have been done and the decision still reached to omit any reference to the wider system. Initiating iteration via the RD is what the CATWOE test is for, but it must be used properly. Whatever decisions are arrived at during an iteration, there should be a consistent pairing of CATWOE and RD.

The inclusion of MD as W, within CATWOE, is a common fault. The 'profit' outcome has probably caused the student to relate the RD to the Managing Director. The meaning of W within CATWOE is to extract the belief contained in words in the RD, not to attribute that belief to an individual. W is a statement of *what the belief is*, and not of *whose belief it is*.

Any individual will probably subscribe to a number of beliefs. Any attribution to an individual will, in any case, be colored by the range of Ws and degrees of commitment to them held by the analyst doing the attribution. In relation to this sparse RD the statement of belief is simply: 'Manufacturing and selling a range of products at minimum cost *will* make a profit'. Within this rather sparse RD the belief is merely a restatement of the whole of the words in the RD. In a richer and more complex RD this would not be the case.

Example 2 – Related to patient care

RD   A hospital-owned system to comfort patients by undertaking regular visits within specified hours.

C   patients

A   relatives

T   provide comfort

W   visiting patients is a good thing to do

O   hospital

E   visiting time

One of the problems with this RD and CATWOE analysis is that different words have been used to describe the CATWOE elements than were used in the RD and there is also considerable ambiguity in the definition. In some cases the differences in the words may be regarded as trivial but as a general rule (given possible semantic problems), the same words should be used.

Thus 'visiting time' may be taken to be the same as 'specified hours' but it may not be, dependent upon who does the specifying. It may not even be a constraint if the system 'decision taker' is the one to do the specifying. The wording of the RD should remove the ambiguity and make this clear. The 'Owner' is 'Hospital' (or someone within the Hospital management structure). This is legitimate in terms of the CATWOE analysis but is it a relevant 'owner'? The wider system (given this 'owner') is apparently within the Hospital management processes and therefore, for the hierarchy to be coherent, we would expect the system also to be within these management processes. This raises the question as to who 'undertakes the regular visits'. The impression that this wording creates (particularly as A appears as relatives), is that the visitor is external to the hospital. However, this is not necessarily the case; it could be an internal visitor. Again this is ambiguity that should be removed.

In relation to the 'transformation process', 'to provide comfort' is not the same as 'to comfort'. One can *provide* by ensuring that someone else does the comforting.

A is specified as 'relatives' but this word does not appear in the RD. Finally the W in this RD (i.e. the belief) is that patients *will be* comforted through regular visits. The W specified in CATWOE is a value judgment about the acceptability of the purpose as a real-world activity. This is totally irrelevant as a technical requirement on the structure of an RD.

As a professional exercise, I could produce a totally defensible RD (in terms of its structure) of a *system to cause unease within a community by random bombing*. To do this, I would not have to believe that this is a good thing to do. The belief that would be contained within the RD is that random bombing *will* cause unease. Whether it is actually a good or bad thing to do is irrelevant to the structure of the RD.

Example 3 – Related to service provision

RD   A consultancy company-owned system, operated by skilled professionals, to satisfy clients' needs for technical advice by undertaking regular training and exploiting developments in new technology

C   clients

A   skilled professionals

T   to satisfy clients need for technical advice

W   keeping up to date with skills and the technology necessary to provide advice

O   consultancy company

E   none specified

The only problem with this RD and CATWOE is that the W (and hence the RD) contains an inconsistency. The actual W contained in the RD is that: 'undertaking regular training and exploiting developments in new technology (Y) *will* satisfy clients' needs for technical advice' (X). It would be possible to undertake training and exploit new technology without having any clients, or without knowing what their needs were. Clearly, doing Y is insufficient to achieve X.

The W expressed in CATWOE sounds fine as a condition but it is not the W expressed in the words of the RD.

A more blatant and obvious example of this same fault appeared in an RD relevant to a manufacturing company. It was stated that the system was: '*To increase company profit by planning to diversify the product range*'.

The outcome of planning is a plan. This will have no effect on profit unless something is done with the plan.

The problems illustrated by these examples can be overcome by less casual use of the CATWOE test, and critical evaluation of what it reveals about the words chosen in the RD. Adherence to a set of general principles and rules will also help.

In the third step, the root definitions are translated into **Human Activity Systems** (HAS). Those are in fact **conceptual models** of the original idea. They develop the root definition further into elements and interactions and make drawings of those. Conceptual models "expand" the root definitions. The elements of the conceptual models are either "verbs" or "arrows". These conceptual models can be more easily communicated to outsiders.

Verbs indicate actions that humans have to undertake in order to realize the root definition. Those verbs are stated in the imperative. **Arrows** combine those verbs. These arrows can give performance information from each of the operational activities, or indicate control actions from the activity.

Examples 3: Conceptual models

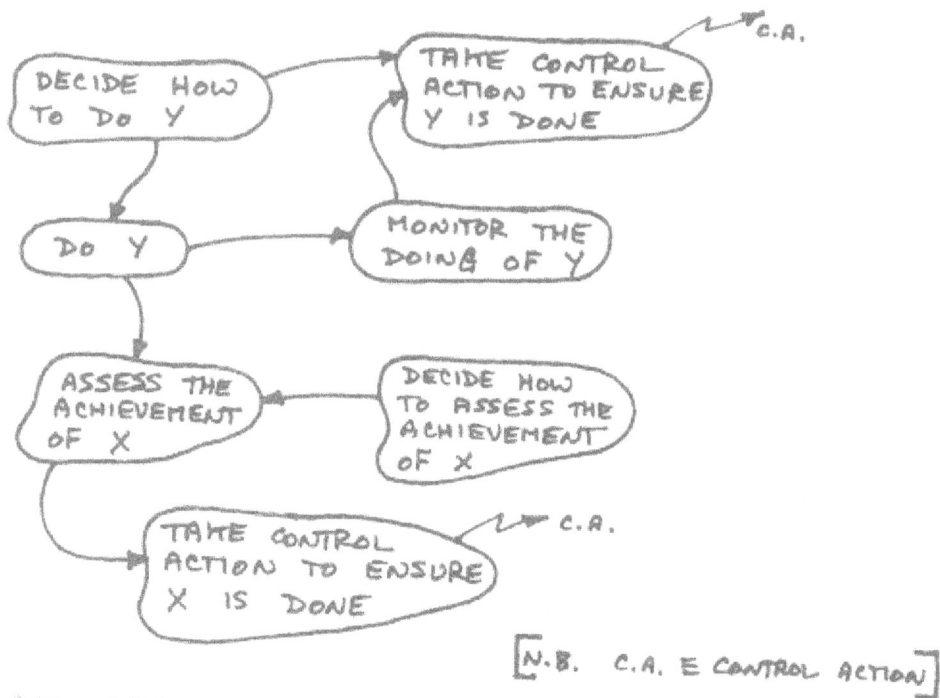

A model of T and W

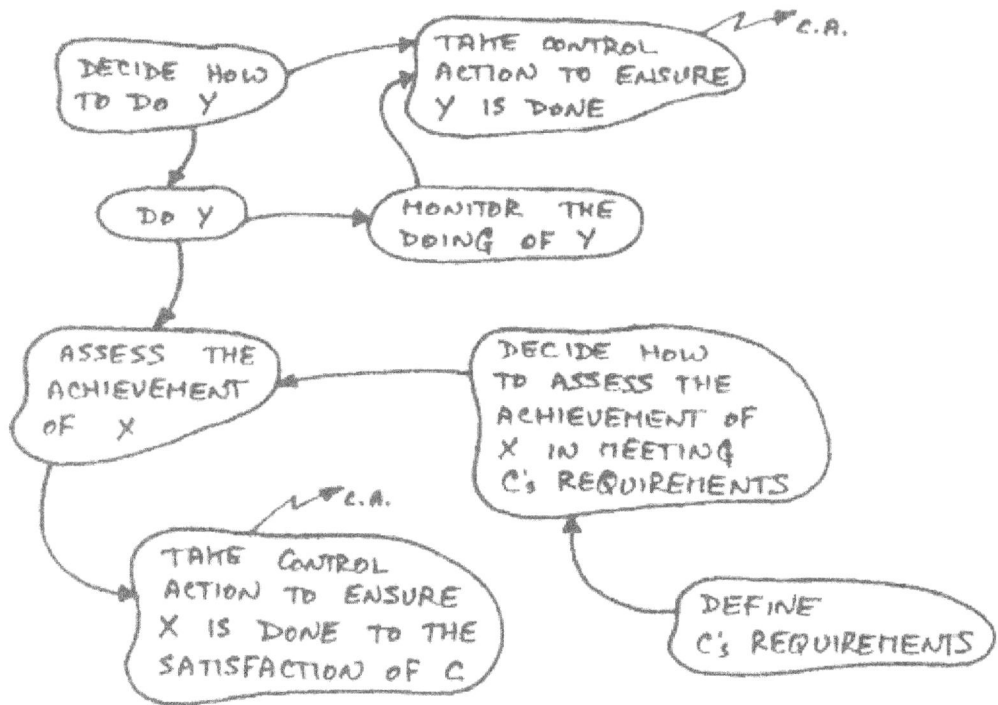

A model of T and W, incorporating C

A model of *T* and *W*, incorporating *C* and *A*

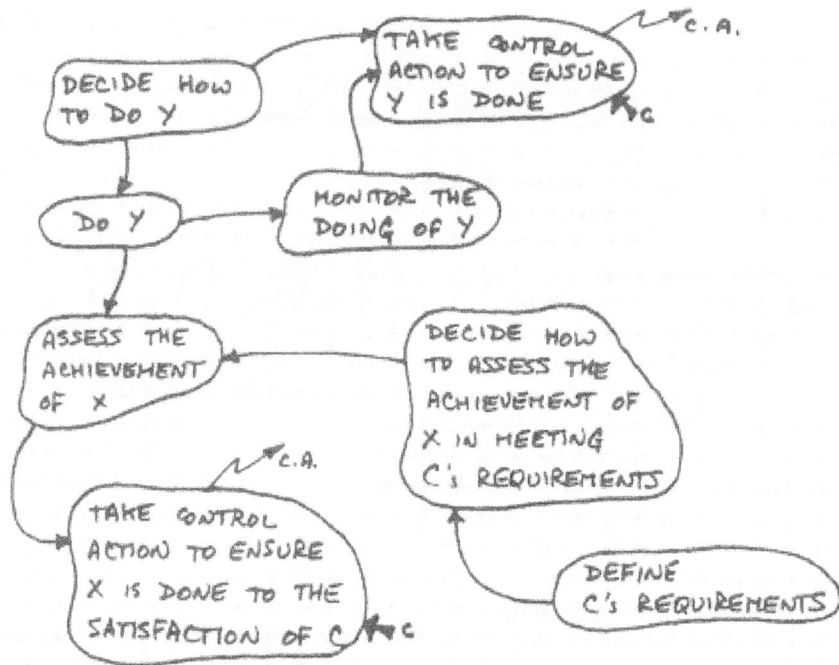

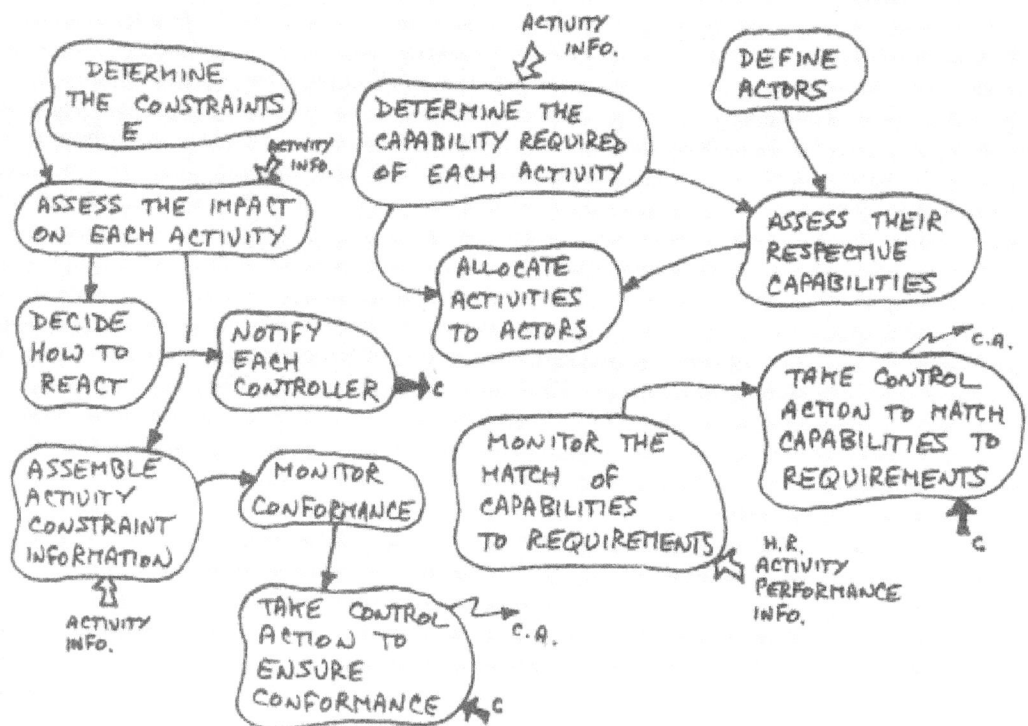

A model of T and W, incorporating C, A and E

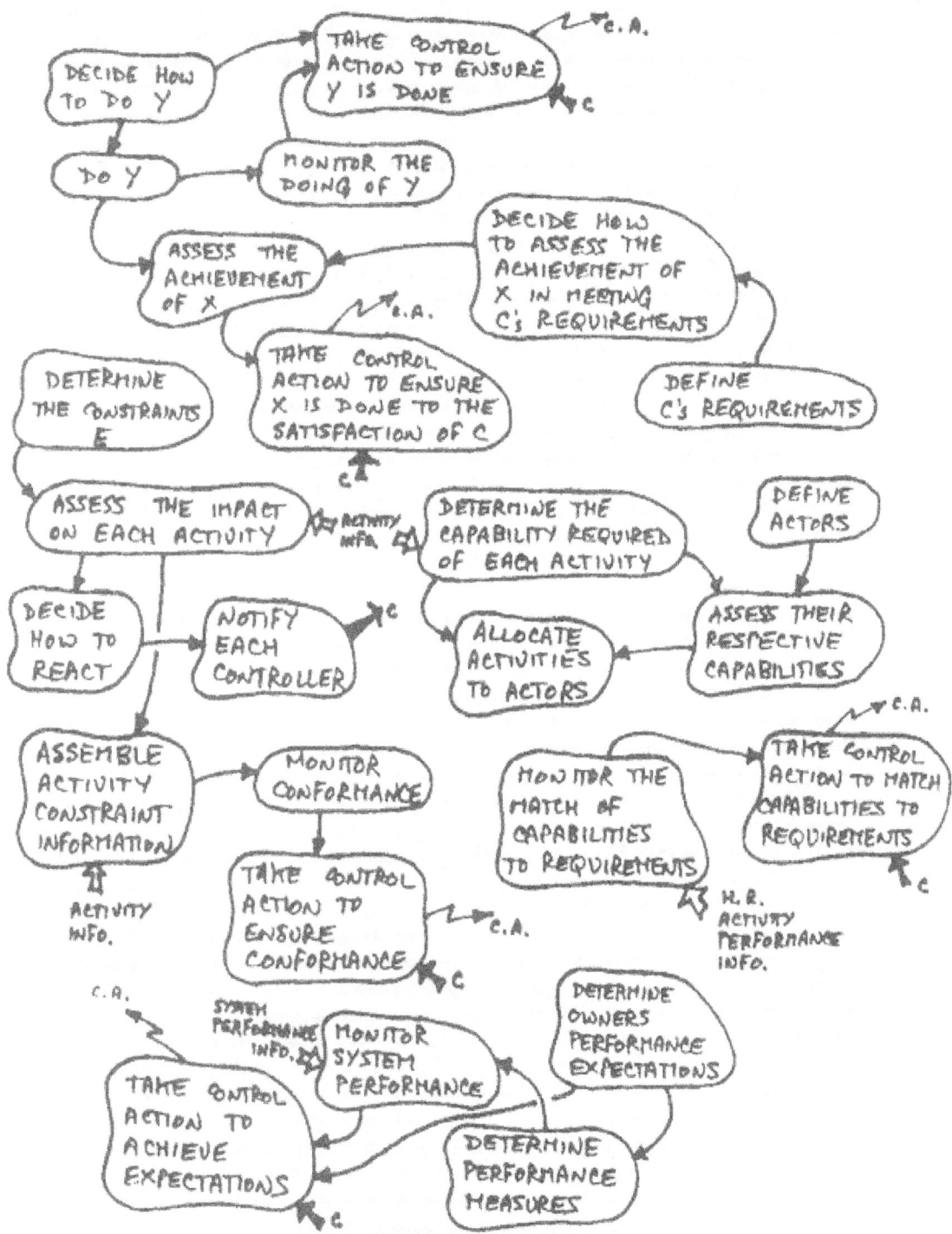

A model of T and W, incorporating C, A, E and O

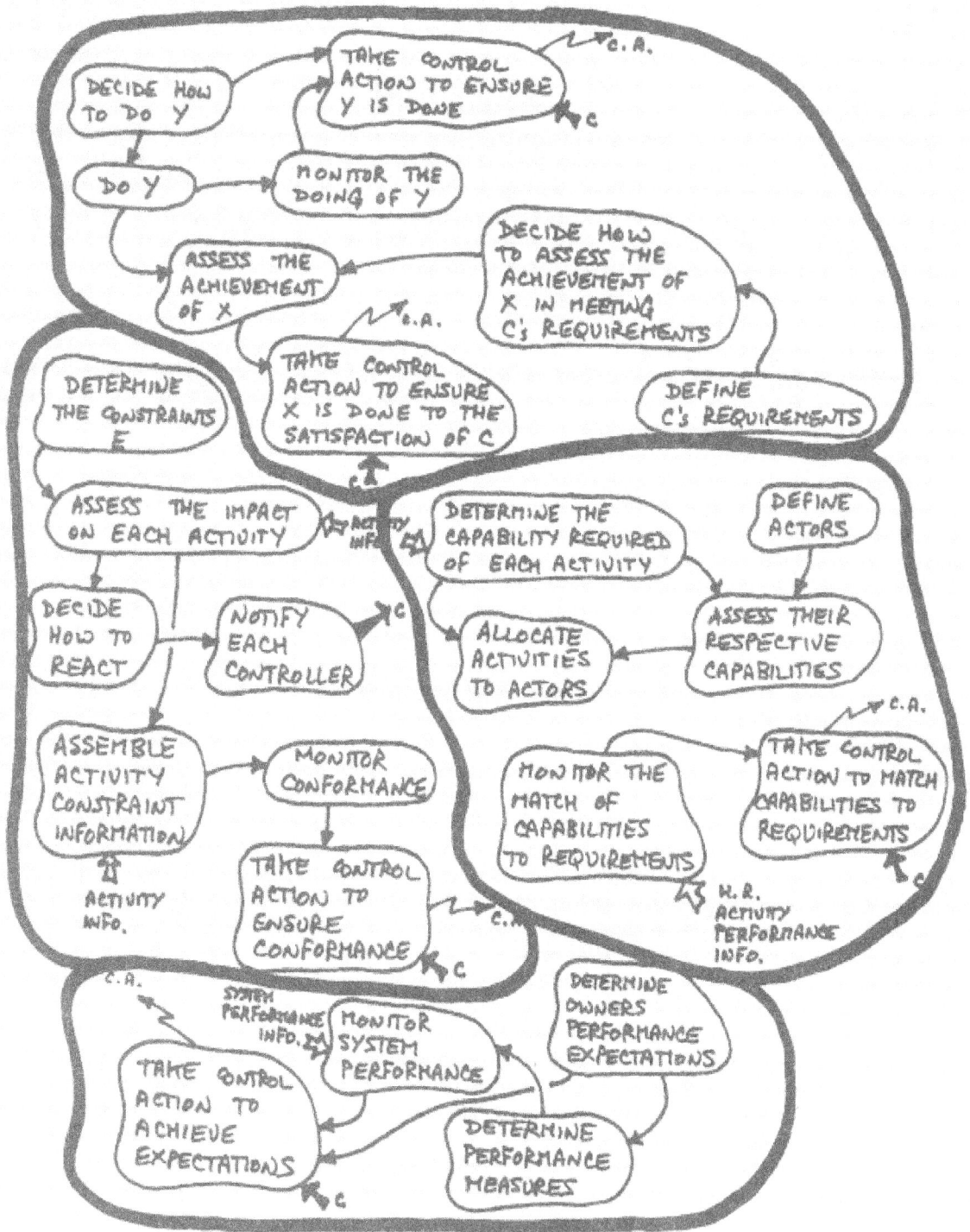

A model of T and W, incorporating C, A, E and O decomposed into subsystems

The outcome of this phase is a drawing that has expanded the initial idea into a representation that depicts the mental model behind the idea, in such a way that it can easily be communicated and taken to the next step, i.e. to check its innovative power.

Assessment of the innovative potential (phase 3)

Many definitions of innovation exist and indeed many have a different focus. In general, however, those definitions either concentrate on the creativity phase, the idea-generation phase, or they would concentrate on the process innovation side, describing how to get from an idea to a realized product or service. A second criterion on which most of the definitions differ is the focus either on breadth or on depth with which innovation is associated. Since we believe that certainly in the first phases, breadth is important, we like to give the West and Farr (1990) definition here:

"Innovation is defined as the intentional introduction and application within a role, group, or organization, of ideas, processes, products or procedures, new to the relevant unit of adoption to significantly benefit the individual, the group, organization or wider society."

In this phase of the project, we are going to try to make an assessment of the innovative potential of the project as it stands now. A possible outcome could be to re-iterate the project (given the outcome of this phase) and aim for new or further idea generation, or to go for the inventory of constraints and capabilities for successful realization inside the company.

In this section a number of lessons learned from existing research are given as a kind of checklist that can help you to assess the innovative potential of your project. Let us start with some general lessons (taken out of standard literature). The next section concentrates more on the learning of more specific, experience-based lessons.

Some general lessons learned about innovation

- Character or culture are human creations, not facts of life. Context, therefore, is important
- All people have creative potential
- One cannot separate creativity from the possibility to create *new* products (what some authors call the ability to transform ideas into viable solutions)
- Creativity is different from creation (production, re-production, etc.)
- Creativity often needs motivation
- Creativity has to do with freedom of choice and choice itself
- Multiplicity is important for creativity; multiple realities always exist
- Recognition of demand is a more frequent factor in successful innovation than recognition of technical potential. In this phase (and not for the first time in the business plan) demand should already be receiving attention
- Training and experience of people right *in* your company are crucial for innovation
- Did we learn any lessons from other (external or internal) innovations?
- Don't innovate for the future, but for the present
- Effective innovation starts small and is often not revolutionary

- Innovation and learning go hand-in-hand; innovation and management is a different ballgame

Questions that should always be addressed with innovation are, in this case particularly with respect to the innovative potential of your project:

- Why (goals)
- What (product-novelty)
- When (timing)
- Where (targeting)
- How (marketing mix)

Here are some identified potential fail factors that should be considered in this stage, when they can still easily be avoided:

- Go for the "better" product (without clients)
- A me-too product (is often too slow)
- Obstruction (unexpected) of the competition
- Products for low-margin markets
- Badly prepared introduction
- Fast introductions
- The newer, the better

- Position a new product as the successor of another one
- Change the positioning of the product (too fast)
- Too low pricing
- Organizational limitations and barriers, like culture, limited managerial support, lack of competencies, etc. Though those aspects get much more attention in the next phase, some initial exploration should take place here.

Potential success factors, that you would like to consider at this stage:

- Intrinsic value of the product
- Structured and well-managed development and introduction process. You should already have a clear idea about this. Maybe a wish list should be made now in this respect
- Understanding the users' needs
- Attention to marketing and publicity
- Efficiency of development
- Effective use of outside technology and external scientific communication
- Seniority and authority of responsible managers – commitment
- Team composition?
- Individual creativity?

The strongest positive correlations with success are:

- Product advantage (costs, innovativeness, quality, satisfying needs)
- Proficiency of pre-development activities (initial brainstorm, screening, thorough market analysis, technical assessment, financial/business analysis)
- Good protocol of all specifications

Inventory of capacities and constraints (phase 4)

Once the concept is ready to be checked against the capacities and constraints of the company, we leave the creativity phase to an extent, and move on into the inventory phase. In this phase the project is assessed against the expected strengths and weaknesses that your company may have in respect of innovation. In some cases the corporate environment, for many different reasons, is somewhat hostile to new, truly innovative projects. This can be due to the organizational structure, the lack of commitment from top management, the culture of the company, etc. Before checking the financial and economic feasibility in the form of a business plan, we first try to create an inventory of the corporate constraints, and of course, the corporate strongholds.

In order to support you in doing this, I again offer some checklists. The first ones are more general in nature and are based on what is commonly known as the NPD (New Product Development) literature. They mostly relate to the expected origination of the further innovation process. Recognizing possible pitfalls early on also affords the possibility to avoid them. The latter checklists are based on research into some real-life projects and share some of those learnings.

Some challenges for the future NPD process of your project:

- Not everything can be realized. Therefore, making trade-offs between different "important" aspects of a new idea is essential. Can you identify these aspects and prioritize them?
- Dynamics: how to deal with changing technologies, preferences, opinions, ecology, economy. Is your project vulnerable to rapid changes?
- Details: small decisions can have large consequences (possibly even on a larger scale)
- Time and timing. How crucial is this?

Some possible fail factors:

- Team that is not empowered enough
- Political (hidden) agendas, on all different levels
- Inadequate sourcing
- Incomplete design team

For the most part, the NPD process that will eventually follow your project is one of uncertainty reduction. NPD is equally a process of seeking and keeping sponsorship. Often, innovation needs sufficient cash. The top 5 critical success factors are as follows:

- Commitment of the top management to the project
- Planning and design
- Involvement of employees in the project
- Education and training
- Internal communication

Did you address these, and if not, it is worth spending some time on it now?

And then, eventually, we come to the NPD process model. Can you detail all (or most) of these steps in what your company should be able to identify and/or deliver for your project to be successful? If you can see constraints, limitations, problems, etc. try to make it clear how they could be solved. Identify the context and conditions necessary for your project to be successful.

1. Development of the concept (basically the steps already undertaken)
2. Choice of the organizational structure (interdisciplinary; functional expertise; speed; availability of people)

3. Identification of client needs (span of the product) (in our approach, this should already have been taken care of in earlier stages of the project). What do they specifically need?
4. Product specification
5. Decompose the planned 'production cycle' into desired functionalities. Who should be involved?
6. Product description: is it possible to detail the product completely (modular; integral)
7. Distinctions like: size, volume, performance features, ergonomics, outlook
8. Production: estimate the production cost (production can also be understood as information handling, computing, etc.)
9. Prototyping (if possible): how would you do that, who should be involved, how would you organize that?
10. Economic analysis, both qualitative and quantitative. Identify the risks (technical, organizational and of the market) involved and identify some go-no-go moments. Make a thorough study of the competitors. Can you identify some possible spin-offs? Keep a close watch on social trends. How does your product give you a competitive advantage? Does it provide you with a better competitive response power? Is the organization able to launch this product, and if not, how will you launch it?

Try and prepare some project planning and management.

It's only an opportunity if you act on it

Some experience-based lessons learned:

The checklist presented here is based on the learnings of a number of real-life innovation projects that have been studied. Since the cases were 'assembled' at the end of the innovation project, some of the issues are clearly related to the process itself. Hence, not all of them are applicable to your particular project. See whether you can learn from some of these learnings in order to improve your own project.

- Reasons for delays often mentioned are: changes in the project team, insufficient resources (availability of people), no clear specifications, insufficient interface between teams, universal optimism and opportunistic planning, outside influences.
- Insufficient project management skills
- Insufficient communication on decisions
- Frustrations of team members
- Unclear responsibilities
- Not all expertise required is available
- Reinvention of the wheel
- Insufficient management commitment that causes stress, pressure, insufficient resources
- Contracting problems if third parties are involved
- No proper risk analysis is available
- Changes in the concept that occur during the project realization are often not checked for risks and consequences
- Market tests are often executed entirely too late

0

3

e

9 Relevance (The concept of the Cassandra tool)

Some Tibetans believe our present world of war, disease, corrupt inequality and environmental desecration, is the self-destructive age of Kali, to be followed by a new age of peace, ethnic harmony, environmental balance, and human dignity, yet to come. This future is Shambhala, sometimes called Shangri-la.

(Laurence Brahm)

Reckless growth, growth for the creation of shareholder value, is increasingly questioned. Or at least, the consequences are. Oil prices are skyrocketing, not only due to an ever-growing demand of oil, but also demand from the emerging economies. We cannot reasonably criticize them since it is our economic model that has created the dream of unlimited growth. However, that same drive for growth is likely to cause economic depression through its recklessness. When this was published in our previous book (Baets and Oldenboom, 2009), at the time of writing, we were not yet in the world crisis that broke out in 2008.

This book has developed an understanding of business thinking and how it could, and should, be rethought. It has defined a number of fairly new managerial concepts, like management by values, co-creation, sustainable performance and sustainability. Above all, it aims to present a coherent new management paradigm, a systemic management paradigm. This paradigm is, on the one hand, embedded in the latest scientific developments and, on the other hand creates space for concepts like corporate social responsibility and sustainable development. It also gives managers the framework within which they are not only able to develop responsibility, but also to make responsibility an important component of sustainable performance. With a systemic approach, as argued in previous chapters, sustainable performance supersedes financial performance.

However, in order to support managers who are willing to make this paradigm shift, there is a need for a methodology – a set of tools that fits the stakeholder paradigm of management. In the appendix we suggest a blueprint for a roadmap: a methodology and a number of checklists. These are designed to help managers to get the process started, to support co-workers, and to give tools for continuous monitoring. The roadmap adopts a very down-to-earth approach to assist managers who have opted for the paradigm shift, with starting the change process.

A real paradigm shift in a company, and a relevant managerial approach that fits this new paradigm, is indeed a major change project. We do not want to repeat here all that has been written on change processes. However, the first step of this change process is the manager's paradigm shift, since it is his or her belief in this new paradigm that will become the driver of the change process. This belief, this view, this energy, this meaning, which the manager aims to give the company, becomes the heartbeat of the company. The appendix only gives a number of tools, but it does not replace the necessary change process – they are only the supporting tools. Inappropriate use of this appendix, and in particular its application without the paradigmatic context, might make the tools useless and even counterproductive. A company interested in this shift, a shift towards responsible management (corporate and individual) that, by definition, will be sustainable (see the Ben Eli definition), aims at sustainable performance. Sustainable performance, in turn, targets fulfillment of all the stakeholder interests, and is a learning and change process that most often needs some support and coaching. The methodology described here is able to give that support, provided that a well-trained consultant-coach (trained in the Cassandra approach) coaches this process.

Laurence Brahm has noted a parallel shift in the world of spirit in noting how some "Tibetans believe our present world of war, disease, corrupt inequality and environmental desecration, is the self-destructive age of Kali, to be followed by a new age of peace, ethnic harmony, environmental balance, and human dignity, yet to come. This future is Shambhala, sometimes called Shangri-la." This chapter is not that concerned with such a meta-theoretical perspective but rather with the role of business in the world. Accordingly, the focus is on social intrapreneurship which, in parallel with social entrepreneurship, re-valorizes the creator, the innovator and the entrepreneur in the manager (instead of the administrator). It aims to make a concrete contribution to society and to realize one or more values. Social intrapreneurship has to do with creation, innovation, learning and making a difference, but always with the purpose of adding value to the stakeholders at large and society. The world would miss a social intrapreneur if he or she would no longer be there. The social intrapreneur makes a difference, not only for the shareholders, but also for all the stakeholders, and for the environment of the company.

Although already suggested, it is worth saying a last time explicitly: Social intrapreneurship, managing for sustainable performance and social responsibility need a new paradigm. This book's project differs from other books around social and environmental responsibility and the like, in two distinct ways. Firstly, it puts all those concepts into the framework of a new paradigm, and secondly, it clarifies that that paradigm shift is the single most important move to make. The rest follows automatically. The mainstream paradigm does not allow mental and financial space for sustainable development or responsible management. Without the shift, responsibility and sustainable development will ultimately end up in the mainstream paradigm as marketing actions, or to put it crudely: corporations are doing no more than attempting to say "look how good and kind we are; we have programs on social responsibility and we deal in fair trade products". Despite the rhetoric and relatively marginal actions, their baseline remains the same. And it is this devastating baseline that eventually, over the long term, makes responsibility in management and sustainable development impossible. The concept of sustainable performance cannot co-exist peacefully with the mainstream paradigm.

This can be clarified in more detail through Draper et al's "Key hallmarks list of a business leader" and, especially, the following "Memorandum of the social innovator" on the necessary qualities.

- A genuine **commitment to contributing value to the economy and the society** is visible at the highest level of the business, with values and sustainability principles present in core strategic goals.
- There is a **clear vision** of the organization in a **future (a long term view)** where sustainability is core to creating value.
- Key sustainable performance indicators are **fully integrated** into the **governance** system of the business.
- **Staff** are encouraged to deliver the sustainability program through effective performance management, incentives and provision of appropriate tools and resources.
- Future **products and services** will deliver value to society, sustainability and profits.

- **Marketing** campaigns and pricing structures help customers make **more sustainable choices**. **Transparency** is a key value.
- Close partnerships with **suppliers** are in place which improve standards and **stimulate innovation**.
- The **environmental impacts (and the stakeholder impact)** of the business, both direct and indirect, are well understood.
- The business has a clear understanding of what it would mean to operate within **environmental limits**.
- There is clear comprehension of the value of **stakeholder engagement**.
- Stakeholders are involved in identifying and prioritizing **material issues, as well as values** of the company at a strategic level.
- The business demonstrates consistency on **public messages** and 'behind the scenes' lobbying, with policy proposals reflecting policies and commitments on sustainability and transparency.
- **Progressive government action** towards a higher degree of sustainability is sought at a national and international level.
- Business **risks and opportunities** associated with sustainable development are well understood and communicated.
- **Environmental** and **social cost accounting methodologies** are recognized and understood by investors and used in describing material realities.
- **Community activities** have strong links to the core business, its brands and its products/services.
- **Reporting** focuses on material issues, and the system for prioritizing these is robust and transparent. The organization doesn't shy away from difficult and sensitive issues.
- The report forms an integral part of management systems, **driving performance**, engaging stakeholders, and challenging the industry.

The five shifts required to facilitate the development of sustainable performance in business are:

Shift 1: Take up of a systemic view of the company by the mainstream

Shift 2: Promote the sustainable performance business model

Shift 3: Valorize the intrapreneur in the manager

Shift 4: Accept that whatever is done should have value for society

Shift 5: Re-engineer the metrics of business

If the reader morally subscribes to this memorandum, the time is ripe for a managerial paradigm shift.

The methodology

The appendix proposes how to operationalize the concepts developed in the book. It offers a set of checklists and questionnaires – discussed in earlier chapters – which, together, act as a kind of roadmap to sustainable performance. This roadmap is available for use either as a step-plan for implementing social intrapreneurship, or alternatively for benchmarking one's own performance, or sustainable performance, in comparison with other companies. However, in order to use it to its full potential, either training or tutoring is necessary. The checklists indeed fit a wider concept (as the book argues in depth) and, without a thorough understanding of this concept, these checklists will be less effective and have less impact.

The Cassandra methodology has five constituent components:

1. **The values and the vision: what is the contribution of the company?**
2. **Benchmarking: from dream to reality (do "we" make a difference?)**
3. **The leadership's checklist: do "I" make a difference?**
4. **Cassandra: a diagnostic for sustainable performance (where are we and where to go from here)**
5. **The learning coach: continuous work on the mutual selves ("on the road")**

the path, and nothing more;

Wanderer, there is no path,

it is created as you walk.

By walking,

you make the path before you,

and when you look behind

you see the path which after you

will not be trod again.

Wanderer, there is no path,

but the ripples on the waters.

Antonio Machado

Those five constituent components form a continuous loop of evaluation, designing, laying down the path by walking (Machado), learning, re-evaluation, re-designing, etc. The appendix itself mainly focuses on assembling a number of checklists and tools that together make up the roadmap.

The main tool we propose is named "Cassandra©". In Greek mythology, Cassandra ('she who entangles men') was a daughter of King Priam and Queen Hecuba of Troy, and her beauty caused Apollo to grant her the gift of prophecy (or, more correctly, prescience). However, when she did not return his love, Apollo placed a curse on her so that no one would ever believe her predictions (Wikipedia). This metaphor could hardly be more illustrative for introducing this shift in paradigm.

Sustainable performance, though it seems to speak for itself, is yet another unknown concept. Unable to find a definition for sustainable performance – rather bizarre in a world filled with discourse about sustainability and responsibility – this chapter offers one. Based on Ben-Eli's core principles, sustainable performance is corporate (or organizational) performance that seeks a dynamic equilibrium in the processes of interaction between a company, the carrying capacity of its stakeholders, and the environment in such a way that the company develops to express its full potential without adversely and irreversibly affecting the carrying capacity of the stakeholders and the environment upon which it depends. As previously argued, this rather new concept needs another context and paradigm but, for application, it also needs metrics.

Cassandra: a holistic diagnostic for sustainable performance and personal development

Within the framework of this book, sustainability, sustainable development, sustainable performance and corporate responsibility, only find a conceptual basis within a holistic view on management. Within classic managerial approaches, other than for personal (or corporate) ethical motivation, there is no reason or space for a company to be responsible or sustainable. The President of the EFMD correctly iterated during the Global Compact Summit in Geneva that the average manager does not automatically think in terms of "responsibility", so if that is to be changed there is a long way to go. This book does not necessarily stress the length of the journey, but rather the taking of different routes. A highly reductionist view on management, focusing primarily, if not exclusively, on short term financial performance, makes sustainability counterproductive. There are no commonly accepted managerial theories that give the manager tools for managing differently.

Some will argue that economics allows for the accounting of any externalities by including, for instance, the cost of pollution. There needs to be a clear distinction between the economic calculations of costs for certain externalities and straightforward management of sustainable development. Calculation of costs for externalities that in fact turn them into an economic good, and allowing them to be traded off, is no solution for sustainable development. It simply shifts the costs of economic development from those with economic power to those without economic power, and at the same time keeps that economic development concentrated in the hands of the economically developed. The market for CO_2 emissions is only one example and resembles the active trade of risky country debt a number of years ago. Indeed a number of international banks have been able to make money on selling high-risk loans, without at any point solving the problem of that same towering country debt. Sustainable development cannot be seen other than within the large network of countries and individuals that are all equally a part of planet Earth. We all have to move forward in co-creation, within a holistic perspective. In certain aspects, it becomes a zero sum game. Sustainable performance and management for sustainable performance therefore needs both new concepts and new diagnostics.

This chapter outlines the development of a diagnostic based on the Wilber holistic model, but adapted to a managerial context. For each of Wilber's quadrants, we identify, with reference to existing management research, a number of items that together co-construct the quadrant. The diagnostic is primarily an inventory and can be further used as a guide for transforming a manager into someone who is capable and prepared for a different way of management. At a later point the book will develop it as a management tool. At this point, the focus is on the manager as a person; the person who is going to be the transformational leader able to manage his or her company or organization, for sustainable performance. The diagnostic analyzes the individual's potential for sustainable managerial performance and is, in fact, a tool for personal development.

The manager scores each question on a 1 to 5 scale of agree/disagree or yes/no. It is clear that not all the questions are equally easy to understand and can be interpreted differently. This tool is used more adequately (and more easily) within a coached framework, but has been successfully tested for non-guided use. High quality coaching and tutoring will always improve its learning potential.

The holistic management quadrants were labeled: values; personal development; mechanistic approaches; and holistic systemic approaches. For the purpose of the development of a diagnostic, we have subdivided each quadrant in two items and we have given the content more of a performance orientation.

The value quadrant is subdivided into the themes of "diversity" and "complexity". Based on the work of de Anca and Vazquez (2007) and Kofman (2006), the diversity theme has been covered by the following questions:

- Do you base your actions on ethical codes?
- Do you sometimes reflect on the sustainability of your actions?
- Do you pay attention to being anti-discriminatory?
- Do your actions reflect Social Responsibility?
- Do we need to take care of all the parties involved in what we do?
- Is assessing someone's work environment important?
- In an organization is it important to pay attention to retention of talent?
- Do you believe that a variety in opinions is a value?
- Do you pay attention to communicating effectively with those around you?
- Should leadership be strongly committed?
- Do you see active interest groups as an asset for society?

The questions for the complexity theme are based on the findings of our own earlier work (Baets, 2006):

- Are you most dynamic and creative at the edge of chaos?
- Does evolution need both the new and extinction?
- Is diversity a prerequisite for the emergence of the new?
- Is radical unpredictability an essential characteristic of any organization?
- Is the self-organizational capacity of any group an indicator for sustainability?
- Is interaction between "individual agents" essential for self-organization?
- Is agency (the action) located at the level of interacting individual entities?

The personal development quadrant is subdivided into the themes of "personal wellbeing" and "leadership and teamwork". The first theme questions the undeniable link between wellbeing, happiness in one's job and the person's contribution to the development of the company. The analysis is based on the work of Chopra (amongst others, his simple guidelines published in 1994), who is an authority on mind-body medical approaches, and retains the following questions:

- Do I value an active approach for the development of individual competencies and skills?
- Do I also value time which is not immediately productive?
- Do I practice a policy of non-judgment on appearances (facts, humans, etc.)?
- Is joy an active element of my professional or societal life?
- Do I feel valued in my professional environment?
- Do I have real responsibility and the space to maneuver?
- Is there space for the realization of my desires in my function/activity?
- Is courage valued in my professional environment?
- Do I feel an essential part of the whole?

The theme of leadership and teamwork is plugged into an alternative source. As discussed in Chapter 7, a number of years ago, Roger Nierenberg (1999), a well-known conductor, made a remarkable TV program in which he put managers in-between the BBC orchestra members in order to have them experience the essence of leadership and teamwork. He conducted small exercises with some of the managers and the orchestra and, while doing so, dealt in a brilliant metaphorical way with the essentials of leadership and teamwork. The questions retained for this theme are:

- Is each individual (surrounding me) well trained and prepared to do his/her job?
- Is a constant sense of awareness essential for success?
- Is my professional environment an intense network of communication?

- Is the purpose in my professional environment always clear and shared?
- Do my managers create space for others?
- Are my managers more concerned with projecting a vision and less with correcting what happened previously?
- Does rigid leadership create confusion?
- Does lack of clarity cause tension and under-performance?
- Do I have an external focus that gives meaning to my work?

The two so-called external quadrants are more classic and better known by most managers. The mechanistic performance has been subdivided into "financial performance" and "innovative potential". Financial performance is not expressed in absolute figures, but rather in comparison with the perceived peer group, and accepts that the financial performance of a person is highly dependent on what he or she perceives to be wealth and a "correct" financial situation. The basic variables are based on Stone's work (1999) and the questions retained are:

- Is my appreciation of my revenue above average in society?
- Is my appreciation of my belongings above average in our society?
- Is my liquidity position above average in society (can I buy what I really want)?
- Do I generate enough cash in order to be financially self-sufficient for what I want to develop?
- Does my cash-flow generation give me a feeling of comfort?

Anticipating that over a certain period of time (this is a longer term diagnostic) the capacity to create and to innovate is essential for performance, the second component of the mechanistic performance quadrant is one's potential to innovate. This is based on innovative potential from the theories of Edward de Bono (as they are commercialized though a network of consultants). In this case, the questions are based on the work of Advanced Practical Thinking Training Inc. (2001).

- Do I actively pay attention to developing new ideas?
- Am I am able to produce creativity on demand?
- Does my professional environment regard idea generation as a key business practice?
- Do I personally develop new ideas on a regular basis?
- Does our leadership structure acknowledge innovative thinking?
- Should an organization have a structured process for evaluating/refining new ideas?
- Does our professional culture value idea assessment/refinement as a core competence?

The final quadrant focuses on systemic performance. Its themes relate directly to systemic concepts of performance such as sustainable development, social responsibility, knowledge management, and organizational learning. As established earlier in the book in more detail, those systemic themes are an essential contribution to sustainable performance and therefore need to be present in a holistic diagnostic. The sustainable development and social responsibility questions are based on the work of Stacey (2000), one of the forerunners in linking strategy with complexity to deal with a complex world.

- Do I value unconditional responsibility?
- Do I value essential integrity?
- Do I value ontological humility (is my basic starting point to be humble)?
- Do I value authentic communication?
- Do I value constructive negotiation?
- Do I value impeccable coordination?
- Do I value conscious responses?
- Do I value emotional mastery?

For the knowledge management and management learning theme, the questions are based on Baets and Van der Linden (2000), where the background of the questions is analyzed in detail.

- Should project managers use more than financial factors to measure success?
- Does the rigidity of processes give people very little possibility for correction?
- Because interaction is important, is harmony between people crucial?
- Are confidence and control two contrary variables?
- Do confidence and motivation have a strong influence on exchange and the creation of knowledge?
- Must confidence levels always be built?
- Does interaction without knowledge prevent learning?
- Does interaction without confidence and motivation prevent learning?
- Do motivation and organization seem to interact positively?
- Is interaction always necessary for the construction of confidence?
- If there are agents at group level who do not cooperate, does the learning of the group stop?

As indicated before, in the Cassandra test the person scores all these questions on a scale of 1 to 5, according to the best of his or her perception. The more honest the answers, the more value the tool will add. The questions are not made in order to be a perfect research tool (though, as explained further, it is correctly tested and validated), but rather to be a good diagnostic. Above all, it is a tool that helps the person develop. In practice this means that the questions are formulated in such a way that ideally someone would want to have an average value of 5 on all the axes. Of course, this situation is idealized and not realistic, but it provides an actionable picture of the themes that need further attention and/or development. An average score per theme is calculated and a raster diagram represents the eight axes, as in the following illustrative figure of a possible case.

Cassandra diagram
The Holistic Diagnoctic for Personal Sustainble Performance

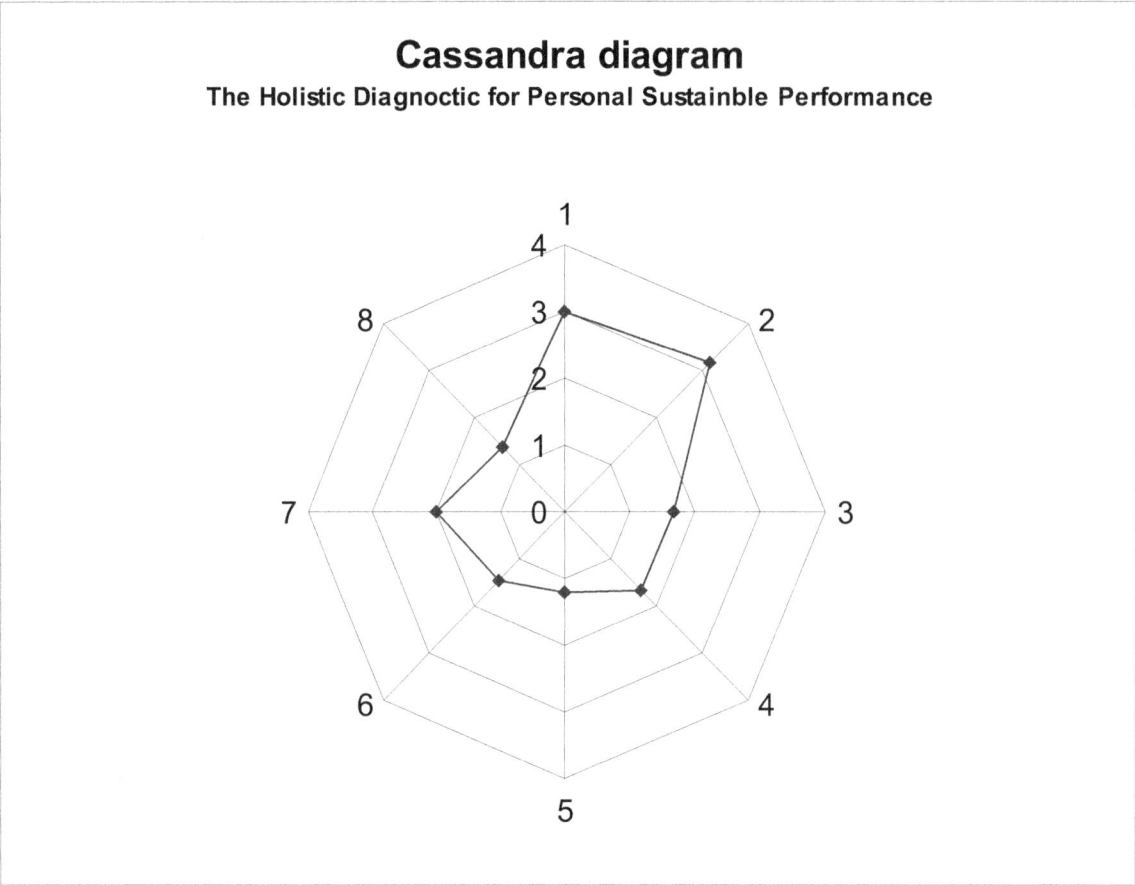

Values

Axis 1: Diversity

Axis 2: Complexity

Personal development

Axis 3: Personal Well Being

Axis 4: Leadership and teamwork

Mechanistic performance

Axis 5: Financial performance

Axis 6: Innovative potential   l

Holistic performance

Axis 7: Sustainable development and social responsibility

Axis 8: Knowledge and learning

If this person would like improve their sustainable performance in leadership (his or her own functioning as a manager), he or she needs to develop their personality in areas other than the values quadrant. In the future we will possibly be able to identify most types of managers and types of development paths. For the time being, the idea of this diagnostic is to give a rich picture of the current situation and suggest possible paths for improvement.

Cassandra, the holistic diagnostic for personal sustainable performance has been tested for its stability and validity. The next section gives further insight into some of the observations made during the testing. Overall, however, the tool seems to be well understood by the user and more importantly, easily used by them. The future will show how it works as a tool for personal development and guidance.

In order to make sustainability a concept that is practically usable for the manager, we have created this diagnostic based on our holistic understanding of sustainability. The tool is oriented to the manager/leader as a person. This is the first step: the personal development trajectory of the learning manager. But the same kind of development needs to be made for the company. The elements developed in this chapter need to be applied company-wide, in order to define a way of management that allows the manager to manage according to a more responsible and more sustainable paradigm; one that is oriented towards sustainable performance. This is the task of the second part of this chapter.

Validity test of the personal version

The Cassandra tool (for personal development) has been construct validated. Detail of this validation can be found in Baets and Oldenboom, 2009. As well as being important to test the construct validity, it served also to demonstrate its novelty, both in subject and in approach (the 8 axes, and the relatively high number of questions compared to more classical approaches). While probably more interesting for the researcher, it should comfort the manager that this tool is sound. The structure invited validation using the technique of Factorial Analysis (FA), based on Malhotra (2004), using data collected amongst Master in Management students, who follow a curriculum within a more systemic management concept.

Seen from the classical point of view of validity of tests, the test results were fine, but at the same time they illustrated how much variance would be lost if it was only limited to a suggested numbers of variables. As argued, and for the reasons discussed, this approach is one of making a picture as diverse as possible, even if that would be less stable from a classic statistical point of view. The conscious option was to prefer richness of information to stability of tests, whatever the latter would mean.

The corporate version of Cassandra

Based on the principles described earlier, a corporate version of Cassandra has been similarly designed. This version depicts the current potential of a company for sustainable performance, and in a second stage, defines a path of sustainable development (a strategy, a vision) and a possible action plan.

The questions raised for the different themes are as follows, and they are each scored on a scale from 1 to 5. At the end, the outcome is represented by the same type of diagram as for the personal version. It is not a quiz and there are no good or bad answers. The more accurate the responses, the more the tool can assist.

Values

Diversity

- Does your company have ethical codes?
- Does your company produce sustainability reports?
- Does your company have anti-discrimination policies?
- Does your company have Corporate Social Responsibility indicators?
- Should your company maintain a dialogue with all stakeholders?
- Do you think that assessing the work environment is important?
- Does your company have a human resources policy that pays attention to talent retention?
- In your company, is variety in opinions considered a value?
- Does your company pay a lot of attention to internal communication?
- Is your company leadership strongly committed?
- Does your company have active interest groups?

Complexity

- Is the dynamic of a company situated at the edge of chaos?
- Does evolution need both the new and extinction?
- Is diversity a prerequisite for the emergence of the new?
- Is radical unpredictability an essential characteristic of business?
- Is the self-organizational capacity of a company an indicator for sustainability?
- Is interaction between "individual agents" essential for self-organization?
- Is agency (the action) located at the level of interacting individual entities?

Personal Development

Personal well-being

- Do we have an active policy and programs for the development of individual competencies and skills?
- Does the company also value time that is not immediately productive?
- Does the company practice a policy of non-judgment on appearances (facts, humans, etc.)?
- Is joy an active element of our corporate life?
- Do I feel valued in my company?
- Do managers in our company have real responsibility and a space to maneuver?
- Is there space for the realization of my desires in my function?
- Is courage valued in the company?
- Do I feel an essential part of the whole?

Leadership and teamwork

- Is each individual well trained and prepared to do his/her job?
- Is a constant sense of awareness essential for success?
- Is our company an intense network of communication?
- Is the purpose in our company always clear and shared?
- Do our managers create space for others?
- Are our managers more concerned with projecting a vision and less with correcting what previously happened?
- Does rigid leadership create confusion?
- Does lack of clarity cause tension and under-performance?
- Do we have an external focus that gives meaning to our work?

Mechanistic performance

Financial performance

- Is our profit margin above average in our industry?
- Is our return on capital employed above average in our industry?
- Is our liquidity position above average in our industry?
- Do we generate enough cash in order to auto-finance our activities and growth?
- Is our cash-flow generation above average in our industry?

Innovative potential

- Do we have a distinct methodology/process in place for developing new ideas?
- Are we able to produce creativity on demand?
- Does our culture regard idea generation as a key business practice?
- Do I personally develop new ideas on a regular basis?
- Do our leadership models and rewards structure acknowledge innovative thinking?
- Do we have a deliberate, structured process for thoroughly evaluating/refining new ideas?
- Does our culture value idea assessment/refinement as a core competence?

Systemic performance

Sustainable development and social responsibility

- Does our company value unconditional responsibility?
- Does our company value essential integrity?
- Does our company value ontological humility?
- Does our company value conscious behaviors?
- Does our company value authentic communication?
- Does our company value constructive negotiation?
- Does our company value impeccable coordination?
- Does our company value conscious responses?
- Does our company value emotional mastery?

Knowledge and learning

- Should project managers use more than financial factors to measure success?
- Does the rigidity of processes give people very little possibility for correction?
- Because interaction is important, is harmony between people crucial?
- Are confidence and control two contrary variables?
- Do confidence and motivation have a strong influence on exchange and the creation of knowledge?
- Must confidence levels always be built?

- Does interaction without knowledge prevent learning?
- Does interaction without confidence and motivation prevent learning?
- Do motivation and organization seem to interact positively?
- Is interaction is always necessary for the development of confidence?
- If there are agents at group level who do not cooperate, does the learning of the group stop?

A case study using the corporate version of Cassandra

Cassandra has been successfully used in a number of corporate workshops, both the personal version and the corporate one. It is often effective to ask individuals to do the personal development version and coach them on that, while, at the same time, asking them to prepare for the seminar by filling out the corporate version. The corporate version is then used as a real-life case, helping to define the way ahead, the actions to take, and once this step is taken, to feed this back into the personal development agenda. This cycle, and the continuous feedback between the personal version and the corporate version has attracted strong participant involvement. However, given its systemic concept, the complexity of the issues raised, and the profound nature of a number of the questions, this does work optimally within an organizational development workshop that includes some personal development coaching. It would be further enhanced if the latter could be continued over time, so that it fed back regularly into a corporate re-evaluation.

An alternative use of the corporate version of Cassandra is to perform a corporate analysis of a company, in order to give advice on the sustainable performance potential of a company (for instance for those considering a possible investment in the company). This type of use is a very welcome approach in courses or general purpose workshops. An illustration of what kind of alternative enriched views the corporate version of Cassandra could lead to, can be found it the following case compiled by one of our part-time MBA students (Carina Richards), and was first published in Baets and Oldenboom, 2009. She created a case study, using published data from Renault Europe Automobiles (REA) and had regular interviews with the director general of the company. At the end of the case study, it was verified and validated by the management of REA. The scores in the Cassandra analysis are her interpretation, based on her research and interviews, and eventually validated by the company.

Although it deals with the company Renault, it is in no way to be understood as either an approval or a rejection of the company or its policies. The case study is intended only to illustrate, for learning purposes, the operation, method and potential of the Cassandra method and, as such, has been simplified in order to show only the essentials, since the actual analysis went much deeper and had far more detail. The case first makes a more classical analysis of the performance of Renault, before using Cassandra to analyze sustainable performance.

Renault Europe Automobiles (Case analysis made by Carina Richards)

"Classical" Analysis

Figures quoted in € million, taken from the Renault 2006 Annual Report

Year	2002	2003	2004	2005	2006
Revenues	36,336	37,525	40,292	41,338	41,528
Operating margin	1,483	1,402	2,115	1,323	1,063
Operating income	1,217	1,234	1,872	1,514	877
Financial expense	(91)	(71)	(331)	(327)	61
Share in net income of Nissan Motor	1,335	1,705	1,689	2,275	1,871
Share in net income of other associates	(4)	155	234	322	389
Pre-tax income	2,457	3,023	3,464	3,784	3,198
Current & deferred tax	(447)	(510)	(561)	(331)	(255)
Net income	2,010	2,513	2,903	3,453	2,943
Net income – minority interests' share	54	33	67	86	74
Net income – Renault share	1,956	2,480	2,836	3,367	2,869
Earnings per share €	7.53	9.32	11.16	13.19	11.17

Key figures 2006

Operating margin
(€ million)

1,063

2006

Workforce
(in units) – at December 31, 2006

128,893

2006

Net income – Renault share
(€ million)

2,869

2006

Revenues – Renault share
(€ million)

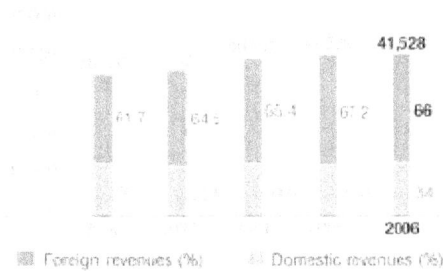

41,528

66

2006

Foreign revenues (%)   Domestic revenues (%)

2006 Commercial results
(Thousand units - Cars + LCVs)

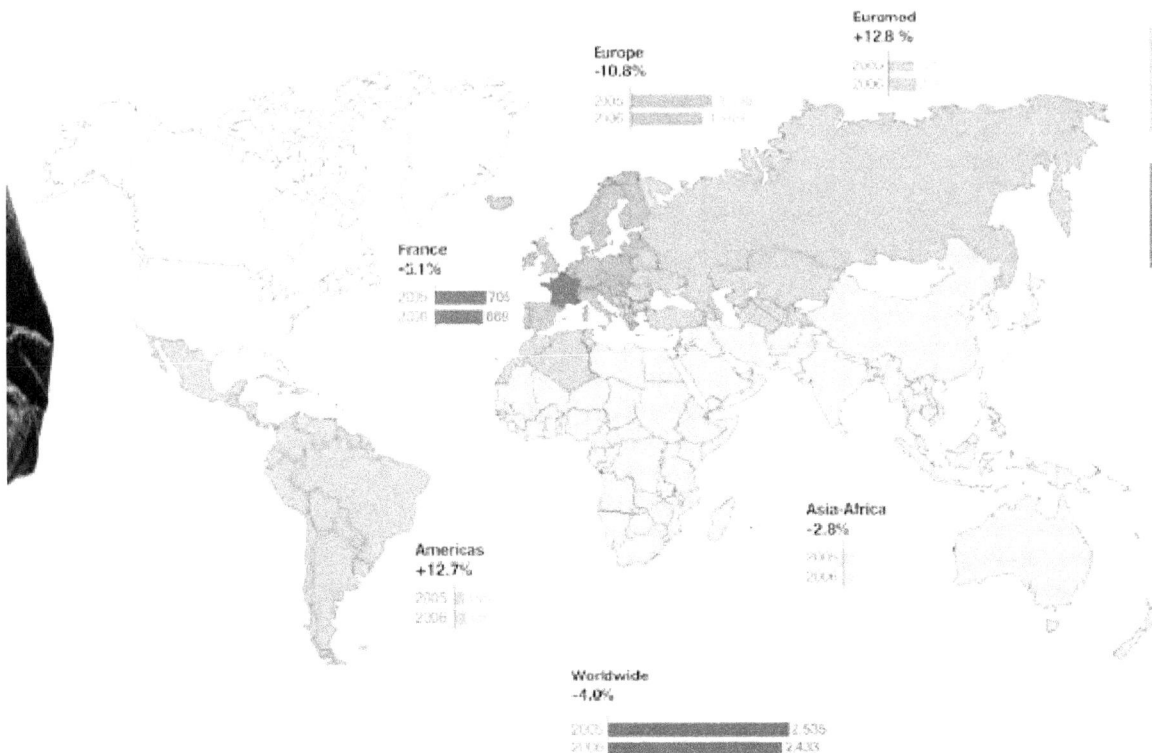

Europe
-10.8%

Euromed
+12.8 %

France
-5.1%

Americas
+12.7%

Asia-Africa
-2.8%

Worldwide
-4.0%

The figures* represent sales in thousands of vehicles.

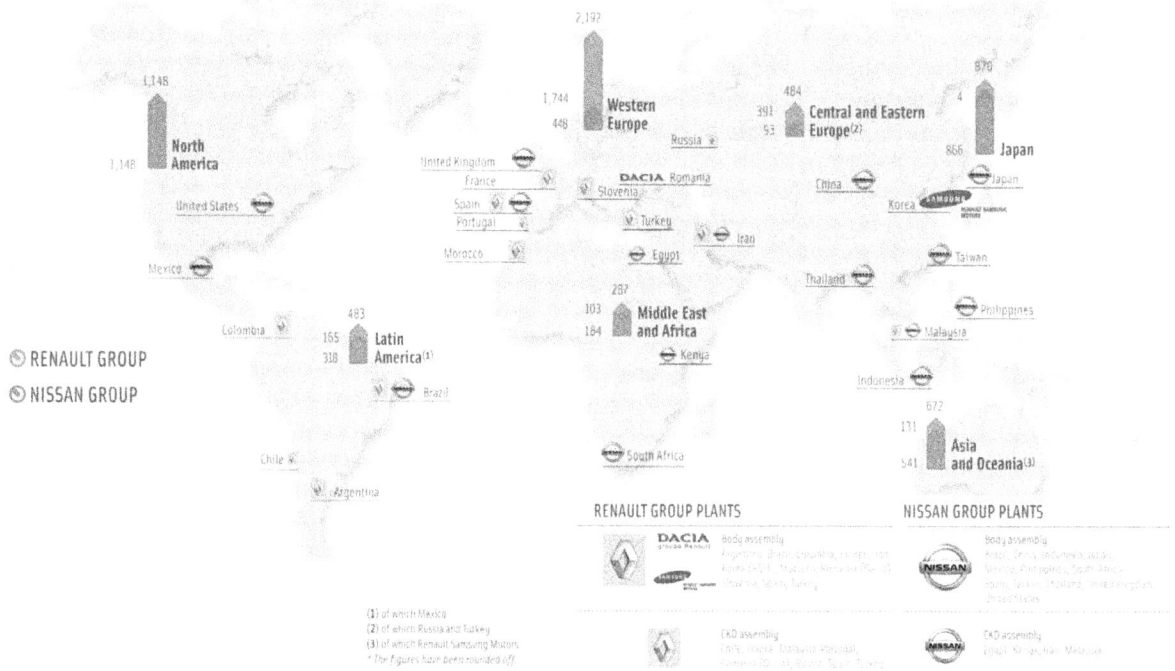

2,192

1,744
448

Western Europe

484
391
53

Central and Eastern Europe(2)

870
4

866

Japan

1,148

3,148

North America

United States

Mexico

United Kingdom
France
Spain
Portugal

Morocco

DACIA Romania
Slovenia

Turkey

Egypt   Iran

China

Korea SAMSUNG

Thailand

Taiwan

Philippines

Malaysia

Colombia

483
165
318

Latin America(1)

Brazil

287
103
184

Middle East and Africa

Kenya

Indonesia

672
171
541

Asia and Oceania(3)

© RENAULT GROUP

© NISSAN GROUP

Chile

Argentina

South Africa

RENAULT GROUP PLANTS

DACIA

SAMSUNG

Body assembly

CKD assembly

NISSAN GROUP PLANTS

NISSAN

Body assembly

NISSAN

CKD assembly

(1) of which Mexico
(2) of which Russia and Turkey
(3) of which Renault Samsung Motors
* The figures have been rounded off.

Alliance Renault-Nissan worldwide sales 2005

Information & indicators

This analysis was drawn from reports and documents published by the Renault Group via its internet site. The assessment was based on financial statements and indicators, and information released concerning the group's strategy and performance, the Renault-Nissan Alliance and future projects and objectives.

Interpretation of findings

Revenues are increasing slightly. The group recorded a slowdown due to the preparation of the launch of new products that will drive the group forward during the second half of 2007.

- Main markets performed sluggishly in 2006:
- The French market declined by 1.9% and the European market grew by 1.3%;
- In Western Europe, the mid-range segment lost 5.5%, mainly to the benefit of the entry-level segment, which gained 6.5%.
- At the same time financial expenses have been reduced despite high cost pressures on raw materials. The group is dedicated to cost control, i.e. manufacturing costs, general expenses, etc. The financial health of the group is sound and its future is clearly promising.
- The operating margin has reached a little over 2.5%, mainly due to cost of raw materials, in particular oil-related products. It is confirmed that these significant increases could not be passed on to sales prices.
- It has reached 2.56% which is the first milestone of the 2009 plan.
- The cross-functional teams have identified opportunities for generating additional operating profits of over €1.5 billion during the 2009 plan period.
- Action plans are being implemented;
- In 2006, cooperation between the cross-functional teams and the functional departments contributed €200 million to operating profits through various measures.
- Dividends to shareholder have already increased from 2.7€ to 3.1€ in 2007. Plans are to reach 4.5€ by 2009.

The Renault-Nissan Alliance

"Our Alliance is a huge competitive advantage, encouraging independence yet also allowing for full synergies between a European and Japanese carmaker," Carlos Ghosn[1].

Principles of the Alliance

Nissan now has a 15% stake in Renault and Renault has increased its holding in Nissan from 36.8% to 44.3%.

"The Renault-Nissan Alliance is built on two independent companies, each with its own corporate culture and brand identity, with a joint strategy of profitable growth and a community of interests."[2]

The Alliance Charter sets out the principles of a shared ambition, mutual trust, respect of each partner's identity, and balance between the two partners – the values that underpin the Alliance – together with respect of a set of operating and confidentiality rules.

- The Alliance is based on trust and mutual respect. Its organization is transparent.
- It ensures:
- clear decision-making for speed, accountability and a high level of performance;
- maximum efficiency by combining the strengths of both companies and developing synergies through common organizations, cross-company teams, shared platforms and components.
- The Alliance attracts and retains talent, providing excellent working conditions and challenging opportunities to enable people to grow and develop a global and entrepreneurial mindset.
- The Alliance generates attractive returns for the shareholders of each company and implements the best established standards of corporate governance.
- The Alliance contributes to global sustainable development.

The value of the Alliance today

- Today the Renault-Nissan Alliance represents 2 global companies linked by cross-shareholdings and "united for performance through a coherent strategy, common goals and principles, results-driven strategies and shared best practices. They respect and reinforce their respective identities and brands"[3];
- Renault has more than doubled its market capitalization (increased by €17.5bn/$22.25bn), and has risen from no. 15 to no. 16 in the industry in terms of corporate value rankings in the industry;
- Nissan has more than quadrupled its market capitalization (increased by 4,854bn Yen/$41.28bn), climbing from no. 7 to no. 4 in the automobile industry value rankings;
- Nissan (pre-Alliance facing near bankruptcy) now has one of the highest operating profit margins in the industry (9.2%);
- Nissan made $4.57bn net profit in 2005/6 (6th consecutive year for record profits);
- in the first 6 months of 2006, Renault Group had increased its sales outside Europe by 10.6%; sales outside Europe now represent 27.7% of total Renault sales, an all-time record;
- collectively, the Alliance has the second highest market capitalization in the motor industry;
- collectively, the Alliance is the second most profitable in the motor industry;
- collectively, the Alliance is now the world's fourth biggest car producer with more than 5.9 million vehicle sales in 2006;
- transparent benchmarking allows 2 culturally diverse companies to share best practices;

- a common platform strategy and shared purchasing strategy have procured massive cost savings; the Alliance saved $1.78bn (the estimated savings when the Alliance was formed) in total synergies in just three years;
- substantial cost savings, claim the management, have been translated into the booming profitability of each company;
- separate companies, management, brands and identities have ensured that Renault and Nissan cars remain distinctive;
- each company has been able to focus on its core competencies, e.g. Nissan in developing new gasoline engines and Renault in developing new diesel engines;
- the new engines are shared but are tuned according to brand: Renault and Nissan engines continue to drive and behave differently, reflecting one of the underlying principles of the Alliance: preservation of individual brand and market identities;
- common B and C Platforms have been developed but here again there has been no negative impact on brand differentiation. For example Nissan's Micra, Cube, Note and Tiida, and Renault's Clio and Modus have all been developed using the shared B Platform – they are very different cars targeting very different customers with as much brand differentiation as cars produced by each company before the Alliance;
- the sharing of platforms has generated about 50% savings in engineering development costs and huge economies of scale advantages.

Recommendation to potential shareholder

Since the year 2000, the Renault Group has doubled its market capitalization and its earnings per share has increased dramatically. Its corporate value has brought the company from No. 15 to No. 6 in just a few years. Collectively, the Renault-Nissan Alliance is the second most profitable business in the motor industry and the fourth biggest car producer in the world. Combined vehicle sales exceeded 5.9 million in 2006. Both Renault and Nissan have ambitious objectives for the future:

Nissan Value Up, April 2005, commitments –

- to reach annual global sales of 4.2 million units in 2008
- to maintain top-level operating profit in the motor industry
- to maintain return on invested capital at or above 20%

Renault Commitment 2009, February 2006, commitments –

- To achieve an operating profit of 6% in 2009.
- To grow and sell an additional 800,000 units in 2009 compared to 2005.
- To position the next Laguna, to be launched in 2007, among the top 3 models in its segment in terms of product and service quality.

With these ambitious objectives in view, together with the strength of the Renault-Nissan Alliance, we strongly recommend that you invest in the Renault Group. Over the last few years, the Renault Group has made significant improvements in terms of revenues and profits:

- Revenues went from 36.336 in 2002 to 41.528 M€ in 2006
- Net income went from 2.010 in 2002 to 2.943 M€ in 2006
- Earnings per share was 7.53€ in 2002 when it was 11.17€ in 2006...

Renault has a strong corporate vision, a coherent strategy and clearly-defined goals. Cross-functional teams have been working effectively to obtain substantial cost savings and have identified further opportunities for generating additional operating profits of over €1.5 billion during the next few years. The group's internationalization plans are already reaping benefits with sales outside Europe increasing by 10.6% in the first half of 2006 alone. Extra-European sales now represent 27.7% of total Renault sales, an all-time record and proof that Renault's global strategy is working.

Despite a drop in performance (decrease in net profits and fall in share value) during 2006 due to the rising costs of raw materials and the company's aging product lines, the Commitment 2009 4-year improvement plan seeks to double the number of new cars it will launch in the coming years.

The Renault-Nissan Alliance seeks to continue its joint projects and activities in each of the areas identified and seek new opportunities, greater synergies and increased profitability. Engineering is seen as one field with high potential for developing additional synergies and the Alliance aims to have 10 shared platforms by 2010.

In short, the company is financially healthy and future prospects are extremely good. The company is on track to further develop and implement its strategy of profitable growth and achieve the objectives it has set itself within the Alliance:

1. To be recognized by customers as being among the best 3 automotive groups in the quality and value of its products and services in each region and market segment;
2. To be among the best three automotive groups in key technologies, each partner being a leader in specific domains of excellence; and
3. To consistently generate a total operating profit among the top three automotive groups in the world, by maintaining a high operating profit margin and pursuing growth.

Huge costs savings, and new high quality, innovative products will enable the Renault Group to honor its 2009 commitments, achieving its objectives of sales growth and profitability in order to secure a satisfactory return on investment for its shareholders.

Cassandra Analysis

Values	
Axis 1: Diversity	**3.4**
Axis 2: Complexity	**3.7**
Personal development	
Axis 3: Personal well-being	**2.2**
Axis 4: Leadership and teamwork	**3.3**
Mechanistic performance	
Axis 5: Financial performance	**3.6**
Axis 6: Innovative potential	**1.7**
Holistic performance	
Axis 7: Sustainable development and social responsibility	**3.0**
Axis 8: Knowledge and learning	**3.7**

Questionnaire findings

Values

Diversity	**Score**
Does your company have ethical codes?	4
Does your company produce sustainability reports?	2
The company has anti-discrimination policies.	4
Does the company have Corporate Social Responsibility indicators?	2
The company should maintain a dialogue with all stakeholders.	5
Assessing the work environment is important.	5
Our company has a human resources policy that pays attention to talent retention.	2
Variety in opinions is a value.	5
The company pays a lot of attention to internal communication.	2
Our leadership is strongly committed.	3
We have active interest groups in the company.	3

Complexity	**Score**
The dynamic of a company is situated at the edge of chaos.	1
Evolution needs both the new and extinction.	4
Diversity is a prerequisite for the emergence of the new.	5
Radical unpredictability is an essential characteristic of business.	3
The self-organizational capacity of a company is an indicator for sustainability.	4
Interaction between "individual agents" is essential for self-organization.	5
Agency (the action) is located at the level of interacting individual entities.	4

Personal Development

Personal well-being	Score
We have an active policy & programs for the development of individual competencies & skills.	1
The company also values time that is not immediately productive.	1
The company practices a policy of non-judgment on appearances (facts, humans, etc.).	2
Joy is an active element of our corporate life.	2
I feel valued in my company.	2
Managers in our company have a real responsibility and a space to maneuver.	2
There is space for the realization of my desires in my function.	2
Courage is valued in the company.	4
I feel an essential part of the whole.	4

Leadership and teamwork	Score
Each individual is well trained and prepared to do his/her job.	1
A constant sense of awareness is essential for success.	5
Our company is an intense network of communication.	3
The purpose in our company is always clear and shared.	2
Our managers create space for the others.	2
Our managers focus more on projecting a vision than correcting what happened in the past.	4
Rigid leadership creates confusion.	5
Un-clarity causes tension and under-performance.	4
We have an external focus that gives meaning to our work.	4

Mechanistic Performance

Financial performance	Score
Our profit margin is above average in our industry.	4*
Our return on capital employed is above average in our industry.	4*
Our liquidity position is above average in our industry.	3
We generate enough cash in order to auto-finance our activities and growth.	4
Our cash-flow generation is above average in our industry.	3
Innovative potential	**Score**
We have a distinct methodology/process in place for developing new ideas.	2
We are able to produce creativity on demand.	2
Our culture regards idea generation as a key business practice.	1
I personally develop new ideas on a regular basis.	2
Our leadership models and rewards innovative thinking.	2
We have a deliberate, structured process for thoroughly evaluating/refining new ideas.	2
Our culture values idea assessment/refinement as a core competence.	1

* Renault Europe Automobiles (France + other countries)

Holistic Performance

Sustainable development and social responsibility	Score
Our company values unconditional responsibility.	2
Our company values essential integrity.	4
Our company values ontological humility.	2
Our company values conscious behaviors.	3
Our company values authentic communication.	2
Our company values constructive negotiation.	2
Our company values impeccable coordination.	4
Our company values conscious responses.	4
Our company values emotional mastery.	4

Knowledge and learning	Score
Project managers use other than financial factors to measure success.	2
The rigidity of processes gives people very little possibility for correction.	4
Interaction is important, so harmony between people is crucial.	4
Confidence and control are two contrary variables.	2
Confidence and motivation have a strong influence on exchange and the creation of knowledge.	5

Confidence must always be built; the level at the start is never enough.	5
Interaction without knowledge does not allow learning.	2
Interaction without confidence and motivation does not allow learning.	5
Motivation and organization seem to interact positively.	4
Interaction is always necessary for the construction of confidence.	4
If there are agents at group level who do not cooperate, the learning of the group stops.	4

The analysis itself

Renault Europe Automobiles (REA) Belgium

- Analysis performed by: Director General REA Belgium
- Number of years in the company (REA France & REA Belgium): 12

- Renault SA Group: automobile manufacturer

    €41bn turnover (2006)

    126,000 employees

- REA Belgium: 100% subsidiary of Renault SA Group

    automobile sales

    €250m turnover (2006)

    380 employees

Interpretation of findings: Values

- Diversity: 3.4

As a large company part of a very large group, it is maybe not surprising (and maybe reassuring?) that REA Belgium (and France) scores highly (4 or 5) on having ethical codes, anti-discrimination policies and maintaining a dialogue with its stakeholders. Although assessing the work environment is important (5), the company scores low (2) on internal communication and on retaining talent. Equally low scores were given to having Corporate Social Responsibility indicators and producing sustainability reports, suggesting that Renault appears to neglect its stakeholders other than its *shareholders*. However, variety in opinions is rated highly (but is this point of view held by the company or the person who performed the assessment?). The fact that the commitment of the leadership and the presence of active interest groups in the company received scores of 3 is maybe of concern for an organization of this size.

All in all, the scores for diversity were varied (strong, weak and average), leading to an overall score barely above average.

- Complexity: 3.7

Concerning complexity, the scores are equally varied. Diversity as a source of creativity is rated highly, as are new ideas and extinction (of the old) for evolution and progress. Interaction between individuals is necessary for action and self-organization. However, radical unpredictability and being at the edge of chaos as elements that are vital in business activity scored non-committal or low, indicating that the notions of control and certainty are important for the company.

Interpretation of findings: Personal development

- Personal well-being: 2.2

In the main, the scores for personal well-being within the company were very low (1–2). There is an absence of active policies and training programs to develop individual competencies and skills, which may well reinforce the typical notion of a large corporate machine manned by a grey and anonymous mass of employees. Time must always be productive and joy is not considered part of working life. Not feeling valued by the company reinforces this, though considering the position of the assessor as a top executive, the findings are particularly worrying. What's more, even a national level general director feels that he does not have real responsibility, space to maneuver or the possibility of self-fulfillment in his professional function. One suspects that valuing courage and feeling nonetheless part of the whole (4) stems from the assessor himself and not his work environment. It would thus be interesting to ask these questions with greater clarity and at other levels of the company. Despite the fact that the company values certain aspects relating to diversity, in practice a policy of non-judgment on appearances is not highly rated.

- Leadership and teamwork: 3.3

The scores for these questions reinforce the findings above. For an automotive company operating in a highly competitive and fast-changing environment, a constant sense of awareness is obviously recognized as being essential for success (5) but employees receive insufficient training and there appears to be a lack of internal communication. Though managers focus more on projecting a vision for the future than correcting the past, the mission is neither clear nor shared. This supports the hypothesis that the approach to management is directive and does not enroll or acknowledge the individual. The fact that rigid leadership creates confusion was corroborated, but we suspect that this was the assessor's view and not that of the company as a whole. Clarity is valued for high performance but the means to achieve clarity are not necessarily employed.

- Financial performance: 3.6

The scores concerning financial performance are relatively high – almost the highest score of the assessment. The company appears to be financially healthy with above-average performance for the industry in terms of profits and return on investment, though liquidity and cash-flow received average scores.

- Innovative potential: 1.7

Where financial performance rated near the top, innovative potential found itself at the very bottom, with an average of only 1.7 overall. Of course we are talking about the sales organization and not R&D, but maybe the company as a whole is suffering from a lack of creativity and innovation. The generation and development of ideas is poorly rated, even amongst top company executives. Innovative thinking is neither encouraged nor rewarded by the company.

Interpretation of findings: Holistic performance

- Sustainable development and social responsibility: 3.0

The scores here are mixed. Impeccable coordination and control score highly whereas humility, authentic communication and constructive negotiation do not. Where integrity is highly valued, unconditional responsibility is not. Conscious behaviors receive a "yes/no" 3 whereas conscious responses receive a positive "yes". Not being sure if the statement "Our company values emotional mastery" was correctly interpreted, we think that what was intended by the score is that it is better to keep one's emotions to oneself, in the case of this particular company.

- Knowledge and learning: 3.7

The findings here are relatively high (top scores for the assessment).

Low scores (2) confirm that success tends to be based on financial criteria and control is a determinant of confidence. However, interaction is considered essential for building confidence and confidence must always be built; confidence and motivation have a strong influence on the exchange and creation of knowledge; and all these are required for learning to take place within an organization (4–5). If processes are too rigid, correction is almost impossible and if people do not relate well to each other and cooperate, learning stops (4).

Though the scores for knowledge and learning were high, we suspect that they reflect a personal rather than company view.

Recommendation to potential shareholder

On the surface the group appears financially sound, with its operating profits and return on investment above average for the industry and glowing reports of its successful alliance with Nissan. It is, however, important to consider what is going on underneath to really get an idea of what the company is about and where it is going. It may have ambitious plans and "seductive" goals but how will these be realized? Is the company doing what is necessary for sustainable performance?

The Cassandra findings indicate that Renault as a company is suffering somewhat from a top-down directive style of leadership and management by objectives that attaches little importance to the well-being and professional/personal development of its employees, and gives little opportunity for learning. Despite the importance of competencies and performance, interaction and knowledge, there is a real lack of training and very poor internal communication.

Though the Renault Group has adopted a series of policies protecting the individual, judgment on appearances is rife and the notion of corporate social responsibility (especially for a company of this size) rates very low. Diversity is recognized but the full potential of the company's tremendous diversity does not appear to be exploited despite its growing global reach into different cultures. For an automobile company where innovation plays a key role, innovative potential is also well below par.

It appears that courage, a strong personality (even a certain aggressiveness) and hard work are required to succeed within the organization, but the level of responsibility conferred to managers is low and there is little space to maneuver, even for top executives. Impeccable coordination and control seems to prevail to the detriment of humility, authentic communication and constructive negotiation.

The general impression given by the analysis is that inside the company motivation and morale are not very high, and creativity and innovation are sorely lacking. Long-term sustainable performance is questionable, the focus being on operational effectiveness and short-term financial results.

Our analysis suggests that investors think twice before investing in the Renault Group. Cassandra suggests examining the Group's values and seeking a deeper understanding of what the company is really doing. And also to consider *how* they are doing it. What the group communicates to the outside world is not necessarily a reflection of what is communicated to people on the inside. So when recent press reports pointed to cracks in the surface, one might well be wise to ask the question: are these caused by growing tensions underneath? Our Cassandra analysis confirms that Renault executives may well be feeling the crunch.

A Renault spokesman stated that employees are concerned about the future and that much of that concern is linked to the company's globalization plans.[4] Three employees of the Renault SA technical design center (Guyancourt Technocenter) have committed suicide. One of the cases has just been recognized as "*un accident de travail*" (workplace accident), but the others are still under investigation. However, they are allegedly due to the excessive pressure placed on Renault personnel, particularly since the company started implementing its restructuring plan. The Renault Contract 2009 has sharply increased the workload, "with a race for deadlines and developing an activity that is becoming more and more complex."[5] Peugeot seems to be suffering a similar fate with 4 suicides reported within a 15 day period. Though "*mal-être sur le lieu de travail*" (ill-feeling in the workplace)is not yet confirmed as the cause of these events, press releases report that the stress levels in the workplace are high and depression amongst employees a real concern. These are serious incidents and require deeper understanding. We should at least ask ourselves what is happening within the European automobile industry: fierce competition is one thing but human life is quite another.

At Renault, the leadership of Carlos Ghosn is being questioned. Notwithstanding his star status in Japan where he masterminded Nissan's extraordinary turnaround, can he do the same in Europe? And can he head 2 distinct organizations simultaneously and successfully? Looking at a photograph of the Renault executive management board, does the collection of rather aged and serious-looking men really inspire confidence? Do they communicate the dynamism of the forward-thinking, innovative company? Or do they project an image of the "old school" approach to management? Anyone thinking of investing in the Renault Group would do well to address these questions and to conduct further investigation before making a decision. Renault has recently started a training program for its middle/top managers entitled "How to manage stress". However, this may be a case of treating the symptoms rather than the cause. Similarly, for the Technocenter, Renault has pledged to hire a further 110 engineers and technicians, host weekly meetings for work teams, better assess workloads and bolster training for technical staff.

From the perspective of this book, "people make the company", and not only the CEO. If the ultimate success of the Renault Group and of the Alliance is not just about cost cutting and profit margins, but about whether the group can produce cars superior to those of the competition, then questions remain: are they on track? Our analysis of the sales organization within the Renault Group confirms that things are not as rosy as they may appear on the surface. And what is happening in Research and Development (R&D) and production? The group's success is undeniably about achieving sustainable competitive advantage but that ultimately depends on the organization's people; and a more holistic understanding of the whole.

Conclusions (by Carina Richards who analyzed this case)

Despite the emphasis placed on internal communication and dialogue, transversal management, cross-functional teams, enrolling and empowering the individual, attracting and retaining talent, benchmarking and transparency, learning, learning from mistakes, etc., a more "classical analysis" may not reveal what is really going on in the Renault Group and, as such, only provide a potential shareholder with a "superficial" view or external/public image of the organization. The final success of a business organization ultimately rests on its people and what is really going on "behind the scenes". This is where a more holistic analysis, such as the Cassandra tool, may be far more useful and revealing.

The Cassandra tool involves measuring for visualization, understanding and learning. These provide insight into how an organization is really functioning and a more accurate picture of its future potential. Herein the notion of shareholder value in real terms: its present capacity for future action and sustainable performance. It highlights the need to understand not only *what* is done but *how*. It also encourages questions about wide-ranging issues concerning the values of a company and the way it operates. Do we like the company? Does the company share our values? Do people enjoy working for the company? Does the company contribute to and support the development of its employees? Is the company socially responsible? Does the company play an active part in protecting the environment for future generations? And so on.

On the other hand, a more "classical" analysis involves measuring for control and profit. It focuses on a limited notion of shareholder value, based on financial measures and external communication. We see only the surface, what has been "accomplished" but rarely how. It encourages us to be concerned only by short-term return on investment: What's in it for me? What can I get out of it financially and how quickly can I get it? I don't really care how, I just care how *much*.

Even when a company may communicate strong human values and to a certain extent, actually live up to them (e.g., the success of the Renault-Nissan Alliance), how widely are these values really felt within the organization itself? And are they adhered to in such a way as to secure long-term sustainable performance? Would we prefer to see a company as a collection of *people* or a collection of *computers*?

Such diametrically different analyses will inevitably give us completely different views of a company: one all-embracing and long-term, the other reductionist and short-term. What we see depends on the way we want to look, and that ultimately depends on the choices we want to make, and hence on us. Cassandra has been designed to reveal such insights at both individual and organizational levels. This chapter has outlined the thinking that informs its construction, the methodology that underpins it, and the kind of results it is capable of generating.

Some afterthoughts

We have given insight into the ontology, the building blocks, the managerial skills and the leadership dimension to start working towards sustainable performance, intrapreneurship and innovation. In this chapter we have defined a tool that allows us to diagnose but equally to follow up on managerial performance. The final step is to redefine the manager as the entrepreneur, the risk taker, the creator and after all, a true leader. Sustainable performance is realized by the manager/entrepreneur, since sustainable performance is not a concept to be administered, but one to be co-created, daily, within the interconnectedness of people inside and outside of the company. The manager/administrator has made different choices. He or she is managing a Newtonian system, a system that would anyway manage itself, even in the absence of the manager/administrator. He or she is controlling a system with very limited shareholder value focus. A multi-criteria approach, or even worse an approach based on value realization is alienated to him or her. Finally we want to define what we call "social intrapreneurship", as a new mode of management.

A new paradigm needs an adapted set of competencies for managers who want to manage in this new paradigm. Management **in** complexity (not **of** complexity), management **in** diversity, management **in** respect for multiple solutions and multiple truths, and management **in** paradoxes: in summary, full color thinking. These are the necessary skills of the manager of today. "Wave or particle?" It only makes a difference in the eye of the observer, in this case, the manager. Machines cannot realize values and cannot make intuitive choices. Machines cannot choose between multiple possible truths; managers who behave and think as machines cannot do so either. Personal involvement, personal development and consciousness in management are all central to this book.

Parallel integrations with quantum science and perennial wisdom can be found in the following quote:

> *First, understand that truly knowing the field, the natural world (prakriti), is not simply a process of listing the myriad items that comprise it. To understand nature itself it is necessary to know something about human consciousness. To know something is to be conscious of it. You become conscious of things in the world (that is, you 'know' things) through the mechanisms of perception in your nervous system – sight, hearing, feeling, mind, and so forth. But the nervous system is itself a part of nature; that which you use to know the world, nature, is also nature. Thus, that which is known cannot really be separated from the knower of it. (Bhagavad Gita, Chapter 13, 5–6)*

Social intrapreneurship for sustainable performance is a similar mind shift, a conscious choice to be part of a larger whole, to be aware, every day, of the interconnectedness of people, nature, in the larger "Gaia". Gaia, as an (ecological) hypothesis that views living and non-living parts of the earth as a complex interacting system that can be thought of as a single organism, is not new age, for those that might still retain that impression. It can no longer be discarded. The reality is clearly visible. The reckless growth worshipped for decades, mainly in Europe and the US, as the "golden calf", is now being taken over by others (e.g., China), and it is rapidly exhausting our resources, natural and human.

The choice is stark: to continue, to do nothing, or to change radically. Changing radically, however, is only possible with a change in ontology of that same Gaia. This book has made an attempt to introduce a new management paradigm, firmly embedded in science, but at the same time, courageous enough to challenge the devastating mainstream ontology. It offers the paradigm and concepts for the manager who is conscious of his or her role in the world, and who would like to make a positive contribution to development, not at any price, but for any person. But the book aims to go further. To change practices also requires new practical tools. A shift often needs a new paradigm; it is a necessary but not sufficient condition. The methodology developed in this book, complements the sufficient condition for change with the managers toolkit to attain it.

We have enjoyed researching this book; we hope you have not only enjoyed reading it but will use it. Paraphrasing the words of Sathya Sai Baba, we hope we have been able to deliver something that is understandable and practical, since as he correctly says, philosophy that cannot be understood and scriptures that are not practical, we have plenty of in the present world. But it is a waste to talk of them. We trust that together we are able to provoke a shift to a more responsible world.

Summarizing this chapter, we would like to state some of the main characteristics of the environment that the leader/innovator is creating, the way they were discovered in this book:

- Creating an open and entrepreneurial culture

- Innovating as a blend of creation and know-how (or rather enacted cognition: action and creation)
- Positioning the generation of social and economic value as central
- Addressing real issues or problems in society
- Providing solutions that really add value
- Forming practical solutions to social problems
- Not living in a competitive world
- Continuously refining and adapting
- Rejecting ideology and disciplinary constraints
- Visioning with a clear plan to realize that vision
- Acting in a highly multi-disciplinary and holistic fashion
- Applying practical, innovative and sustainable approaches
- Grounding their activities in values and processes
- Correctly differentiating between the need for cash flow (working capital), which is an entrepreneurial concern, and the demand for profit, which is an issue of reporting, taxes, share value, etc.

The main concerns/activities of the leader/innovator would be:

- Creative and innovative leadership
- Bringing management back to its essence (i.e. being the creator of value, real value added for the society, or the economy)
- What can be done with experiences (the concept of learning)
- How the creation of value takes time
- Generating value for all, not money for a few
- Taking a risk: professional management does not incur any risk any more (the manager, having a view on strategy and not on creation, is no longer the driver for creativity and innovation, but rather for risk avoidance and certainty)
- Being open to share their knowledge and learning
- Being fully accountable for what they do
- Having a clear vision; that drives the social innovator
- Success related to leadership (and not much to management)
- Removing barriers
- Pragmatic vision
- Achieving systemic and sustainable social change
- Strongly believing in the natural capacity of all people to contribute meaningfully to economic and social development
- Trusting that motivation is a stronger driver than skills
- Showing passion that drives others

- Strongly using market principles
- Determined action
- Breaking away from constraints imposed by ideology of field or discipline
- Taking risks that others would not dare to take
- Achieving high standards
- Using appropriate follow up systems: quantitative and qualitative
- Acting as a learning organization
- Healthy impatience, especially with bureaucracies
- Drive for change
- Ambition and persistence
- Committing their lives to their projects
- Being user friendly, understandable, and ethical
- Setting out with the assumption of competence

Social intrapreneurship, as we have defined and detailed it, is definitely a method for personal and organizational development. For those who would like to use the methodology, training seminars can be organized. Workbooks are also available with the checklists for easy use in real life situations. For more detail, please contact the authors

---

Meanwhile back in the Serengeti, Giraffe prances around coat gleaming eyes bright…

Hyena: Looking good Giraffe!

Giraffe: I have a date with Cassandra

Hyena: Who's Cassandra, one of the zebras you were hanging out with last summer?

Giraffe: For the last time, I only walked with the zebras in the last migration because the other giraffes left early. And I like company.

Hyena: Whatever you say. So who is Cassandra?

Giraffe: Cassandra is my date with destiny.

Hyena: I'm confused, who are you dating?

Appendix: Blueprint of a workbook

The methodology

This appendix references and revisits a number of issues and points of discussion from chapters throughout the book and then proposes ways to operationalize the concepts developed throughout the preceding chapters. It offers a set of checklists and questionnaires – discussed in earlier chapters – which, together, act as a kind of roadmap to sustainable performance. This roadmap is available for use, either as a step plan for implementing social intrapreneurship, or alternatively for benchmarking one's own performance, or the sustainable performance, in comparison with other companies. However, in order to use it to its full potential, either training or tutoring is necessary. The checklists indeed fit a wider concept (as the book argues in depth) and, without a thorough understanding of this concept, the checklists themselves will be less effective and have less impact.

The methodology has five constituent components:

- **The values and the vision: what is the contribution of the company?**
- **Benchmarking: from dream to reality (do we make a difference?)**
- **The leadership's checklist: do I make a difference?**
- **Cassandra: a diagnostic for sustainable performance (where are we and where to go)**
- **The learning coach: continuous work on the mutual selves ("on the road")**

> **Wanderer, your footprints are**
>
> the path, and nothing more;
>
> Wanderer, there is no path,
>
> it is created as you walk.
>
> By walking,
>
> you make the path before you,
>
> and when you look behind
>
> you see the path which after you
>
> will not be trod again.
>
> Wanderer, there is no path,
>
> but the ripples on the waters.
>
> Antonio Machado

Those five constituent components form a continuous loop of evaluation, designing, laying down the path by walking (Machado), learning, re-evaluation, re-designing, etc. The remainder of this appendix will mainly focus on assembling a number of checklists and tools that together make up the roadmap.

The roadbook to social intrapreneurship

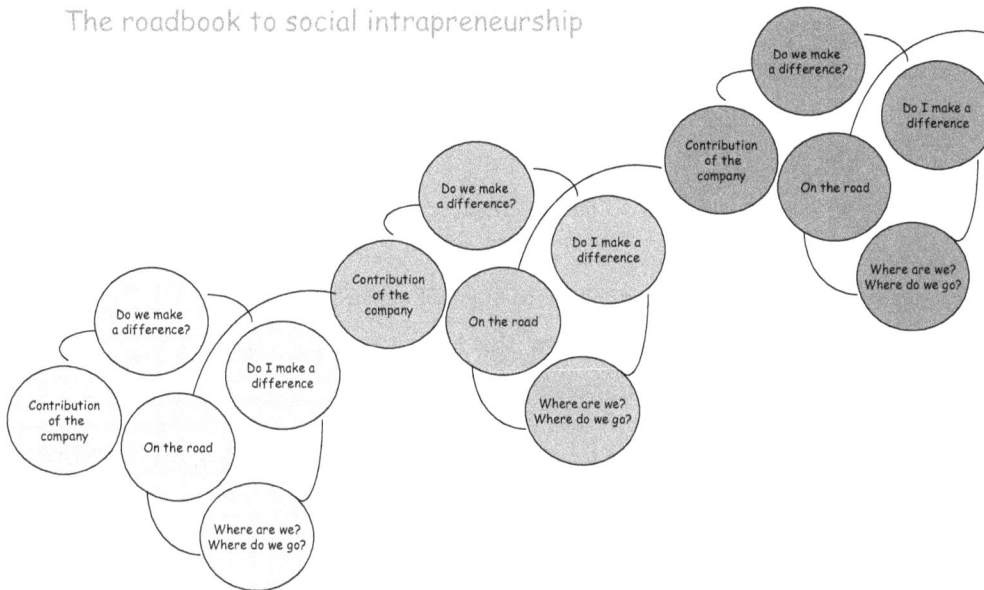

The values and the vision: what is the contribution of the company?

Sustainable performance starts in the lower right quadrant of Wilber's systemic model, (i.e. with the identification of the (shared) values). Since, very often, they remain hidden or unknown, and since they are the drivers of the sustainable performance process, the first step involves making them explicit and discussing how far they are shared. It is important to answer the question "What are the values of the company?" and/or "What does it contribute to society?". If the company would not exist anymore, what would society miss? If the creation of employment would be a value for a company, then bankruptcy would certainly cause a loss of value. However, this would imply that the creation of jobs would be a core value of the company (and not a necessary resource constraint). Sustainable performance will be driven by those shared values.

A first stage might just, in order to make it easy for people to start choosing, start from a very exhaustive list of possible values. In a second stage, those values would be negotiated in order to find out what the shared values are. Once these are agreed, they can be translated into personal development issues like leadership and learning.

It does not take that much of an effort to come up with a whole list of possible corporate values such as: liability, availability of information, involvement, reliability, conflict resolution, consensus, creativity, democratic process, sustainability, ecological awareness, honesty, ethics, organization as a family, decency, shared identity, shared vision, shared values, equal opportunities, community services, harmony, humor/pleasure, innovation, integrity, quality of living, long term perspective, emphasis on global thinking, nature conservation, humility, mutual support, openness, training possibilities, optimism, personal growth, personal satisfaction, personal freedom, political involvement/activism, recreation possibilities, respect, respect for the law, risk minded, social justice, social cohesion, social responsibility, social security, solidarity, spirituality, strategic alliances, strict moral/religious rules, tolerance, transparency, responsibility, diversity, making a difference, faith, public health and security, prosperity, continuing improvement, peaceful cooperation, friendship, freedom of expression of opinion, conscience of values, world peace, employment and many other values. This list is not in any way presented as exhaustive but as suggestive, and a means to sparking discussion.

Once the real shared values are identified (via an iterative process of workshops or brainstorm session), the next stage is to start questioning how they can be translated into the necessity for personal development and leadership. This questioning should answer how far an employee (any employee but at the same time all employees) is involved and engaged. Only conscious employees, as Kofman calls them, are able to really contribute to the realization of the values. Afterwards, a conscious manager needs a space (a workspace) that gives the possibility, the support, and the drive for the conscious employee to contribute to the realization of values.

Kofman, when talking about the necessity for personal involvement and/or engagement, and personal development, uses seven qualities to distinguish conscious from unconscious employees. Together with each employee (or manager) the task is to try and see how far this person has come in becoming a conscious manager and if not, how this could be changed. The first three are character attributes: unconditional responsibility, essential integrity and ontological humility. The next three are interpersonal skills: authentic communication, constructive negotiation and impeccable coordination. The seventh quality is an enabling condition for the previous six: emotional mastery.

In other words, the idea is that each employee/manager evaluates him or herself on those seven qualities.

- Unconditional responsibility
- Essential integrity
- Ontological humility
- Authentic communication
- Constructive negotiation
- Impeccable coordination
- Emotional mastery

Once comfortable with the fact that employees/managers are conscious (and therefore able to contribute to the realization of values), the next step is to consider the supportiveness of the environment for enabling that realization.

Buckingham and Coffman's studies of organizational effectiveness produced an interesting checklist. According to them, exceptional managers create a workplace in which employees emphatically answered 'yes' to the following questions:

25. Do I know what is expected of me at work?
26. Do I have the materials and equipment I need to do my work right?
27. At work, do I have the opportunity to do what I do best every day?
28. In the last seven days, have I received recognition or praise for doing good work?
29. Does my supervisor, or someone at work, seem to care about me as a person?
30. Is there someone at work who encourages my development?
31. At work, do my opinions seem to count?
32. Does the mission/purpose of my company make me feel my job is important?
33. Are my co-workers committed to doing high-quality work?
34. Do I have a best friend at work?
35. In the last six months, has someone at work talked to me about my progress?
36. This last year, have I had opportunities at work to learn and grow?

It is almost enough to count the number of *yes* responses to get an idea of the organizational effectiveness, or the degree to which employees and managers feel supported by the company in their endeavor to realize the corporate values.

Benchmarking: from dream to reality (do we make a difference?)

Imagine an organization that has been able to identify values or the anticipated valued added of its existence or activity. The next step in our continuing journey is to establish some kind of benchmark. Compared to other companies, activities or industries, does the organization deliver something that is not yet delivered elsewhere? Can a number of elements, which would give a certain concrete idea of the direction to follow, be identified? Would they really be different, and capable of setting the industry standard? This kind of benchmarking is not done for competitive reasons or for finding blue ocean strategies (as in Kim and Mauborgne, 2005), but for helping to identify the difference that makes a real difference – in a very detailed and down-to-earth fashion. It is this analysis that will help enable our marketing support, our commercial argumentation, our commercial message, etc. It will help to translate values, mission and value added into communication (internal, as well as external).

In a two-step procedure, the first performs a rather classical benchmark analysis. The second attempts to evaluate the innovative potential. Is it possible to ensure that what is offered is a real innovation (rather than just a copy of an existing product or service)? Does the proposal have the potential to innovate the market, the industry, and to make a social difference? In aspiring to this new development what resources are needed?

For the first step, we base our analysis on an extended version of Kim and Mauborgne's (2005) blue ocean concept. For the second step we use part of an innovation roadmap methodology (designed earlier within the innovative learning-by-doing platform and approach, for practicing managers to learn about management while creating and while managing, and captured under the framework known as the Innovation School). The roadmap itself contains more steps than the ones used here, but these are restricted to the most essential ones that fit the methodology proposed in this chapter.

The **first step** is based on the following figure that is based on the blue ocean concept. The blue ocean strategy invites a company to develop products and services that tap into a blue ocean (an ocean without fierce competition, where it is pleasant to live, compared to a red ocean of "bloody" competition). The approach proposes to ask the following four questions:

5. Which factors that the industry takes for granted should be eliminated?
6. Which factors should be raised well above the industry's standard?
7. Which factors should be reduced well below the industry's standard?
8. Which factors should be created that the industry never previously offered?

The answers to these questions give an idea of how the company, new product, or whatever, positions itself in the market. Equally, the answers, especially to the fourth, give an initial indication on the innovative potential of the company, service, etc. Though these factors can be identified individually, this is typically an exercise done in an animated workshop, since some of the questions might be rather challenging.

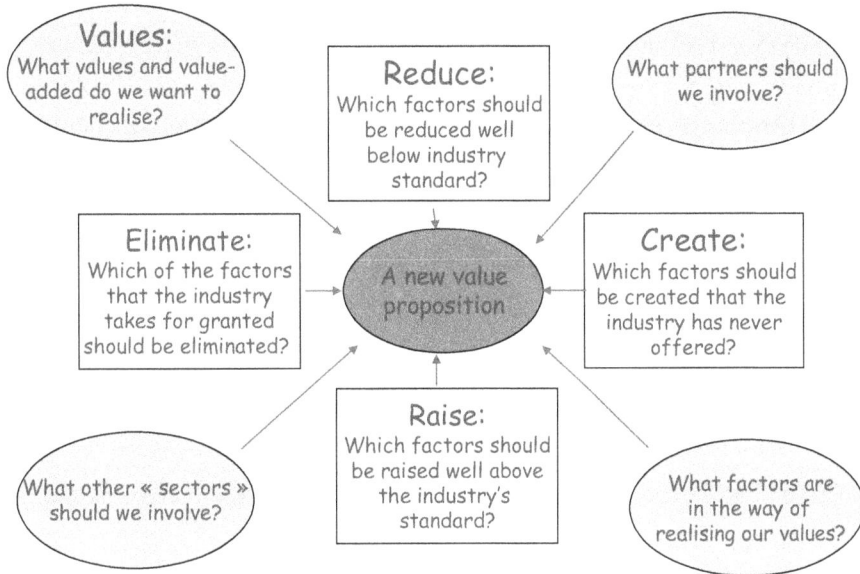

Values:
What values and value-added do we want to realise?

Reduce:
Which factors should be reduced well below industry standard?

What partners should we involve?

Eliminate:
Which of the factors that the industry takes for granted should be eliminated?

A new value proposition

Create:
Which factors should be created that the industry has never offered?

What other « sectors » should we involve?

Raise:
Which factors should be raised well above the industry's standard?

What factors are in the way of realising our values?

However, we want to extend the blue ocean approach with another additional four questions that position the company (or its new product or service) within a broader network (of partners). We also want to relate to the specific purpose of realizing values, and demand a more intense and varied innovation focus:

- What values and valued added do we want to realize, compared to what exists (this time)?
- What factors are in the way of realizing those values?
- What partners (companies, organizations) should we involve?
- What other "sectors" should we involve in our activities?

It is worth recalling that one of the remarkable observations in social entrepreneurship is that companies and services are often not limited to one specific sector or industry. The social intrapreneurship advocated here aims to realize the same openness to others, and to enroll solutions into a holistic focus on the value added of the company (that will be reinforced by the use of Cassandra later on).

The **second step** in the process from dream to reality involves introspection on the innovative potential of the value added to be created, and on identifying a reasonable list of resource issues that would be related to the value added that is aspired to. The realization of this step is based on the "Innovation Roadmap", a methodology designed and used for guiding innovation processes of any kind.

The original aim of the Innovation Roadmap was to support the manager in the development of a grounded business plan for a creative idea. In that process, the main focus is on the translation of the idea into a project that can be communicated to, and shared with others. Attention is also given to the screening of the innovative potential of the proposal, before translating it into the necessary resource inventory. Eventually, that resource inventory, with proposed solutions for any possible snags, is translated into a business plan that investigates and reports on the economic and financial viability of the project.

Creation, innovation, and intrapreneurship are skills, capacities and approaches that are typical for anyone seeking to remain competitive. During a project, the Innovation Roadmap supports the manager in order to facilitate the discovery of one's own approach. The support that the roadmap gives should be seen as a structure and checklist; one will still need to walk the talk. One needs – as Machado says – *to lay down the path in walking.*

In the overall innovation literature, a clear distinction is made between the phase of creativity and the follow-up phase that is commonly addressed as the innovation phase (detailed planning and production). The first phase receives low priority (in the innovation literature), though most of that literature also agrees that success and failure of new product development is often already 'genetically imprinted' at the start of the so-called innovation process, which is based on the quality of the creativity phase. A second commonly identified reason for failure can be found in the process of the creation phase. Where we certainly stress the importance of time and effort spent on the first creativity phase, we do require at least an inventory of the resources and limitations to overcome for the inventory phase, rather than the creation phase.

In short, based on what common theories suggest, an innovation process contains roughly five different phases:

1. Idea generation
2. From idea to real world (how to translate an idea into a concept that can be communicated)
3. Assessment of the innovative potential (and the commercial feasibility) of the project
4. Inventory of the internal capacities and constraints in order to assess technical feasibility
5. The economic (and mainly financial) feasibility – the business plan

Though a certain progression in time seems logical (certainly in the first three phases), some feedback loops will emerge as necessary and are extremely effective in adding value. However, at a certain point in time, and after a number of feedback loops, one should continue in the development phase and the economic viability study. The following diagram depicts the process, which will be detailed – with the help of some checklists and relevant issues/questions – further on in this appendix.

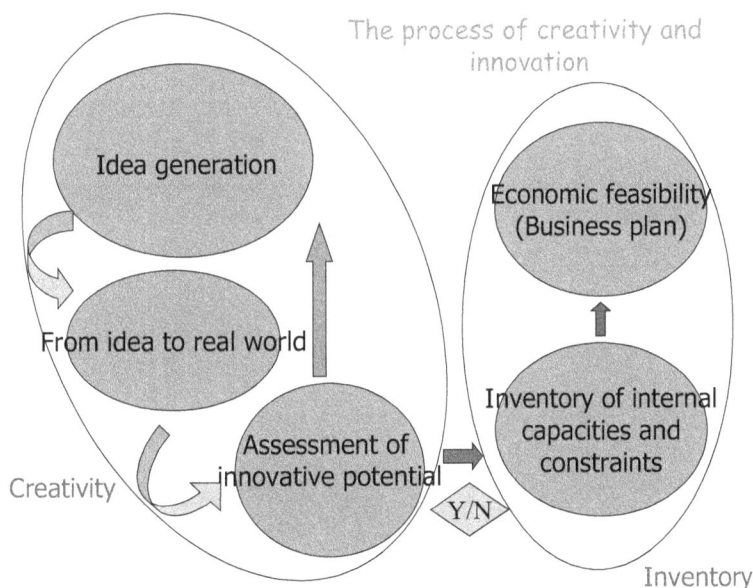

The process of creativity and innovation

For the purpose of social intrapreneurship, we use only the third and fourth stage of the entire Innovation Roadmap. The figure above establishes the context of the approach. The innovation process starts with a phase of idea generation and/or creativity. This is the phase in which the wildest dreams can be transformed into ideas. Very often, this process gains momentum when undertaken in groups creatively (rather than by individuals).

A difficult step, very often, is then to translate the ideas into the real world. The idea can be clear in the mind of the idea-owner(s), but requires translation into a form that can be communicated to wider audiences. That is not a typical problem for the innovation process, but it is of paramount importance and key to further successful development. In order to support this vital step, techniques like soft systems methodology (SSM) are designed to transform ideas into the real world, with the aim of eventually designing Information Systems.

Once the idea is translated from the owner's mind into a form that can be communicated (with sentences, activities, to-do lists), its innovative potential has to be assessed. It is difficult to evaluate the innovative potential of an idea when it is not somehow embedded into a message and descriptions on paper. Therefore, this step can only be undertaken after the 'translation' from idea into activities.

The logical progression from idea generation, via translation into a communicative action and description in order to evaluate its innovative potential, is a cycle that does not necessarily immediately generate the eye-catching new product or service. Frequently, it is the insertion of a feedback loop that brings the process back to the phase of idea generation. Creativity and innovation very often proceed via a process of incremental steps, rather than individual earth-shattering breakthrough ideas. Indeed, this feedback loop often needs to be taken a number of times but the cycle of three phases remains the backbone of the creativity process.

In our social intrapreneurship approach, we take up the Innovation Roadmap methodology, presuming that a workable form of the project or the entire company is available.

Once a "go" decision is taken, the next phase involves researching the internal capacities and constraints that are key to a future successful implementation. In this phase an inventory is made of resources and constraints and, in case constraints would hinder the process, possible solutions need to be considered. Needless to say it is possible, though not indicated on the figure, to have additional feed-back loops bringing you back from the inventory phase into (again) the idea generation phase (and its subsequent steps). The more the innovation process can be kept dynamic, the higher the chances for innovative products. This fourth phase can also be integrated into the social intrapreneurship approach.

Finally, the economic and financial feasibility study converts ideas, capacities, and constraints into a business plan. The business plan very often acts as the communication tool for going to market in order to find support, finance, etc. for proposals, and should be considered as such. It is also a communication tool and should, therefore, be made attractive and clear. Though the business plan deals with the economics and financials of the project, most of those are already identified earlier on in the process. Therefore, we suggest that the business plan is more about financial feasibility and justification, than about economic viability which, implicitly, has already played a role much earlier in the process. Therefore, it is rather an outcome than an input. The important role of the business plan as communication tool, in the process from development to real market, needs to be kept in mind.

Assessment of the innovative potential

Many definitions of innovation exist and each has a different focus. In general, however, they tend either to concentrate on the creativity phase, the idea generation phase, or the process innovation side (that describes how to get from an idea to a realized product or service). A second criterion on which most of the definitions differ is the focus either on the breadth or on the depth with which innovation is associated. Certainly, in the first phases, breadth is important, and this is captured by West and Farr's definition of innovation "*as the intentional introduction and application within a role, group, or organization of ideas, processes, products or procedures, new to the relevant unit of adoption to significantly benefit the individual, the group, organization or wider society.*"

Their definition of innovation also fits strongly with the concept of social intrapreneurship. In fact, in this definition, social intrapreneurship becomes a perfect example of an innovation. Accordingly, this part of the Innovation Roadmap can assess, at this stage, the innovative potential of the project. Possible outcomes could be to re-iterate the project (given the outcome of this phase) and select a new idea or, alternatively, to opt for the inventory of constraints and capabilities for successful realization inside the company and to continue the procedure.

Lessons learned from existing research are presented as useful checklists that can help in assessing the innovative potential of the project. This next section provides some general lessons (taken out of standard literature) and is followed by a section focused more on specific, experience-based learnings.

Some general lessons learned about innovation (that the user should turn into questions about his or her company or project)

- Character and culture are human creations, not facts of life. Context is therefore important
- All people have creative potential
- One cannot separate creativity and the possibility of generating new products (sometimes called the capability to transform ideas into viable solutions)
- Creativity is different from creation (production, re-production, etc.)
- Creativity often needs motivation
- Creativity has to do with freedom of choice and choice itself
- For creativity, multiplicity is important because multiple realities always exist
- Recognition of demand is a more frequent factor in successful innovation than recognition of technical potential. Already in this phase (and not for the first time in the business plan) demand requires some attention
- Training and experience of people inside your company are crucial for innovation
- Were any lessons learned from other (external or internal) innovations?
- Don't innovate for the future, but for the present
- Effective innovation starts small and is often not revolutionary
- Innovation and learning go hand-in-hand; innovation and management are a different ballgame

The recommendation is to make a list of those lessons that the company does explicitly take into account (and comment on them, describe their context, etc.), and those that might need more attention. Not all of them are always equally applicable.

Questions that should always be addressed concern the innovative potential of the project:

- Why (goals)?
- What (product-novelty)?
- When (timing)?
- Where (targeting)?
- How (marketing mix)?

Certain identified potential fail factors are worth considering during this stage, when they can still easily be avoided:

- Go for the "better" product (without clients)
- A me-too product (is often too slow)
- Obstruction (unexpected) of the competition
- Products for low-margin markets
- Badly prepared introduction
- Fast introductions
- The newer, the better
- Position a new product as the successor of another one
- Change the positioning of the product (too fast)
- Pricing too low
- Organizational limitations and barriers such as culture, limited managerial support, lack of competencies. Though those aspects get much more attention in the next phase, some initial exploration should take place here.

Moreover, those observations should be turned into questions that merit responses, comments and contextualizing.

Potential success factors worth considering at this stage (are they present in the company, project or product?) include:

- Intrinsic value of the product
- Structured and well-managed development and introduction process, insofar as there is already a clear idea about this (perhaps a wish list could be made)
- Understanding the needs of users
- Attention to marketing and publicity
- Efficiency of development
- Effective use of outside technology and external scientific communication
- Seniority and authority of responsible managers – commitment
- Team composition
- Individual creativity

The strongest positive correlations with success are:

- Product advantage (costs, innovativeness, quality, satisfying needs)
- Proficiency of pre-development activities (initial brainstorm, screening, thorough market analysis, technical assessment, financial/business analysis)
- Good protocol of all specifications

Ticking all those questions/issues should ensure a reasonable potential to add value to the market.

Inventory of capacities and constraints

Once the concept is ready to be evaluated against the capacities and constraints of the company, the creativity phase gives way to the inventory phase. In this phase the project is assessed against the expected strengths and weaknesses that your company has in respect of innovation. In some cases, the corporate environment, for many different reasons, is somewhat hostile to new, truly innovative projects. This can be due to a range of factors from the organizational structure, through the lack of commitment from top management, to the culture of the company itself.

Support in this phase can again be provided by a few checklists. The first ones are more general in nature and are based on what is commonly known as the NPD (New Product Development) literature. They mostly relate to the establishment of the additional innovation process. By recognizing possible pitfalls early on, firms can possibly avoid them. The latter checklists, and some of their learnings, are based on research into some real-life projects.

Some challenges for the future NPD process of your project:

- Not everything can be realized. Therefore, making trade-offs between different "important" aspects of a new idea is essential. Attempt to identify these aspects and prioritize them.
- Dynamics: how to deal with changing technologies, preferences, opinions, ecology, economy. Is your project vulnerable to rapid changes?
- Details: small decisions can have large consequences (possibly even on a larger scale)
- Time and timing. How crucial are these?

Some possible fail factors:

- Team that is not empowered enough
- Political (hidden) agendas, on various levels
- Inadequate sourcing
- Incomplete design team

In essence, the NPD process, which will eventually follow your project, is an uncertainty reduction process. NPD also involves seeking and keeping sponsorship. Often, innovation needs sufficient cash, and the following additional success factors are critical:

- Commitment from the top to the project
- Planning and design
- Involvement of employees in the project
- Education and training
- Internal communication

If these are not addressed, then this is the stage to spend some time on them.

The introduction of social intrapreneurship is, at the end of the day, a large change management project, as well as a new 'concept' development project, hence the deployment of lessons learned in the new product development experience. For certain cases and companies, this phase might be less adequate. The book leaves it to the judgment of the reader, or the consultant using this methodology, to decide whether this might be a value adding part of the process.

Some experience-based lessons learned:

The checklist presented here is based on the learnings of a number of real-life innovation projects that have been studied. Since the cases were 'assembled' at the end of the innovation project, some of the issues are clearly related to the process itself. Not all of them are applicable to any particular project. For improving a social intrapreneurship change process, certain lessons will add more value:

- Reasons for delays often mentioned are: changes in the project team, insufficient resources (availability of people), no clear specifications, insufficient interface between teams, universal optimism and opportunistic planning, outside influences
- Insufficient project management skills
- Insufficient communication on decisions
- Frustration of team members
- Unclear responsibilities
- Not all expertise required is available
- Reinvention of the wheel
- Insufficient management commitment that contributes to stress, pressure, and insufficient resources
- Contracting problems if third parties are involved
- No proper risk analysis available
- Changes in the concept that occur during the project realization are often not checked for risks and consequences
- Market tests are often executed far too late

Having detailed all of this, and deciding to go for it, the next areas of focus are the leadership's checklist and the management diagnostics.

The leadership's checklist: do I make a difference?

As argued earlier, the role of the leader, and what it might involve, is vital for successful social intrapreneurship. Accordingly, this section limits itself to repeating the 'leadership's checklist' developed in an earlier chapter, which contains the list's context and interpretation.

This checklist has been designed to help identify how close one is to becoming a real leader, instead of just a manager. Part of this checklist will be used in the overall holistic diagnostic tool 'Cassandra' that was also developed in an earlier chapter. An honest and detailed reflection on this checklist allows its users to progress consciously on the way to sustainable leadership.

- Are we able to take many decisions in parallel?
- Are we able to balance between activity and restraint; or we capable of "slow" management?
- Do we base our leadership on the belief in each individual's ability to perform his task?
- Do we consider any "instrument" we use as an extension of our enacted leadership?
- Do we engage all our senses?
- Do we see management as an incredible act of coordination (and not control)?
- Are we really able to work together in a team?
- Do we have a constant sense of awareness?

- Are we aware that organizations are made up of positions, and that there is a different level of information related to each position?
- Are we aware that only the leader has the global view and do we act accordingly?
- Are we assuming the responsibility of the "podium" we occupy?
- Are we aware that the orchestra doesn't really need the conductor?
- Do we accept the self-organizational capacity of the organization?
- Do we see the company as an intense network of communication?
- Do we behave like the conductor who sends signals and receives signals back; are we open to receiving these signals back?
- The energy that makes the company turn ultimately comes from its purpose. Do we have a purpose and do we manage the related energy in that sense?
- The energy, created by the purpose, is conveyed via the people. Do we manage people accordingly?
- As managers, do we create the space for the others?
- As managers, do we say what should be done (rather than what should not be done)?
- As managers, do we project a vision? Or do we rather correct people's behavior?
- Are we aware that power always goes with responsibility and do we take responsibility for that power?
- Are we able to perform "slow" management, knowing that there is a response time?
- Leadership is committing to what has not yet happened. Is that our daily practice?

- The leader should commit first. Do we do that?
- Rigid leadership creates confusion. Are we flexible enough in our leadership style?
- Rigid leadership chops off the line (the purpose). Can we identify when we chop off the line?
- Unnecessary movements can create confusion. Do we actively limit confusing messages and actions?
- Lack of clarity causes tension and under-performance with people. Do we strive always to be crystal clear in our communication?
- Are we aware of the areas where we are rather internally oriented (e.g. to the technicality of processes)? Do we see where this limits our client focus?
- Are we sufficiently externally focused? Are we aware that it is the external focus (the desire to serve a client that is waiting and paying for your service) that gives meaning to our work?

Cassandra: a diagnostic for sustainable performance (where are we and where to go)

With the adapted leadership necessary for social intrapreneurship, we are now able to deal with the diagnostics through Cassandra (discussed in an earlier chapter). Cassandra serves a triple purpose: it gives an instantaneous picture of the situation; it allows the identification of the development path (where to go to); and it is a follow-up tool to guide that development. Cassandra has two versions. The first is a personal (development) version for any individual manager who would like to self-manage (or be coached) about his or her potential for sustainable performance (as a manager). At the same time, the second version makes it possible to monitor corporate sustainable performance. Both checklists are re-iterated here. They are integrated into a tool (as described earlier) that allows visualization of the results. The checklist could be further developed into more advanced reporting tools. Questions are scored on a scale of 1 to 5. Of course, these questions can equally be used as a simple checklist.

The questions in the corporate version: what is the sustainable performance level and potential of the company?

Values

Diversity

- Does your company have ethical codes?
- Does your company produce sustainability reports?
- Does the company have anti-discrimination policies?
- Does the company have Corporate Social Responsibility indicators?
- Should the company maintain a dialogue with all stakeholders?
- Assessing the work environment is important
- Our company has a human resources policy that pays attention to talent retention
- Variety in opinions is a value
- The company pays a great deal of attention to internal communication
- Our leadership is strongly committed
- We have active interest groups in the company

Complexity

- The dynamic of a company is situated at the edge of chaos
- Evolution needs both the new and extinction
- Diversity is a prerequisite for the emergence of the new
- Radical unpredictability is an essential characteristic of business
- The self-organizational capacity of a company is an indicator for sustainability
- Interaction between "individual agents" is essential for self-organization
- Agency (the action) is located at the level of interacting individual entities

Personal Development

Personal well being

- We have an active policy and programs for the development of individual competencies and skills
- The company also values time that is not immediately productive
- The company practices a policy of non-judgment on appearances (facts, humans, etc.)
- Joy is an active element of our corporate life
- I feel valued in my company
- Managers in our company have a real responsibility and space to maneuver
- There is space for the realization of my desires in my function
- Courage is valued in the company
- I feel an essential part of the whole

Leadership and teamwork

- Each individual is well trained and prepared to do his/her job
- A constant sense of awareness is essential for success
- Our company is an intense network of communication
- The purpose in our company is always clear and shared
- Our managers create space for others
- Our managers are more concerned with projecting a vision and less with correcting what happened previously
- Rigid leadership creates confusion
- Lack of clarity causes tension and under-performance
- We have an external focus which gives meaning to our work

Mechanistic performance

Financial performance

- Our profit margin is above average in our industry
- Our return on capital employed is above average in our industry
- Our liquidity position is above average in our industry
- We generate enough cash in order to auto-finance our activities and growth
- Our cash-flow generation is above average in our industry

Innovative potential

- We have a distinct methodology/process in place for developing new ideas
- We are able to produce creativity on demand
- Our culture regards idea generation as a key business practice
- I personally develop new ideas on a regular basis
- Our leadership model rewards innovative thinking
- We have a deliberate, structured process for thoroughly evaluating/refining new ideas
- Our culture values idea assessment/refinement as a core competence

Systemic performance

Sustainable development and social responsibility

- Our company values unconditional responsibility
- Our company values essential integrity
- Our company values ontological humility
- Our company values conscious behaviors
- Our company values authentic communication
- Our company values constructive negotiation
- Our company values impeccable coordination
- Our company values conscious responses
- Our company values emotional mastery

Knowledge and learning

- Project managers use more than financial factors to measure success
- The rigidity of processes gives people very little possibility for correction
- Interaction is important, so harmony between people is crucial
- Confidence and control are two contrary variables
- Confidence and motivation have a strong influence on exchange and the creation of knowledge
- Confidence must always be built; the level at the start is never enough
- Interaction without knowledge does not allow learning
- Interaction without confidence and motivation does not allow learning
- Motivation and organization seem to interact positively
- Interaction is always necessary for the construction of confidence
- If there are agents at group level who do not cooperate, the learning of the group stops

The questions of the personal (development) version: what is the individual manager's potential to take up the role of the leader in sustainable performance?

Values

Diversity

- Do you base your actions on ethical codes?
- Do you sometimes reflect on the sustainability of your actions?
- You pay attention to being anti-discriminatory?
- Do your actions reflect a sense of social responsibility?
- We need to take care of all the parties involved in what we do
- Assessing someone's work environment is important

- In an organization it is important to pay attention to the retention of talent
- Variety in opinions is a value
- You pay attention to effectively communicating with those around you
- Leadership should be strongly committed
- Active interest groups are an asset for society

Complexity

- You are most dynamic and creative at the edge of chaos
- Evolution needs both the new and extinction
- Diversity is a prerequisite for the emergence of the new
- Radical unpredictability is an essential characteristic of any organization
- The self-organizational capacity of any group is an indicator for sustainability
- Interaction between "individual agents" is essential for self-organization
- Agency (the action) is located at the level of interacting individual entities

Personal development

Personal well being

- I value an active approach to the development of individual competencies and skills
- One should also value time that is not immediately productive
- I practice a policy of non-judgment on appearances (facts, humans, etc.)
- Joy is an active element of my professional or societal life
- I feel valued in my professional environment
- I have a real responsibility and space to maneuver
- There is space for the realization of my desires in my function/activity
- Courage is valued in my professional environment
- I feel an essential part of the whole

Leadership and teamwork

- Each individual (surrounding me) is well trained and prepared to do his/her job
- A constant sense of awareness is essential for success
- My professional environment is an intense network of communication
- The purpose in my professional environment is always clear and shared
- My managers create space for others
- My managers are more concerned with projecting a vision and less with correcting what happened previously
- Rigid leadership creates confusion
- Lack of clarity causes tension and under-performance
- I have an external focus that gives meaning to my work

Mechanistic performance

Financial performance

- My appreciation of my revenues is above average in society
- My appreciation of my belongings is above average in our society
- My liquidity position is above average in society (I can spend what I really want)
- I generate enough cash in order to be financially self-sufficient for what I want to develop
- My cash-flow generation gives me a comfortable feeling

Innovative potential

- I actively pay attention to developing new ideas
- I am able to produce creativity on demand
- My professional environment regards idea generation as a key business practice
- I personally develop new ideas on a regular basis
- Our leadership model rewards innovative thinking
- An organization should have a structured process for evaluating/refining new ideas
- Our professional culture values idea assessment/refinement as a core competence

Systemic performance

Sustainable development and responsibility

- I value unconditional responsibility
- I value essential integrity
- I value ontological humility (My basic starting point is to be humble)
- I value authentic communication
- I value constructive negotiation
- I value impeccable coordination
- I value conscious responses
- I value emotional mastery

Knowledge and learning

- Project managers should use more than just financial factors to measure success
- The rigidity of processes gives people very little possibility for correction
- Interaction is important, so harmony between people is crucial
- Confidence and control are two contrary variables
- Confidence and motivation have a strong influence on exchange and the creation of knowledge
- Confidence must always be built; the level at the start is never enough
- Interaction without knowledge does not allow learning
- Interaction without confidence and motivation does not allow learning
- Motivation and organization seem to interact positively
- Interaction is always necessary for the construction of confidence
- If there are agents at group level who do not cooperate, the learning of the group stops

After Cassandra has been used to make the diagnostic in either version, it immediately visualizes the areas where most progress is necessary. From that observation onwards we can define a path to follow in order to develop towards the desired goal. Then, after a certain time, we could re-use Cassandra to check whether we did indeed progress towards our goals. Alternatively we could use part (or all) of the Cassandra tool to build a management tool for continuous monitoring and/or corrective action

The learning coach: continuous work on the mutual selves ("on the road")

The last element of the methodology for social intrapreneurship focuses on the role of the manager as a learning coach. This is the process that we need to install in order to generate the supporting methodology and to maintain momentum. We would like to define the "learning coach" as a **contract** and a contract **follow-up** about a methodology and a developmental trajectory. Each and every individual involved in the process has to identify a personal developmental trajectory and a series of management competencies that they would like to develop, using all possible activities as a tool for that development. These can be considered as a learning contract that a manager or employee can sign with him or herself and, if applicable, with his or her coach. Such a learning contract is visualized in the following diagram.

The learning contract

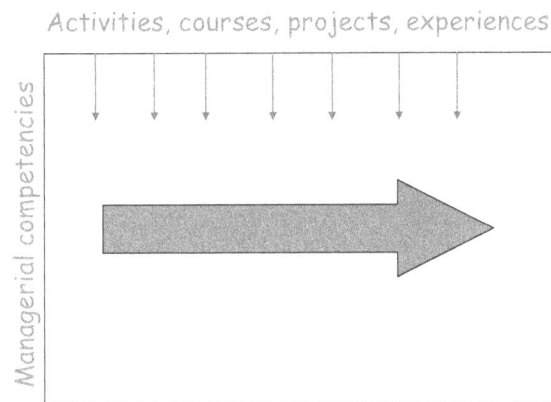

Activities, courses, projects, experiences

Managerial competencies

A learning contract can be seen as a contract about his or her learning that the learner signs with him or herself (but of course in practice, at the same time with his or her educational support or coach). However, in case of any coaching or tutoring or formal training, this learning contract will have a third party involved to sign up: the coach, trainer or tutor. Areas to be addressed can be gathered from the following quote: "What is it what I expect to learn: in this course, in this activity, in this question?" If somebody chooses to enroll for a course, what does that person expect to learn? And what does he or she commit to focus on for learning? To what can the coach, the tutor, or the manager hold the learner accountable? The same type of questions should be asked before starting a coaching session. What is the person's ambition to learn? Is he or she committed to focusing on achieving that ambition? Can the coach keep the learner accountable for that focus?

In a managerial context, that focus, or learning goal, could easily be expressed as a series of managerial competencies that the learner wants to acquire. Then many different activities can take place that are, in themselves, tools allowing the learner to progress in their learning. These tools could be courses or activities (whether job related or not). In fact, the nature of the activity is much less important. Any activity has the potential to contribute to the creation of learning moments for the "conscious" learner.

During the learning or coaching process, it is part of the exercise to validate the progress in the learning contract. Has there been progress in the acquisition of some desired managerial competencies? If yes, what others are desired? If not, why not? And what needs to be done to improve the learning? In fact, an assessment is regularly made on the progress of the realization of the learning contract (see the description of the nature and content of the learning contract in the figure above).

Secondly, the learning coach is a technique, a methodology of co-coaching, which can easily be trained, importantly, in order to improve the efficiency of co-coaching in companies. Co-coaching could take place between managers at the same level, but it could equally be used by a manager in his role as a coach for his co-workers. Co-coaching is the technique that might help the learner on a day-to-day basis (and not only via tutoring or coaching) to progress.

The aim is that the participants (managers, learning individuals) learn in order to realize their individual learning goals, based on personal responsibility (that we should have developed by now). The anticipated result is that managers are better able than before to manage their personal development plan. The methodology consists of a number of steps briefly described here, although it might need some initial coaching to get started.

At the beginning of the learning trajectory, there is an intake interview that roughly deals with the following questions that aim to guide the participant to explore their own current feelings:

Who am I?

What goal do I want to reach, or what do I want to learn?

What do I need for that?

How do I anticipate reaching that?

When do I want to have reached this?

The aim is to translate, in a very detailed and down-to-earth way, a number of individual wishes, intentions and expectations. Based on the results, a personal learning coach is (ideally) appointed. In a corporate setting, this might be the "learning coach" who takes this role on him or herself. Next the participants start working on the more content-driven parts of their job (in fact on any activity, assignment, or possibly even a course), though always using a learning-by-doing approach. In this context, a course can never be a simple teacher-driven knowledge transfer. Personal development can only flourish when learners are confronted with new insights, preferably challenging insights. This combination of new insights and personal development is an on-going process. The earlier identified trinity of insight, form and meaningfulness (science, art and spirituality) is the guiding principle for the entire methodology and approach.

During the intake, one could use competency criteria and behavioral criteria in order to facilitate the interview (see example below). The knowledge and innovation approach advocated in this book is clearly and exclusively one that is based on competency development. Possible interesting competencies for a manager to review are: courage, initiative, independence, the capacity to deal with stress, the capacity to convince, organizational sensitivity, cooperation, flexibility, ambition, and energy. Of course, these criteria need to be adapted to each company or organization, and to what each individual wants to learn.

During the progress of the (job related) assignments, or what could be called projects, the participants can share different (virtual) meeting places. This can be illustrated through the metaphor of a house, in which different groups of participants can serve as each other's mirrors and sounding boards concerning their own learning. All this takes place in a self-organizing way. Within the different "houses" there are different "rooms" and it is the people inside who decide whom they allow in. Hence somebody knocks on the door, and possibly someone opens it. The further details of the organization are less important here.

The sounding board function needs to be understood as follows. We consider here a triangular situation in which somebody is confronted with what he considers to be a problem – comparable to the "problematique" in Soft Systems Methodology). That is the basis of the triangle. A third person comes into the game and that person can take a number of roles. The first classical role, indicated by the blue arrow, is that the third person gives his advice concerning the problem. The third person takes the role of the consultant and, in fact, takes over the problem instead of allowing the person to learn. The second possible role that the third person can take is indicated by the red arrow and is the one of the therapist. The third person gives advice on the behavior and decisional power of the person in question. Often this does not help the person to learn, since the therapist (consultant) again takes over, but now he takes over the learning potential. The role of learning coach that we suggest is illustrated by the green arrow. The coach encourages the person to learn-by-doing and to solve the problem by himself. The coach allows the person to take full responsibility and only mirrors certain observations, contextual information, etc.

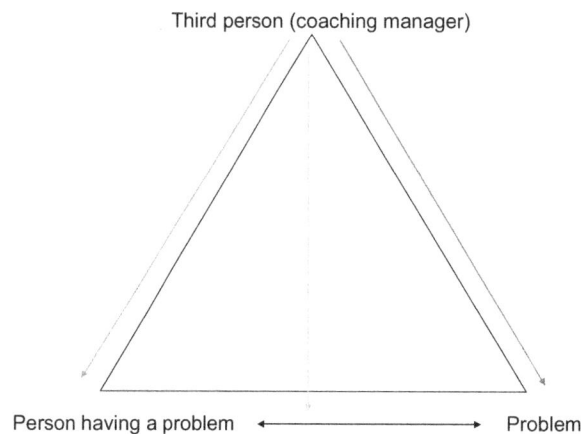

Third person (coaching manager)

Person having a problem ←——————————→ Problem

This approach of being, or becoming, a learning coach is not evident and needs to be trained. Therefore such an approach, which has been used successfully for many years in certain "schools" of personal development, needs some initial training/coaching from a professional, after which, in principle, everybody could take on this role of learning coach amongst his or her peers. The attempt of the professional is not to stay in the picture for the entire learning loop, but rather to pass on the competencies for becoming a learning coach.

The role of the coach is hopefully clear now: to stimulate, to activate, to motivate, to inspire and to raise enthusiasm. The pillar of this approach is and remains the responsibility of the learner for his or her own personal learning. The learner decides where to go, taking the steering wheel in hand. The learner reacts to what is offered, but also creates (first). The learner respects others' opinions and listens to others. The learner contributes to the learning processes of other participants and respects the privacy of the others. In practice this list is longer, but this gives some insight into the basic rules of the game.

This rather external approach to personal learning and development can only succeed if the emotional component in this process is not ignored. Learning without emotions is like training a monkey for the circus.

Again, it is suggested that a set of managerial competencies be developed to help make this process more concrete. In certain cases companies have identified the managerial competencies their managers require. In other cases, these competencies need to be defined. However, monitoring the process of the learning coach will need some kind of tool, some identifiable goals and competencies that the learner aims to develop. In order to give some possible suggestions for such a list, the following offers an example of a list of managerial competencies appropriate for developing a manager with the ambition to be able to manage within a more systemic context, in other words, for a social intrapreneur (the list is not exhaustive):

- Analytical skills
- Problem solving skills
  - Identification of variables and constraints
  - Identification of information sources
  - Information management
  - Creation of solutions and their prioritization

- Project management skills
  - Scenario building
  - Identification of multidimensional solution spaces
  - Risk management
  - Structuring and controlling

- Vision development
  - Understanding the economic context
  - Anticipation of competitive evolution
  - Imagination and creation of innovative actions
  - Production of coherence/holism

- Managing performance
  - Management of indicators
  - Translation of ideas into actions that create value
  - Management of information, and IS

- Client orientation
  - Don't produce for yourself
  - Master and develop quality
  - Satisfy customers (internal and external)

- **Accepting diversity as a creative power**
  - Avoid ethnocentric thinking
  - Make use of cultural diversity
  - Use diversity as a constructive principle
  - Learn about diversity (cultural, religious)
  - Facilitate networking

- **Decision making skills**
  - Operationalizing
  - Installation of a Management Information System
  - Anticipation, correction, and analysis
  - Propose actions

- **Communication skills**
  - Management of communication supports
  - Organization of communication flows
  - Anticipation of communication needs

- Groupworking
  - Mastery of team-oriented parameters and attitudes
  - Understanding and identification of each other's role
  - Enrich roles
  - Anticipate hurdles
  - Share knowledge and experience
  - Flexibility
  - Adaptability

- Leadership/Motivation
  - Propose and assume responsibility
  - Create synergy
  - Listen
  - Construct
  - Convince
  - Motivate
  - Support and back up your co-workers

- Coaching
  - Evaluate
  - Inform
  - Organize and support workplace learning

- Respect for the human being
  - Cultivate an open mind
  - Be aware of and accept differences
  - Be tolerant and show humility
  - Be sensitive to context

- Self-motivation
  - Be able to motivate yourself in all circumstances
  - Be involved, more and more

- Creativity/Innovation
  - Be open to, and apply change
  - Dare to innovate
  - Embrace complexity and variety (don't limit)
  - Be a continuous "learner"
  - Allow and support others to learn continuously

- **Entrepreneurship**
  - Be an entrepreneur
  - Be an actor in development

- **Management learning**
  - Progress your own "knowing"
  - Learn from your errors
  - Incorporate continuous learning

- **Personal mission**
- **Stress Management**
  - Time management
  - Conflict management
  - Prioritization of difficulties and opportunities

- **Social responsibility and sustainable orientation**
  - Take societal responsibility for your actions
  - Societal/environmental engagement

- **Ethical mission**

www.ingramcontent.com/pod-product-compliance
Lightning Source LLC
Chambersburg PA
CBHW081806200326
41597CB00023B/4162